MW01110128

WAKING UP IN HEAVEN

WAKING UP IN HEAVEN

WAKING UP *IN HEAVEN*

A Contemporary Edition of Centuries of Meditation

THOMAS TRAHERNE

edited by David Buresh

hesedpress

WAKING UP IN HEAVEN: A Contemporary Edition of *Centuries of Meditation*
PUBLISHED BY HESED PRESS
P.O. Box 186
Spencerville, MD 20868-0186

Hesed Press Web Site: http://www.hesedpress.com

hesedpress

ISBN   0-9721602-0-5
         0-9721602-1-3 (pbk.)

The Library of Congress Control Number: 2002096955

Jacket and book design by Mark Rowland

Printed in the United States of America

Dedication in Traherne's original manuscript:

This book unto the friend of my best friend
As of the wisest love a mark I send,
That she may write my Maker's praise therein
And make herself thereby a Cherubin.

This edition dedicated to:

Carolyn, Maddie, Katya, and Olivia —
Four Queens of the Universe
& Heiresses of Heaven

CONTENTS

Acknowledgments   ix

Preface: An Experience & A Quest   xiii

Introduction: My Friendship with Thomas Traherne   xvii

SECTION I: MY CHALLENGES TO YOU   I

1. Consider Secret Influences on Your Soul   3

2. Think Well   6

3. Enjoy the World Like Never Before   13

4. Understand What You Want   25

5. Claim the World as Your Inheritance   31

SECTION II: MY TALKS WITH JESUS   35

6. The Cross of Christ is the Gate of Heaven: 37
   An Introduction to My Prayers

7. Thanking Jesus For All the Treasures He Has Given Us   41
   in the World

8. Thanking Jesus For His Love & For Himself   46

9. Requesting That I Grow in Jesus' Love   53

10. Requesting That I Become Like Jesus   58

SECTION III: MY VISION OF THE WORLD   69
   . . . Where All the Riches of God's Kingdom Appear

11. The World Serves Us   71

12. God Can Be Seen in the World   79

13. Let God's Love Restore Your Person to Greater Beauty   86

14. See God's Love in the Trinity   95

15. Extend Your Love to All Objects   IOI

16. Go Out of Yourself with the Power of Your Soul   III

17. Rest & Delight in the Greatness of Your True Self   I25

SECTION IV: THE STORY OF MY PERSONAL JOURNEY   135
18. My Childhood & Adolescence   137
19. My Years at the University   162
20. My Years in the Country   169
21. My Mentor, David   184

SECTION V: PRINCIPLES FOR YOUR OWN JOURNEY   207
22. The Principle of Two Kinds of Christians   209
23. Principles of Retirement and Solitude   216
24. Principles of Charity   221
25. Principles of Our Free Choice & Effort   230
26. Principles of Self-Love   238
27. Principles for Loving Others   243
28. Principles Related to Love & the Soul   249

SECTION VI: CONTINUING BEYOND BOUNDS
OR RESTRAINTS   275
29. Infinite Room For Our Imaginations   277
30. Traveling Into God's Eternity & Omnipresence   281

EPILOGUE
Thomas Traherne & the Discovery of *Centuries of Meditation*   285

APPENDICES   291
Appendix A: Notes   293
Appendix B: Scripture References   295
Appendix C: Bibliography   299
Appendix D: Detailed Table of Contents   301
Appendix E: Statement of Editorial Guidelines   321

ACKNOWLEDGMENTS

This book has been, and always will be, Thomas Traherne's book. For the pleasure and privilege of putting it into the hands of a new generation of readers, I have many to thank.

First of all, as my teacher, Rosalie deRosset encouraged my imagination and affirmed my intuition in a way that prepared me to appreciate Traherne when I first encountered him. She also offered valuable suggestions in the last stages of this project. I hope that I can, in my lifetime, affect one other person the way that her teaching and friendship has affected me and hundreds of other students.

Leanne Payne's PCM schools and books gave me the courage to complete this creative project. Without Mrs. Payne and her team, this book would never have materialized.

My wife and best friend, Carolyn, has encouraged my enthusiasm for Traherne ever since I met her in college. She refused to let me give up on this project and read countless drafts of various sections. Her intelligent and creative feedback, along with her patience, are stamped on the pages of this book. She is an extraordinary friend. I am also deeply grateful to my three daughters—Maddie, Katya, and Olivia—who have been exceptionally patient with me in my effort to complete this book. Katya, thank you for asking me to tell you stories about Thomas Traherne.

Professor George A. Panichas's teaching and writing have been an inspiration for me since my days as an undergraduate at the University of Maryland. He encouraged me to continue pursuing Traherne, and his 'critical meditations' on Dostoevsky and Simone Weil have been important models for ways in which to deepen the experience of reading great works of literature.

I am grateful to Fred and Christie Morse for their great friendship, encouragement, and kindness—and to Fred for his teaching on the spiritual disciplines.

I am grateful for everyone who took the time to look at early drafts of this book. In particular, I am indebted to Rosie, Carolyn, Katherine Brown, Maureen McNulty, Neil Livingstone, and Jeff Kline, who intuited the type of edition I was attempting to create and helped me gain clarity. They gave me penetrating feedback and valuable direction. I finally felt a sense of closure when Maureen McNulty generously applied her skill to the final editing of the supplemental sections.

It has been a great pleasure and honor to work with Mark Rowland on the design of this book's cover and layout. He has encouraged me to view this as an artistic venture, and I am grateful for his patience during the last year of this project.

I owe much thanks to my many friends at Cedar Ridge Community Church. I am grateful for the privilege of having Brian McLaren as my Pastor and friend for many years. He has been a gracious and gifted teacher and writer, and he has encouraged me in my own writing aspirations. His tendency towards the 'Way of Affirmation' reflects much of Traherne's love for God's creation. I am also grateful for several pastors who have used their gifts to encourage spiritual growth in me and many others at CRCC: Gene Maynard, Lisa Holloway, and Stephen Shields. Gene offered special encouragement in the final stages of this project and opened the door to many more devotional classics. Many men have been strong, supportive brothers to me, including Kevin Barwick, Mark Buckingham, Steve Shandy, and the men who have been part of 'The Entrepreneurs' over the years (Mark, Scott, Craig, Fred, John, Mike, Bruce, Barry, Eric, Tom, Chris, & Jon David).

My parents, brother, and sister have been a consistent encouragement to me and a source of strength. My brother, Scott, has been a mentor, and my sister, Sue, a friend and cheerleader. My mother and father, Stella and Ted Buresh, have been exceptionally generous and supportive.

In the course of this project, I have been inspired by the vision of the Renovaré organization (led by Richard Foster) and its commitment to reviving Christian spiritual classics. I am grateful for Lyle SmithGraybeal's friendship and his encouragement to complete this project.

I am thankful for the many people who have prayed with me for this book. In working on this edition, I have cried out many times, "Jesus, help me!" In closing, I cry out, in the spirit of Thomas Traherne, "Soli Deo Gloria!"

PREFACE:
AN EXPERIENCE & A QUEST

"Contemplation is a form of knowing arrived at not by thinking but by seeing, intuition."[1] —Josef Pieper

Clearing a Trail

Over the last twenty years, many of my friends have enthusiastically set out to read *Centuries of Meditation*, only to give up in frustration. Unfortunately, they lacked a clear path to guide them through the book. It's no wonder. Traherne left us with no book title or section headings or chapter titles or paragraph breaks. Furthermore, the original version was filled with "thee's" and "thou's" and, by today's standards, irregular punctuation usage. So, my friends walked away from their reading with a few extraordinary quotes, but with no concrete, lasting experience.

I shared in my friends' frustration; yet a burning desire to know Traherne more intimately raged like a wildfire inside of me. I knew he had more to offer than a mere collection of quotes. And my suspicion that he was leading his readers on a carefully planned trail drove me to create this version of *Centuries of Meditation*. In it, I have attempted to clear the path and post markers, while resurrecting Traherne's voice as our guide.

An Experience and A Quest

Thomas Traherne wanted readers to experience his book as much as to read it. At the beginning of *Centuries*, we are invited on a quest to discover heaven on earth. Will we accept? If so, the gate is open. With map in hand and conversing with us as we walk, Traherne leads us out of our man-made world, continually enticing us with a taste of what lies further down the road. He allows us to eavesdrop on his talks with Jesus.

When we arrive at the edge of paradise, Traherne surveys the land, describing for us what he sees. What initially appear to be worthless rocks come into focus as precious stones; seemingly common peasants turn out to be kings and queens. Traherne pours every ounce of his being into convincing us that we are heirs of this land. His contagious vision of the world arouses feelings of joy within us and affirms our longing for greatness.

Traherne then turns to his personal experience, reminiscing about his life in this kingdom—from birth through adulthood. Finally, as he prepares to send us off on our own, he offers us principles for our journey and describes one final vision to remind us what is possible.

Traherne's Questions & His Influence on Three 20th Century Leaders

Throughout his quest, Traherne wrestles with important spiritual formation questions:

> How do we change our thinking and understand
>   our desires?
> How can we talk with Jesus?
> How can we enjoy the world and every person in it?
> How can we love people the way Jesus does?
> How can we see all the treasures God has given
>   us in creation?
> How can we overcome our sins and be restored?
> How can we fill our lives with joy and beauty?

He doesn't offer us simple answers; rather he shows us how to find God in the subtle and commonplace wonders of creation, in the boundless soul of every person, and in the Trinity itself.

Three of the most prominent Christian writers of the 20th century—C. S. Lewis, Thomas Merton, and Dorothy Sayers—found joy in their encounter with Thomas Traherne. In 1961, just two years before his death, C. S. Lewis recommended Traherne as a counterpoint to another devotional master—Thomas à Kempis: "The *Imitation* is very severe. . . . A good book to balance it is Traherne's *Centuries of Meditation. . .* There is all the gold & fragrance!"[2] Lewis sensed that while Thomas à Kempis helps us leave the world made by men, Thomas Traherne helps us enjoy the world made by God.

In the same year, on the other side of the Atlantic, Thomas Merton wrote one of the most insightful descriptions of Traherne's *Centuries* that I have ever come across:

"[Traherne] can speak in theological symbols that echo the intuitions of Julian of Norwich about the Redemption. . . . He can also be more difficult, more philosophical. . . . In either case, what is important is not a theory, not an abstract proposition, but a concrete experience, expressed now in the context of theological mystery, now in philosophical language. Yet in every case we must penetrate immediately to the central intuition, a basic Eucharistic and primitive Christian theology of praise."[3]

Before her death in 1957 at the age of sixty-four, Dorothy Sayers—the brilliant novelist, poet, dramatist, and essayist—confessed that she wanted to better develop the Way of Affirmation as it was specifically illustrated in the writings of Traherne, Dante, Blake, and Wordsworth. She perfectly characterized what Traherne offers alongside these other great poets:

". . . the Way [of Affirmation], though neglected and overgrown, has not been left wholly uncharted. Dante is its pioneer, Blake its prophet; **Traherne has supplied it with a manual of devotion.** . . ."[4]

Twenty years after these twentieth-century giants recommended Traherne, I came across this treasure myself and, for the first time, encountered a voice that gave me permission to claim the world as my inheritance and enjoy the friendship of God. My prayer is that you will have a similar experience with *Waking Up in Heaven*.

David Buresh
Silver Spring, MD

INTRODUCTION:
MY FRIENDSHIP WITH THOMAS TRAHERNE

The Mistake

Thomas Traherne has been my friend—and one of my greatest sources of joy—for the last twenty years. I would never have pursued Traherne if it had not been for my experience in an English 101 class, which, for awhile, anyway, I chalked up to some sort of administrative oversight. It happened during my freshman year at a small, conservative college in Chicago.

In August of 1981, my older brother and I tossed my suitcases into the back of our parents' VW Bus and drove 600 miles from our home in suburban Baltimore to downtown Chicago. I had been eager to attend this school ever since visiting my brother there four years earlier. But unlike my brother, who had already graduated with highest honors, I was plagued with self-doubt and had resigned my self to dwelling in the ranks of the "B" students. Moving to Chicago was, for me, an act of reckless abandon, considering my fear of the unknown. I felt like a freakish amalgam of desire and fear. I wanted to go to India as a missionary, and yet, everyday conversations terrified me. It wasn't uncommon for me to obsess for hours over an innocent, good-hearted teasing.

On the first day of the semester, I sat in a classroom on the second floor of a twelve-story brick building, gazing out the window at the high-rises in Cabrini Green, a nearby housing project, and envisioning the movements of gang members. A ringing bell startled me back to reality just as my English 101 teacher—an attractive, energetic woman in her early 30's—stepped briskly through the door and dropped a stack of books on the table. She surveyed the room and grinned.

We were, of course, the "B" class. Yet, she began lobbing questions: "Who is your favorite poet?" We responded with blank stares. She threw another one at us: "Have you guys ever journaled?" We responded with even blanker stares. It wasn't that we had never read poetry, but it was not the type of poetry found in the *Norton Anthology*. As for journals, all we could think of were our dads' *Wall Street Journals* or our mothers' *Ladies Home Journals*—and we didn't dare write in those.

If our inexperience dismayed her, Miss deRosset showed no signs. For three mornings a week over the next two semesters, she treated us like the "A" class. We went toe-to-toe with C. S. Lewis, T. S. Eliot, Dostoevsky, Alan Paton, Gerard Manley Hopkins, Solzhenitsyn, Flannery O'Connor and others. We came to feel that we really understood these brilliant writers. We fell in love with journaling. We even got an occasional paper printed in the college newspaper. One thing was for sure—we couldn't get enough! Miss deRosset had coaxed us into believing that no author or writing project was beyond us.

Summer School

During the spring semester, I mapped out my plans for the summer break. I planned to earn some of the next year's tuition by working a graveyard shift desk job downtown, which left my days free to pursue my new-found love of literature. I asked Miss deRosset for names of colleges in the Chicago area that offered the best summer school literature classes. She pointed me to Wheaton College in the western suburbs. Soon I was enrolled in three classes—including one on the 18th Century English Romantic poets and one on the New England poets.

The spring semester ended in early May. A week later, as soon as my graveyard shift ended at 7:30 on Monday morning, I bolted out the door and practically ran down LaSalle Drive, over the Chicago River, and across to Northwestern Station, where I caught the Union Pacific/West Line train to Wheaton. When I finally stepped onto the lawn of Wheaton's suburban campus and looked up at the imposing, limestone edifice on a hill, it was only the confidence I had gained in Miss deRosset's class that propelled me forward—into the "A" class.

Throughout the summer, Professor Wayne Martindale saturated my imagination with the enthusiastic and optimistic voices of Byron and Blake and Wordsworth and Coleridge and Dickinson and Frost. These poets boldly painted the world as a friendly, albeit complex, place. Midway through the first session, when we had to select a topic for a paper, I walked across campus to the undergraduate library to begin my research.

In the process of combing the stacks, I came across a recently-published book with an intriguing cover. It was a collection of life-long letters from C.S. Lewis to one of his best friends, Arthur Greaves, entitled *They Stand Together*. I signed it out along with several books for my research paper. As soon as the the train left the Wheaton station that afternoon, I began skimming through Lewis's letters. Halfway through the book, I came across an exceptionally enthusiastic letter written when Lewis was 31 years old. In this correspondence, dated July 8th, 1930, Lewis wrote:

"Almost ever since the Vac. began I have been reading a little every evening in Traherne's Centuries of Meditations (Dobell. About 7/—. Lovely paper). I forget whether we have talked of it or not. I think he suffers by making out everything much too easy and really shirking the problem of evil in all its forms: at least, as far as I have got, for it is unfair to say this of a book not yet finished. But apart from this he has extraordinary merits. What do you think of the following; — 'The world . . . is the beautiful frontispiece to Eternity' — 'You never enjoy the world aright till the sea itself floweth in your veins, till you are clothed with the heavens and crowned with the stars . . . till you can sing and rejoice and delight in God as misers do in gold' — 'I must lead you out of this into another world to learn your wants. For till you find them you will never be happy' — 'They (i.e. Souls) were made to love and are dark and vain and comfortless till they do it. Till they love they are idle or misemployed. Till they love they are desolate.' But I could go on quoting from this book forever." [1]

I immediately flipped back to the index to see where else Lewis might have referenced this fellow whom 'he could go on quoting forever'. I found four other such letters, dated July 29th, 1930; August 28th, 1930; December 23rd, 1941; and November 12th, 1961. These letters spanned 31 years of Lewis's life and showed no loss of enthusiasm in Traherne's book.

The next day, I rushed to the library before my class and signed out a copy of *Centuries of Meditation*. As I began reading it on the train, I felt many of my fears temporarily melt in the rush of joy and hope and desire beyond what even the Romantic poets or the Scriptures had invoked in me. I had a feeling of entitlement to joy that was previously elusive. My soul began to heal on the train that June afternoon. The Romantics and the New England poets and the Bible had planted the seeds that Traherne was now bringing to fruition.

My Advocate

I kept Traherne's *Centuries* checked out of the library for the rest of the summer, and then bought several used copies (a Dobell edition and a Margoliouth edition) as soon as the summer sessions were over. A day didn't pass over the next year without my having reread portions of my new treasure. Traherne felt to me like my champion, an advocate for joy in my life.

The next spring, when given the assignment to write a paper on an influential person in Church history, I leaped at this excuse to write something about Traherne. It was my first chance to research Traherne's life and writings in greater depth. I was a little surprised at how little I found about him in Church history books. On the other hand, when I turned to literary book and journals, I found a wealth of material. I titled my paper, "Thomas Traherne: Yet to Come Into His Own," which hinted at my confusion as to why this man was such a well-kept secret.

A couple of months later, I flew to India with five other college students for the summer. On a train enroute from Bangalore to New Delhi, I read *Centuries of Meditation* again. I remember looking out the train window as we passed by village after village, wondering to myself if Traherne's vision of the world made any sense there. In some ways, it made even more sense in India than it did in America. Nevertheless, I wanted Traherne to make sense wherever I went.

Pursuing Traherne in Maryland

After flying back to the U.S. and completing my studies at Moody Bible Institute in Chicago, I returned to Maryland and enrolled at the University of Maryland, College Park. I began with courses in Agriculture, because I still had ambitions of going to India as a missionary. However, I eventually switched my major to my true passion, English literature, and immediately registered for all the 17th-century literature classes available to undergraduates. I wanted to learn more about the milieu in which Traherne lived and wrote. I discovered Milton and Herbert and Bunyan, who spoke to my imagination in a similar way as Traherne.

Several of my professors modeled the value of spending an entire decade or more meditating on the works of one or two authors: Professor George A. Panichas did this with Dostoevsky and Simone Weil, Professor Lewis Lawson with Walker Percy, and Professor Verlyn Flieger with J. R. R. Tolkien. These teachers were giants who graciously shared their mentors with me and with all of their students. Professor Panichas, in particular, confirmed that Traherne was an author worthy of a decade or two of my attention.

I applied to graduate school at Maryland, with the intention of doing thesis work on Traherne. I was confident that there were oceans to be explored in *Centuries of Meditation* and my dream was to swim wide and deep within those oceans. Graduate school seemed like the natural place to pursue this. I was accepted into the program, but at the same time, I fell in love with my future wife, and life took a very different turn. I decided to take a full-time job in the computer industry and get married.

Traherne in the Shadows

Traherne remained one of my favorite writers, but my passion for his vision mellowed. For the next ten years, I raced from business prospect to business prospect, often sleeping overnight at my desk in the office, trying to prove my worth as a salesman and a breadwinner. These years mirrored a description from Traherne's own autobiography:

> "Being swallowed up therefore in the miserable gulf of idle talk and worthless vanities, thenceforth I lived among dreams and shadows, like a prodigal son feeding upon husks with swine. A comfortless wilderness full of thorns and troubles the world was, or worse: a waste place covered with idleness and play, and shops, and markets, and taverns."

It wasn't until 1998, when I sat hunched over on the edge of my bed in a psychiatric hospital, after having admitted myself for suicidal depression, that my mad, endless rush around the Washington Beltway came to a halt long enough for me to acknowledge the hole in my life.

My Recommitment to *Centuries*

As one important part of my road to recovery, I attended a conference led by Leanne Payne the following spring in Virginia Beach, Virginia.

During this week, Mrs. Payne prayed for the presence of Christ to heal me and then instructed me to write down in my journal what I felt God was telling me over the next few days. That night in my hotel room, I rested my back against several pillows at the head of my bed and began writing in my black marble composition book. I recorded, in a stream of consciousness, everything I was saying to God. After a half hour of writing, I looked back at my own handwriting and saw the following sentences: "Today, I sense Jesus wants to tell me a little more what he wants to do with my life. . . . I think the writings of Traherne will always be an important part of my life that I need to share." In the process of sharing Traherne, I would have the opportunity to deepen my friendship with him and once again open the door for joy to return to my life.

Trying to Follow Traherne's Overgrown Trail

At first, I worked off of a hunch. I suspected that Traherne's book was organized in such a way that it could lead a reader not only to understand how Traherne viewed the world, but to actually learn how to view the world in the same way. It wasn't long before I began finding clues throughout *Centuries of Meditation*, hinting at a journey to this place, from which there was no return. Once we got to this place, we would see the same world that we saw before, but in a completely different way: Traherne's way.

I could not confirm my hunch until I did some cleanup work. I wrote down descriptive titles for each of Traherne's sections and subsections. Then, iteration by iteration, I updated the verb forms, the pronouns, the capitalization, the punctuation, and paragraph breaks. Finally, the journey lay charted before me. I could finally experience this book and let it change the way I viewed the world and all of its creatures.

C. S. Lewis: Surprised By Traherne

In the course of my journey with Traherne, I have played a little game. The idea came from C. S. Lewis's comment about *Centuries of Meditation* that first turned me on to Traherne: "I could go on quoting from this book forever." Because Lewis blurted this out on his first reading of *Centuries of Meditation* at the age of 31, I couldn't help but wonder if Lewis did in fact go on quoting from *Centuries* for the rest of his life. Thus the game: to see how often and how long Lewis quoted this poet. Every time I have picked up a Lewis book for the first time since then, I have flipped through the index and then the contents to see if I could find any Traherne quotes or references. (I call it a game to mask the eccentricity of this habit.)

The results of my game thus far have resulted in the following chronology of Lewis's quotes and references to Traherne:

1930: Lewis mentions and quotes Traherne in three letters to Arthur Greaves.

1940: Lewis mentions Traherne in a letter to a former pupil.

1940: Lewis quotes Traherne in *The Problem of Pain*.

1941: Lewis mentions Traherne in a letter to Arthur Greaves.

1942: Lewis quotes and mentions Traherne in *Preface to Paradise Lost*.

1943: Lewis quotes Traherne in *The Abolition of Man*.

1944: Lewis mentions Traherne in his Introduction to Sister Penelope's translation of *The Incarnation of the Word of God*, reprinted later as the essay, "On the Reading of Old Books."

1947: Lewis mentions Traherne in his Introduction to *George MacDonald: An Anthology*.

1949: Lewis mentions Traherne in a letter to Rhona M. Bodle.

1951: Lewis mentions Traherne in a letter to Ruth Pitter.

1954: Lewis mentions Traherne in *English Literature in the*

Sixteenth Century, Excluding Drama.

1955: Lewis quotes Traherne in *Surprised by Joy.*

1960: Lewis mentions Traherne in his Preface to a new edition of
The Screwtape Letters with Screwtape Proposes a Toast.

1961: Lewis mentions Traherne in a letter to Mrs. Margaret Gray.

1961: Lewis mentions Traherne in a letter to Arthur Greaves.

1963: Lewis mentioned Traherne in his last book, *Letters to
Malcolm: Chiefly on Prayer.* Lewis died later this year.

In addition to these dates, it is interesting that he began quoting Traherne
a year before his 'conversion' to Christianity (marked by his late night
'Mythopoeia' conversation with J. R. R. Tolkien and Owen Barfield) and
that he enthusiastically referenced him up until 1963. Some of Lewis's references to *Centuries* in 1930 provide reasonable proof that Traherne may
have been very influential in Lewis's conversion. Traherne helped convince
Lewis that he would be able to enjoy the world more deeply through a rela-
tionship with Jesus.

    This game has expanded to other members of Lewis's society.
Owen Barfield, in *Saving the Appearances*, likened Traherne to David's
Psalms and indirectly to Walt Whitman. Dorothy Sayers wrote enthusiastically about Traherne at the end of her life and linked him to Charles
Williams, another intimate friend of Lewis. These discoveries shed light on
the extent of Traherne's influence, and each one fuels my enthusiasm for
the next.

    And so the game continues.

I.
MY CHALLENGES TO YOU

CHAPTER 1

CONSIDER SECRET INFLUENCES ON YOUR SOUL

Truths You Love Without Knowing Them

An empty book is like an infant's soul, in which anything may be written. It is capable of all things, but contains nothing. I have a mind to fill this with profitable wonders.

And since love made you put it into my hands, I will fill it with those truths you love without knowing them. I will fill it with those things which, if it be possible, shall show my love to you in communicating most enriching truths—and show my love to truth in exalting her beauties in such a soul.

Attraction to Unknown Things

Do not wonder that I promise to fill it with those truths you love but know not; for though it be a maxim in the schools that there is no love of a thing unknown, yet I have found that things unknown have a secret influence on the soul, and like the center of the earth unseen violently attract it. We love we know not what, and therefore everything allures us.

As iron at a distance is drawn by the loadstone, there being some invisible communications between them, so is there in us a world of love to something, though we know not what in the world that should be. There are invisible ways of conveyance by which some great thing touches our souls, and by which we tend to it. Do you not feel yourself drawn by the expectation and desire of some great thing?

Making You Possessor of the World

"I will open my mouth in parables, I will utter things that have been kept secret from the foundation of the world."[1] Things strange, yet common; incredible, yet known; most high, yet plain; infinitely profitable, but not esteemed.

Is it not a great thing that you should be heir of the world?[2] Is it not a great enriching truth—in which the fellowship of the mystery, which from the beginning of the world has been hid in God, lies concealed![3]

The thing has been from the creation of the world but has not been explained in such a way that the interior beauty should be understood. It is my design therefore in such a plain manner to unfold it that my friendship may appear in making you possessor of the whole world.

Advancing Gently

I will not by the noise of bloody wars and the dethroning of kings advance you to glory, but by the gentle ways of peace and love. As a deep friendship meditates and intends the deepest designs for the advancement of its objects, so does it show itself in choosing the sweetest and most delightful methods, whereby not to weary but please the person it desires to advance. Where love heals, its tenderness is expressed in balms and cordials. It hates corrosives and is rich in its administrations.

Even so, God designing to show his love in exalting you has chosen the ways of ease and repose by which you should ascend. And I after his similitude will lead you into paths plain and familiar, where all envy, rapine, bloodshed, complaint and malice shall be far removed, and nothing appear but contentment and thanksgiving. Yet will the end be so glorious that angels dare not hope for so great a one till they had seen it.

Communing with God

The fellowship of the mystery that has been hid in God since the creation is not only the contemplation of the work of his love in the redemption, though that is wonderful, but the end for which we are redeemed: a communion with him in all his glory.

For which cause St. Peter says, "The God of all grace has called us to his eternal glory by Jesus Christ."[4] His eternal glory by the method of his divine wisdom being made ours, and our fruition of it the end for which our Saviour suffered.

Seated in the Highest Happiness

True love as it intends the greatest gifts intends also the greatest benefits. It contents not itself in showing great things unless it can make them greatly useful. For love greatly delights in seeing its object continually seated in the highest happiness.

Unless therefore I could advance you higher by the uses of what I give, my love could not be satisfied in giving you the whole world. But because when you enjoy it you are advanced to the throne of God and may see his love, I rest well pleased in bestowing it.

It will make you to see your own greatness, the truth of the Scriptures, the amiableness of virtue, and the beauty of religion. It will enable you to contemn the world and to overflow with praises.

CHAPTER 2

THINK WELL

Two Worlds

To condemn the world and to enjoy the world are things contrary to each other. How then can we condemn the world which we are born to enjoy?

Truly there are two worlds. One was made by God, the other by men. That made by God was great and beautiful. Before the Fall it was Adam's joy and the temple of his glory. That made by men is a Babel of confusions: invented riches, pomps and vanities, brought in by sin.

"Give all," says Thomas à Kempis, "for all." Leave the one that you may enjoy the other.

Thinking Well

What is more easy and sweet than meditation? Yet in this has God commended his love, that by meditation it is enjoyed.

As nothing is more easy than to think, so nothing is more difficult than to think well. The easiness of thinking we received from God, the difficulty of thinking well proceeded from ourselves.

Yet in truth, it is far more easy to think well than ill, because good thoughts be sweet and delightful; evil thoughts are full of discontent and trouble. So that an evil habit and custom have made it difficult to think well, not nature. For by nature nothing is so difficult as to think amiss.

Imagining the World

Is it not easy to conceive the world in your mind? To think the heavens fair? The sun glorious? The earth fruitful? The air pleasant? The sea profitable? And the giver bountiful?

Yet these are the things which it is difficult to retain. For could we always be sensible of their use and value, we should be always delighted with their wealth and glory.

Enjoying the World

To think well is to serve God in the interior court: to have a mind composed of divine thoughts, and set in frame, to be like him within. To conceive aright and to enjoy the world is to conceive the Holy Ghost and to see his love, which is the mind of the Father.

And this more pleases him than many worlds, could we create as fair and great as this. For when we are once acquainted with the world, you will find the goodness and wisdom of God so manifest therein, that it was impossible another or better should be made. Which being made to be enjoyed, nothing can please or serve him more than the soul that enjoys it. For that soul accomplishes the end of his desire in creating it.

The Reason We were Created

Love is deeper than at first it can be thought. It never ceases but in endless things. It ever multiplies. Its benefits and its designs are always infinite.

Were you not holy, divine, and blessed in enjoying the world, I should not care so much to bestow it. But now in this you accomplish the end of your creation, and serve God best, and please him most, I rejoice in giving it.

For to enable you to please God is the highest service a man can do you. It is to make you pleasing to the king of heaven that you may be the darling of his bosom.

Prizing All Things

Can you be holy without accomplishing the end for which you are created? Can you be divine unless you be holy? Can you accomplish the end for which you were created unless you be righteous? Can you then be righteous unless you be just in rendering to things their due esteem?

All things were made to be yours, and you were made to prize them according to their value: which is your office and duty, the end for which you were created, and the means whereby you enjoy. The end for which you were created is that, by prizing all that God has done, you may enjoy yourself and him in blessedness.

God's Thoughts

To be holy is so zealously to desire, so vastly to esteem, and so earnestly to endeavour it, that we would not for millions of gold and silver decline, nor fail, nor mistake in a tittle. For then we please God when we are most like him.

We are like him when our minds are in frame. Our minds are in frame when our thoughts are like his. And our thoughts are then like his when we have such conceptions of all objects as God has, and prize all things according to their value.

For God prizes all things rightly, which is a key that opens into the very thoughts of his bosom. It seems arrogance to pretend to the knowledge of his secret thoughts. But how shall we have the mind of God unless we know his thoughts? Or how shall we be led by his divine spirit till we have his mind?

His thoughts are hidden, but he has revealed to us the hidden things of darkness. By his works and by his attributes we know his thoughts, and by thinking the same, are divine and blessed.

Prizing Things in their Proper Places

When things are ours in their proper places, nothing is needful but prizing to enjoy them. God therefore has made it infinitely easy to enjoy, by making everything ours, and us able so easily to prize them.

Everything is ours that serves us in its place. The sun serves us as much as is possible, and more than we could imagine. The clouds and stars minister unto us, the world surrounds us with beauty, the air refreshes us, the sea revives the earth and us. The earth itself is better than gold because it produces fruits and flowers.

And therefore in the beginning was it made manifest to be mine, because Adam alone was made to enjoy it. By making one, and not a multitude, God evidently showed one alone to be the end of the world and every one its enjoyer. For every one may enjoy it as much as he.

God Made the World for Every Individual

Such endless depths live in the divinity and in the wisdom of God, that as he makes one, so he makes every one the end of the world; and the supernumerary persons being enrichers of his inheritance.

Adam and the world are both mine. And the posterity of Adam enrich it infinitely.

Souls are God's jewels, everyone of which is worth many worlds. They are his riches because his image, and mine for that reason. So that I alone am the end of the world, angels and men being all mine. And if others are so, they are made to enjoy it for my further advancement.

God only being the giver and I the receiver. So that Seneca philosophized rightly when he said, *Deus me dedit solum toti Mundo, ét totum Mundum mihi soli*: "God gave me alone to all the world, and all the world to me alone."

Everything Points in the Same Direction

That all the world is yours, your very senses and the inclinations of your mind declare. The works of God manifest, his laws testify, and his word proves it. His attributes most sweetly make it evident. The powers of your soul confirm it.

So that in the midst of such rich demonstrations, you may infinitely delight in God as your Father, friend, and benefactor; in yourself as his heir, child, and bride; in the whole world as the gift and token of his love; neither can anything but ignorance destroy your joys. For if you know yourself, or God, or the world, you must of necessity enjoy it.

God Delights in Giving

To know God is life eternal. There must therefore some exceeding great thing be always attained in the knowledge of him.

To know God is to know goodness. It is to see the beauty of infinite love; to see it attended with almighty power and eternal wisdom; and using both those in the magnifying of its object. It is to see the king of heaven and earth take infinite delight in giving.

Whatever knowledge else you have of God, it is but superstition. Which Plutarch rightly defined to be an ignorant dread of his divine power without any joy in his goodness. He is not an object of terror, but delight.

To know him therefore, as he is, is to frame the most beautiful idea in all worlds. He delights in our happiness more than we, and is of all other the most lovely object. An infinite Lord, who having all riches, honors, and pleasures in his own hand, is infinitely willing to give them unto me. Which is the fairest idea that can be devised.

The Heavens Within the World

The world is not this little cottage of heaven and earth. Though this be fair, it is too small a gift. When God made the world he made the heavens, and the heavens of heavens, and the angels, and the celestial powers. These also are parts of the world; so are all those infinite and eternal treasures that are to abide forever after the Day of Judgment.

Neither are these some here and some there, but all everywhere, and at once to be enjoyed. The world is unknown till the value and glory of it is seen; till the beauty and the serviceableness of its parts is considered.

When you enter into it, it is an unlimited field of variety and beauty, where you may lose yourself in the multitude of wonders and delights. But it is a happy loss to lose oneself in admiration at one's own felicity and to find God in exchange for oneself. Which we then do when we see him in his gifts, and adore his glory.

God's Presence and Eternity Are Our Companions

You never know yourself till you know more than your body. The image of God was not seated in the features of your face, but in the lineaments of your soul. In the knowledge of your powers, inclinations, and principles, the knowledge of yourself chiefly consists. Which are so great that even to the most learned of men, their greatness is incredible; and so divine, that they are infinite in value.

Alas the world is but a little center in comparison of you. Suppose it millions of miles from the earth to the heavens, and millions of millions above the stars, both here and over the heads of our Antipodes. It is surrounded with infinite and eternal space. And like a gentleman's house to one that is traveling, it is a long time before you come unto it, you pass it in an instant, and leave it forever.

The omnipresence and eternity of God are your fellows and companions. And all that is in them ought to be made your familiar treasures. Your understanding comprehends the world like the dust of a balance, measures heaven with a span, and esteems a thousand years but as one day.[5] So that great, endless, eternal delights are only fit to be its enjoyments.

Loving God with All the Powers of Your Soul

The laws of God, which are the commentaries of his works, show them to be yours because they teach you to love God with all your soul and with all your might. Whom if you love with all the endless powers of your soul, you will love him in himself, in his attributes, in his counsels, in all his works, in all his ways; and in every kind of thing wherein he appears, you will prize him, you will honor him, you will delight in him, you will ever desire to be with him and to please him. For to love him includes all this.

You will feed with pleasure upon everything that is his. So that the world shall be a grand jewel of delight unto you: a very paradise and the gate of heaven. It is indeed the beautiful frontispiece of eternity; the temple of God and palace of his children.

The laws of God discover all that is therein to be created for your sake. For they command you to love all that is good, and when you see well, you enjoy what you love. They apply the endless powers of your soul to all their objects, and by ten thousand methods make everything to serve you.

They command you to love all angels and men. They command all angels and men to love you. When you love them, they are your treasures; when they love you, to your great advantage you are theirs; all things serve you for serving them whom you love, and of whom you are beloved.

The entrance of his words gives light to the simple.[6] You are magnified among angels and men; enriched by them, and happy in them.

CHAPTER 3
ENJOY THE WORLD LIKE NEVER BEFORE

Valuing Present Mercies

By the very right of your senses you enjoy the world. Is not the beauty of the hemisphere present to your eye? Does not the glory of the sun pay tribute to your sight? Is not the vision of the world an amiable thing? Do not the stars shed influences to perfect the air? Is not that a marvelous body to breath in? To visit the lungs, repair the spirits, revive the senses, cool the blood, fill the empty spaces between the earth and heavens; and yet give liberty to all objects?

Prize these first and you shall enjoy the residue: glory, dominion, power, wisdom; honor, angels, souls, kingdoms, ages. Be faithful in a little and you shall be master over much.[7]

If you be not faithful in esteeming these, who shall put into your hands the true treasures? If you be negligent in prizing these, you will be negligent in prizing all. For there is a disease in him who despises present mercies, which till it be cured, he can never be happy. He esteems nothing that he has, but is ever gaping after more, which when he has he despises in like manner. Insatiableness is good, but not ingratitude.

Man's Soul is Insatiable

It is of the nobility of man's soul that he is insatiable. For he has a benefactor so prone to give that he delights in us for asking.

Do not your inclinations tell you that the world is yours? Do you not covet all? Do you not long to have it, to enjoy it, to overcome it?

To what end do men gather riches, but to multiply more? Do they not, like Pyrrhus the King of Epire, add house to house and lands to lands that they may get it all? It is storied of that prince, that having conceived a purpose to invade Italy, he sent for Cineas, a philosopher and the King's friend, to whom he communicated his design and desired his counsel.

Cineas asked him to what purpose he invaded Italy?

He said, "To conquer it."

"And what will you do when you have conquered it?"

"Go into France," said the King, "and conquer that."

"And what will you do when you have conquered France?"

"Conquer Germany."

"And what then?" said the philosopher.

"Conquer Spain."

"I perceive," said Cineas, "you mean to conquer all the world. What will you do when you have conquered all?"

"Why then," said the King, "we will return and enjoy ourselves at quiet in our own land."

"So you may now," said the philosopher, "without all this ado."

Yet could he not divert him till he was ruined by the Romans.

Thus men get one hundred pound a year that they may get another, and having two covet eight, and there is no end of all their labor because the desire of their soul is insatiable. Like Alexander the Great they must have all, and when they have got it all, be quiet. And may they not do all this before they begin? Nay it would be well, if they could be quiet.

But if after all, they shall be like the stars that are seated on high but have no rest, what gain they more, but labor for their trouble? It was wittily feigned that that young man sat down and cried for more worlds to conquer.

So insatiable is man, that millions will not please him. They are no more than so many tennis balls in comparison of the greatness and highness of his soul.

God's Treasures are Free

The noble inclination whereby man thirsts after riches and dominion is his highest virtue, when rightly guided; and carries him as in a triumphant chariot to his sovereign happiness.

Men are made miserable only by abusing it. Taking a false way to satisfy it, they pursue the wind; nay, labor in the very fire, and after all reap but vanity.

Whereas, as God's love, which is the fountain of all, did cost us nothing, so were all other things prepared by it to satisfy our inclinations in the best of manners, freely, without any cost of ours.

Seeing therefore all satisfactions are near at hand, by going further we do but leave them; and wearying ourselves in a long way round about, like a blind man, forsake them. They are immediately near to the very gates of our senses. It becomes the bounty of God to prepare them freely: to make them glorious, and their enjoyment easy.

For because his love is free, so are his treasures. He therefore that will despise them because he has them is marvelously irrational; the way to possess them is to esteem them.

And the true way of reigning over them is to break the world all into parts, to examine them asunder, and, if we find them so excellent that better could not possibly be made and so made they could not be more ours, to rejoice in all with pleasure answerable to the merit of their goodness.

We being then kings over the whole world, when we restore the pieces to their proper places, being perfectly pleased with the whole composure. This will give you a thorough grounded contentment, far beyond what troublesome wars or conquests can acquire.

The Fruition of the World

Is it not a sweet thing to have all covetousness and ambition satisfied, suspicion and infidelity removed, courage and joy infused? Yet is all this in the fruition of the world attained. For thereby God is seen in all his wisdom, power, goodness, and glory.

Everything in the World is Yours

Your enjoyment of the world is never right till you so esteem it, that everything in it is more your treasure than a king's exchequer full of gold and silver. And that exchequer yours also in its place and service.

Can you take too much joy in your Father's works? He is himself in everything. Some things are little on the outside, and rough and common, but I remember the time when the dust of the streets were as pleasing as gold to my infant eyes, and now they are more precious to the eye of reason.

Spiritually Enjoying the Service of Things

The services of things and their excellencies are spiritual, being objects not of the eye but of the mind, and you more spiritual by how much more you esteem them.

Pigs eat acorns, but neither consider the sun that gave them life, nor the influences of the heavens by which they were nourished, nor the very root of the tree from whence they came. This being the work of angels, who in a wide and clear light see even the sea that gave them moisture, and feed upon that acorn spiritually while they know the ends for which it was created, and feast upon all these as upon a world of joys within it; while to ignorant swine that eat the shell, it is an empty husk of no taste nor delightful savour.

Seeing the Love of God in Everything

You never enjoy the world aright till you see how a sand exhibits the wisdom and power of God, and prize in everything the service which they do you, by manifesting his glory and goodness to your soul far more than the visible beauty on their surface or the material services they can do your body.

Wine by its moisture quenches my thirst, whether I consider it or not; but to see it flowing from his love who gave it unto man, quenches the thirst even of the holy angels. To consider it is to drink it spiritually. To rejoice in its diffusion is to be of a public mind. And to take pleasure in all the benefits it does to all is heavenly, for so they do in heaven.

To do so is to be divine and good, and to imitate our infinite and eternal Father.

Waking Up in Heaven

Your enjoyment of the world is never right till every morning you awake in heaven, see yourself in your Father's palace, and look upon the skies, the earth, and the air as celestial joys, having such a reverend esteem of all, as if you were among the angels. The bride of a monarch in her husband's chamber has no such causes of delight as you.

Till the Sea Flows in Your Veins

You never enjoy the world aright till the sea itself flows in your veins, till you are clothed with the heavens and crowned with the stars and perceive yourself to be the sole heir of the whole world, and more than so, because men are in it who are every one sole heirs as well as you.

Till you can sing and rejoice and delight in God, as misers do in gold, and kings in sceptres, you never enjoy the world.

Delighting in God's Goodness to All

Till your spirit fills the whole world, and the stars are your jewels;

till you are as familiar with the ways of God in all ages as with your walk and table;

till you are intimately acquainted with that shady nothing out of which the world was made;

till you love men so as to desire their happiness with a thirst equal to the zeal of your own;

till you delight in God for being good to all;

you never enjoy the world.

Till you more feel it than your private estate, and are more present in the hemisphere, considering the glories and the beauties there, than in your own house;

till you remember how lately you were made and how wonderful it was when you came into it;

and more rejoice in the palace of your glory than if it had been made but today morning.

A Mirror of Infinite Beauty

Yet further, you never enjoy the world aright till you so love the beauty of enjoying it, that you are covetous and earnest to persuade others to enjoy it. And so perfectly hate the abominable corruption of men in despising it, that you had rather suffer the flames of hell than willingly be guilty of their error.

There is so much blindness and ingratitude and damned folly in it. The world is a mirror of infinite beauty, yet no man sees it. It is a temple of majesty, yet no man regards it. It is a region of light and peace, did not men disquiet it. It is the paradise of God. It is more to man since he is fallen than it was before.

It is the place of angels and the gate of heaven. When Jacob waked out of his dream, he said, "God is here, and I knew it not. How dreadful is this place! This is none other than the house of God, and the gate of heaven."[8]

Ingratitude

Can any ingratitude be more damned than that which is fed by benefits? Or folly greater than that which bereaves us of infinite treasures? They despise them merely because they have them, and invent ways to make themselves miserable in the presence of riches.

They study a thousand newfangled treasures, which God never made, and then grieve and repine that they be not happy. They dote on their own works and neglect God's, which are full of majesty, riches, and wisdom. And having fled away from them because they are solid, divine, and true, greedily pursuing tinselled vanities, they walk on in darkness and will not understand.[9] They do the works of darkness, and delight in the riches of the Prince of Darkness, and follow them till they come into eternal darkness.

According to that of the Psalmist, "All the foundations of the earth are out of course."[10]

Hideous Riches of Darkness

The riches of darkness are those which men have made during their ignorance of God Almighty's treasures, that lead us from the love of all to labor and contention, discontentment and vanity.

The works of darkness are repining, envy, malice, covetousness, fraud, oppression, discontent, and violence. All which proceed from the corruption of men and their mistake in the choice of riches; for having refused those which God made, and taken to themselves treasures of their own, they invented scarce and rare, insufficient, hard-to-be-gotten, little, movable, and useless treasures. Yet as violently pursued them as if they were the most necessary and excellent things in the whole world.

And though they are all mad, yet having made a combination they seem wise; and it is a hard matter to persuade them either to truth or reason. There seems to be no way but theirs, whereas God knows they are as far out of the way of happiness as the East is from the West.

For by this means, they have let in broils and dissatisfactions into the world and are ready to eat and devour one another, particular and feeble interests, false proprieties, insatiable longings, fraud, emulation, murmuring and dissension being everywhere seen, theft and pride and danger and cousenage, envy and contention drowning the peace and beauty of nature, as waters cover the sea. Oh how they are ready to sink always under the burden and cumber of devised wants! Verily, the prospect of their ugly errors is able to turn one's stomach, they are so hideous and deformed.

Neglecting the Heavens & the Stars

Would one think it possible for a man to delight in gauderies like a butterfly and neglect the heavens? Did we not daily see it, it would be incredible. They rejoice in a piece of gold more than in the sun; and get a few little glittering stones and call them jewels. And admire them because they be resplendent like the stars, and transparent like the air, and pellucid like the sea.

But the stars themselves which are ten thousand times more useful, great, and glorious they disregard. Nor shall the air itself be counted anything, though it be worth all the pearls and diamonds in ten thousand worlds. A work of God so divine by reason of its precious and pure transparency, that all worlds would be worth nothing without such a treasure.

Our Inheritance

The riches of the light are the works of God which are the portion and inheritance of his sons, to be seen and enjoyed in heaven and earth, the sea, and all that is therein: the light and the day, great and fathomless in use and excellency, true, necessary, freely given, proceeding wholly from his infinite love.

As worthy as they are easy to be enjoyed; obliging us to love him and to delight in him, filling us with gratitude, and making us to overflow with praises and thanksgivings. The works of contentment and pleasure are of the day.

So are the works which flow from the understanding of our mutual serviceableness to each other, arising from the sufficiency and excellency of our treasures: contentment, joy, peace, unity, charity, etc., whereby we are all knit together and delight in each others' happiness. For while everyone is heir of all the world, and all the rest his superadded treasures, all the world serves him in himself, and he delights in them as his superadded treasures.

A Paradise & A Prison

The common error which makes it difficult to believe all the world to be wholly ours, is to be shunned as a rock of shipwreck or a dangerous quicksands. For the poison which they drank has infatuated their fancies, and now they know not—neither will they understand—they walk on in darkness. All the foundations of the world are out of course.[11]

It is safety not to be with them, and a great part of happiness to be freed from their seducing and enslaving errors. That while others live in a Golgotha or prison we should be in Eden, is a very great mystery. And a mercy it is that we should be rejoicing in the temple of heaven while they are toiling and lamenting in hell—for the world is both a paradise and a prison to different persons.

Open Eyes

The brightness and magnificence of this world, which by reason of its height and greatness is hidden from men, is divine and wonderful. It adds much to the glory of the temple in which we live. Yet it is the cause why men understand it not. They think it too great and wide to be enjoyed.

But since it is all filled with the majesty of his glory who dwells in it, and the goodness of the Lord fills the world, and his wisdom shines everywhere within it and about it, and it abounds in an infinite variety of services; we need nothing but open eyes to be ravished like the cherubims. Well may we bear the greatness of the world, since it is our storehouse and treasury. That our treasures should be endless is a happy inconvenience—that all regions should be full of joys and the room infinite wherein they are seated.

In the Best of Manners

You never enjoy the world aright till you see all things in it so perfectly yours that you cannot desire them any other way, and till you are convinced that all things serve you best in their proper places.

For can you desire to enjoy anything a better way than in God's image? It is the height of God's perfection that hides his bounty, and the lowness of your base and sneaking spirit that makes you ignorant of his perfection. (Everyone has in him a spirit with which he may be angry.)

God's bounty is so perfect that he gives all things in the best of manners—making those to whom he gives so noble, divine, and glorious, that they shall enjoy in his similitude. Nor can they be fit to enjoy in his presence or in communion with him, that are not truly divine and noble. So that you must have glorious principles implanted in your nature: a clear eye able to see afar off, a great and generous heart apt to enjoy at any distance, a good and liberal soul prone to delight in the felicity of all, and an infinite delight to be their treasure. Neither is it any prejudice to you that this is required, for there is great difference between a worm and a cherubim. And it more concerns you to be an illustrious creature than to have the possession of the whole world.

Every Soul a Treasure

Your enjoyment is never right till you esteem every soul so great a treasure as our Savior does, and that the laws of God are sweeter than the honey and honeycomb because they command you to love them all in such perfect manner.[12]

For how are they God's treasures? Are they not the riches of his love? Is it not his goodness that makes him glorious to them? Can the sun or stars serve him any other way than by serving them? And how will you be the Son of God but by having a great soul like unto your Father's?

The laws of God command you to live in his image, and to do so is to live in heaven. God commands you to love all like him because he would have you to be his Son, all them to be your riches, you to be glorious before them, and all the creatures in serving them to be your treasures, while you are his delight, like him in beauty, and the darling of his bosom.

Free from Trivial Things

Socrates was wont to say, "They are most happy and nearest the gods that needed nothing." And coming once up into the Exchange at Athens, where they that traded asked him, "What will you buy; what do you lack?" After he had gravely walked up into the middle, spreading forth his hands and turning about, "Good Gods," said he, "who would have thought there were so many things in the world which I do not want!" And so left the place under the reproach of nature.

He was wont to say that happiness consisted not in having many, but in needing the fewest things. For the gods needed nothing at all, and they were most like them that least needed.

We needed heaven and earth, our senses, such souls and such bodies with infinite riches in the image of God to be enjoyed; which God of his mercy having freely prepared, they are most happy that so live in the enjoyment of those, as to need no accidental trivial things, no splendors, pomps, and vanities.

Socrates, perhaps being an heathen, knew not that all things proceeded from God to man, and by man returned to God; but we that know it must need all things as God does that we may receive them with joy and live in his image.

CHAPTER 4

UNDERSTAND WHAT YOU WANT

Wants & Supplies in Heaven

As pictures are made curious by lights and shades, which without shades could not be, so is felicity composed of wants and supplies, without which mixture there could be no felicity. Were there no needs, wants would be wanting themselves, and supplies superfluous, want being the parent of celestial treasure. It is very strange: want itself is a treasure in heaven and so great a one that without it there could be no treasure.

God did infinitely for us when he made us to want like gods that like gods we might be satisfied. The heathen deities wanted nothing and were therefore unhappy, for they had no being. But the Lord God of Israel, the living and true God, was from all eternity and from all eternity wanted like a god. He wanted the communication of his divine essence and persons to enjoy it. He wanted worlds, he wanted spectators, he wanted joys, he wanted treasures. He wanted, yet he wanted not, for he had them.

What God Wants

This is very strange that God should want. For in him is the fullness of all blessedness: he overflows eternally. His wants are as glorious as infinite: perfective needs that are in his nature, and ever blessed because always satisfied. He is from eternity full of want or else he would not be full of treasure.

Infinite want is the very ground and cause of infinite treasure. It is incredible, yet very plain. Want is the fountain of all his fullness.

Want in God is treasure to us. For had there been no need he would not have created the world, nor made us, nor manifested his wisdom, nor exercised his power, nor beautified eternity, nor prepared the joys of heaven. But he wanted angels and men, images, companions. And these he had from all eternity.

Learning Your Wants

Infinite wants satisfied produce infinite joys, and in the possession of those joys are infinite joys themselves. The desire satisfied is a tree of life. Desire imports something absent and a need of what is absent.

God was never without this tree of life. He did desire infinitely, yet he was never without the fruits of this tree, which are the joys it produced.

I must lead you out of this, into another world to learn your wants. For till you find them you will never be happy, wants themselves being sacred occasions and means of felicity.

God's Treasures

You must want like a god that you may be satisfied like God. Were you not made in his image?

He is infinitely glorious because all his wants and supplies are at the same time in his nature from eternity. He had, and from eternity he was without, all his treasures. From eternity he needed them and from eternity he enjoyed them. For all eternity is at once, in him, both the empty durations before the world was made and the full ones after.

His wants are as lively as his enjoyments and always present with him. For his life is perfect and he feels them both. His wants put a lustre upon his enjoyments and make them infinite. His enjoyments being infinite crown his wants and make them beautiful even to God himself. His wants and enjoyments being always present are delightful to each other, stable, immutable, perfective of each other, and delightful to him. Who being eternal and immutable, enjoys all his wants and treasures together.

His wants never afflict him; his treasures never disturb him. His wants always delight him; his treasures never cloy him. The sense of his wants is always as great as if his treasures were removed, and as lively upon him.

The sense of his wants, as it enlarges his life, so it infuses a value and continual sweetness into the treasures he enjoys.

Being Sensible of Your Wants

This is a lesson long enough, which you may be all your life in learning and to all eternity in practicing. Be sensible of your wants that you may be sensible of your treasures. He is most like God that is sensible of everything.

Did you not from all eternity want someone to give you a being? Did you not want one to give you a glorious being? Did you not from all eternity want someone to give you infinite treasures? And someone to give you spectators, companions, enjoyers? Did you not want a Deity to make them sweet and honorable by his infinite wisdom?

What you wanted from all eternity, be sensible of to all eternity. Let your wants be present from everlasting. Is not this a strange life to which I call you? Wherein you are to be present with things that were before the world was made?

And at once present, even like God, with infinite wants and infinite treasures. Be present with your want of a Deity and you shall be present with the Deity. You shall adore and admire him, enjoy and prize him; believe in him and delight in him, see him to be the fountain of all your joys, and the head of all your treasures.

Prize What You Need and Have

It was his wisdom made you need the sun. It was his goodness made you need the sea. Be sensible of what you need or enjoy neither. Consider how much you need them, for thence they derive their value.

Suppose the sun were extinguished or the sea were dry. There would be no light, no beauty, no warmth, no fruits, no flowers, no pleasant gardens, feasts, or prospects, no wine, no oil, no bread, no life, no motion. Would you not give all the gold and silver in the Indies for such a treasure?

Prize it now you have it, at that rate, and you shall be a grateful creature. Nay, you shall be a divine and heavenly person. For they in heaven do prize blessings when they have them. They in earth, when they have them, prize them not. They in hell prize them when they have them not.

Heaven & Hell

To have blessings and to prize them is to be in heaven; to have them and not to prize them is to be in hell, I would say, upon earth; to prize them and not to have them is to be in hell. Which is evident by the effects.

To prize blessings while we have them is to enjoy them and the effect thereof is contentation, pleasure, thanksgiving, happiness. To prize them when they are gone: envy, covetousness, repining, ingratitude, vexation, misery.

But it was no great mistake to say that to have blessings and not to prize them is to be in hell. For it makes them ineffectual, as if they were absent. Yea, in some respect it is worse than to be in hell. It is more vicious and more irrational.

Seeing & Enjoying What We Want

They that would not upon earth see their wants from all eternity, shall in hell see their treasures to all eternity. Wants here may be seen and enjoyed, enjoyments there shall be seen, but wanted. Wants here may be blessings; there they shall be curses. Here they may be fountains of pleasure and thanksgiving; there they will be fountains of woe and blasphemy.

No misery is greater than that of wanting in the midst of enjoyments, of seeing and desiring yet never possessing. Of beholding others happy, being seen by them ourselves in misery.

They that look into hell here may avoid it hereafter. They that refuse to look into hell upon earth, to consider the manner of the torments of the damned, shall be forced in hell to see all the earth and remember the felicities which they had when they were living. Hell itself is a part of God's kingdom, to wit his prison. It is fitly mentioned in the enjoyment of the world. And is itself by the happy enjoyed as a part of the world.

Ingratitude & Envy

The misery of them who have and prize not, differs from others who prize and have not. The one are more odious and less sensible, more foolish and more vicious; the senses of the other are exceeding keen and quick upon them, yet are they not so foolish and odious as the former. The one would be happy and cannot; the other may be happy and will not. The one are more vicious; the other more miserable.

But how can that be? Is not he most miserable that is most vicious? Yes, that is true. But they that prize not what they have are dead; their senses are laid asleep, and when they come to hell they wake, and then they begin to feel their misery. He that is most odious is most miserable, and he that is most perverse is most odious.

Living in Heaven

They are deep instructions that are taken out of hell, and heavenly documents that are taken from above.

Upon earth we learn nothing but vanity. Where people dream and loiter and wander and disquiet themselves in vain to make a vain show, but do not profit because they prize not the blessings they have received.[13]

To prize what we have is a deep and heavenly instruction. It will make us righteous and serious, wise and holy, divine and blessed. It will make us escape hell and attain heaven, for it will make us careful to please him from whom we have received all, that we may live in heaven.

Our Wants Bond Us to God

Wants are the bands and cements between God and us. Had we not wanted, we could never have been obliged. Whereas now we are infinitely obliged because we want infinitely.

From eternity it was requisite that we should want. We could never else have enjoyed anything. Our own wants are treasures. And if want be a treasure, sure everything is so.

Wants are the ligatures between God and us, the sinews that convey senses from him into us, whereby we live in him and feel his enjoyments. For had we not been obliged by having our wants satisfied, we should not have been created to love him. And had we not been created to love him, we could never have enjoyed his eternal blessedness.

CHAPTER 5
CLAIM THE WORLD AS YOUR INHERITANCE

How You Inherit Everything

Love has a marvelous property of feeling in another. It can enjoy in another as well as enjoy him. Love is an infinite treasure to its object, and its object is so to it.

God is love, and you are his object. You are created to be his love, and he is yours. He is happy in you when you are happy, as parents in their children. He is afflicted in all your afflictions.[14] And whosoever touches you touches the apple of his eye.

Will not you be happy in all his enjoyments? He feels in you; will not you feel in him? He has obliged you to love him. And if you love him, you must of necessity be heir of the world, for you are happy in him. All his praises are your joys, all his enjoyments are your treasures, all his pleasures are your enjoyments.

In God you are crowned, in God you are concerned. In him you feel, in him you live and move and have your being, in him you are blessed.[15] Whatsoever therefore serves him, serves you and in him you inherit all things.

As Rich as God

O the nobility of divine friendship!

Are not all his treasures yours, and yours his? Is not your very soul and body his? Is not his life and felicity yours? Is not his desire yours?

Is not his will yours? And if his will be yours, the accomplishment of it is yours, and the end of all is your perfection. You are infinitely rich as he is, being pleased in everything as he is. And if his will be yours, yours is his. For you will what he wills, which is to be truly wise and good and holy. And when you delight in the same reasons that moved him to will, you will know it. He willed the creation not only that he might appear but be, wherein is seated the mystery of the eternal generation of his Son. Do you will it as he did, and you shall be glorious as he.

He willed the happiness of men and angels not only that he might appear, but be good and wise and glorious. And he willed it with such infinite desire, that he is infinitely good: infinitely good in himself and infinitely blessed in them. Do you will the happiness of men and angels as he did, and you shall be good and infinitely blessed as he is. All their happiness shall be your happiness as it is his.

He willed the glory of all ages, and the government and welfare of all kingdoms, and the felicity also of the highest cherubims. Do you extend your will like him and you shall be great as he is and concerned and happy in all these. He willed the redemption of mankind, and therefore is his Son, Jesus Christ, an infinite treasure. Unless you will it too, he will be no treasure to you.

Verily you ought to will these things so ardently that God himself should be therefore your joy because he willed them. Your will ought to be united to his in all places of his dominion.[16] Were you not born to have communion with him? And that cannot be without this heavenly union. Which, when it is what it ought, is divine and infinite. You are God's joy for willing what he wills.

He loves to see you good and blessed. And will not you love to see him good? Verily, if ever you would enjoy God, you must enjoy his goodness: all his goodness to all his hosts in heaven and earth. And when you do so, you are the universal heir of God and all things. God is yours and the whole world. You are his and you are all, or in all, and with all.

Having Everything

He that is in all and with all, can never be desolate. All the joys and all the treasures, all the counsels and all the perfections, all the angels and all the saints of God are with him. All the kingdoms of the world, and the glory of them, are continually in his eye. The patriarchs, prophets, and apostles are always before him. The councils and the fathers, the bishops and the doctors, minister unto him. All temples are open before him, the melody of all choirs revives him, the learning of all universities employs him, the riches of all palaces delight him, the joys of Eden ravish him, the revelations of St. John transport him, the creation and the day of judgment please him, the hosannas of the church militant and the hallelujahs of the saints triumphant fill him, the splendor of all coronations entertain him, the joys of heaven surround him, and our Saviour's cross, like the center of eternity, is in him; it takes up his thoughts, and exercises all the powers of his soul, with wonder, admiration, joy, and thanksgiving.

The omnipotence of God is his house, and eternity his habitation.

Being Present Throughout Eternity

The contemplation of eternity makes the soul immortal. Whose glory it is, that it can see before and after its existence into endless spaces. Its sight is its presence. And therefore in the presence of the understanding endless, because it's sight is so. O what glorious creatures should we be could we be present in spirit with all eternity! How wise would we esteem this presence of the understanding to be more real than that of our bodies!

When my soul is in Eden with our first parents, I myself am there in a blessed manner. When I walk with Enoch and see his translation, I am transported with him. The present age is too little to contain it. I can visit Noah in his ark and swim upon the waters of the deluge. I can see Moses with his rod and the children of Israel passing through the sea. I can enter into Aaron's tabernacle and admire the mysteries of the holy place. I can travel over the land of Canaan and see it overflowing with milk and honey.

I can visit Solomon in his glory, and go into his temple, and view the sitting of his servants, and admire the magnificence and glory of his kingdom.

No creature but one like unto the holy angels can see into all ages. Sure this power was not given in vain, but for some wonderful purpose, worthy of itself to enjoy and fathom. Would men consider what God has done, they would be ravished in spirit with the glory of his doings. For heaven and earth are full of the majesty of his glory. And how happy would men be could they see and enjoy it!

II.
MY TALKS WITH JESUS

CHAPTER 6

THE CROSS OF CHRIST IS THE GATE OF HEAVEN: AN INTRODUCTION TO MY PRAYERS

But above all these our Saviour's cross is the throne of delights—that center of eternity, that tree of life in the midst of the paradise of God!

Journeys of the Soul

There are we entertained with the wonder of all ages. There we enter into the heart of the universe. There we behold the admiration of angels. There we find the price and elixir of our joys.

As on every side of the earth all heavy things tend to the center; so all nations ought on every side to flow in unto it. It is not by going with the feet, but by journeys of the soul, that we travel thither. By withdrawing our thoughts from wandering in the streets of this world to the contemplation and serious meditation of his blood sufferings.

Where the carcase is thither will the eagles be gathered together.[17] Our eyes must be towards it, our hearts set upon it, our affections drawn, and our thoughts and minds united to it.

"When I am lifted up", says the Son of Man, "I will draw all men unto me."[18] As fishes are drawn out of the water, as Jeremiah was drawn out of the dungeon,[19] as St. Peter's sheet was drawn up into heaven;[20] so shall we be drawn by that sight from ignorance and sin and earthly vanities, idle sports, companions, feast and pleasures, to the joyful contemplation of that eternal object.

But by what cords? The cords of a man and the cords of love.[21]

What Attracts Us?

As eagles are drawn by the scent of a carcase, children are drawn together by the sight of a lion. As people flock to a coronation and as a man is drawn to his beloved object, so ought we.

As the sick are drawn by the credit of a physician, as the poor drawn by the liberality of a king, as the devout drawn by the fame of the holy, and as the curious drawn by the noise of a miracle, so ought we.

As the stones were drawn to the building of Thebes by the melody of Amphion, as the hungry are drawn with the desire of a feast, and the pitiful drawn to a woeful spectacle, so ought we.

What visible chains or cords draw these? What invisible links allure? They follow all or flock together of their own accord. And shall not we much more!

Who would not be drawn to the gate of heaven were it open to receive him? Yet nothing compels him, but that which forces the angels, commodity and desire. For those are things which the angels desire to look into. And of men it is written, "They shall look on him whom they have pierced."[22] Verily the Israelites did not more clearly see the brazen serpent upon the pole in the wilderness than we may our Saviour upon the cross. The serpent was seen with their eyes; the slayer of the serpent is seen with our souls. They had less need to see the one than we to see the other.

The Gate of Heaven

The cross is the abyss of wonders, the center of desires, the school of virtues, the house of wisdom, the throne of love, the theatre of joys, and the place of sorrows. It is the root of happiness and the gate of heaven.

The Cross is the Center of Eternity

Of all the things in heaven and earth it is the most peculiar. It is the most exalted of all objects. It is an ensign lifted up for all nations, to it shall the Gentiles seek, his rest shall be glorious. The dispersed of Judah shall be gathered together to it from the four corners of the earth.[23]

If love be the weight of the soul and its object the center, all eyes and hearts may convert and turn unto this object—cleave unto this center and by it enter into rest.

There we might see all nations assembled with their eyes and hearts upon it.

There we may see God's goodness, wisdom, and power, yea his mercy and anger displayed.

There we may see man's sin and infinite value. His hope and fear, his misery and happiness.

There we might see the rock of ages and the joys of heaven.[24]

There we may see a man loving all the world, and a God dying for mankind.

There we may see all types and ceremonies, figures and prophecies. And all kingdoms adoring a malefactor: an innocent malefactor, yet the greatest in the world.

There we may see the most distant things in eternity united; all mysteries at once couched together and explained.

The only reason why this glorious object is so publicly admired by churches and kingdoms and so little thought of by particular men is because it is truly the most glorious. It is the rock of comforts and the fountain of joys. It is the only supreme and sovereign spectacle in all worlds. It is a well of life beneath, in which we may see the face of heaven above; and the only mirror wherein all things appear in their proper colors: that is, sprinkled in the blood of our Lord and Saviour.

A Flame that Illuminates the World

The cross of Christ is the Jacob's ladder by which we ascend into the highest heavens. There we see joyful patriarchs, expecting saints, prophets ministering, apostles publishing and doctors teaching, all nations concentering and angels praising.[25]

That cross is a tree set on fire with invisible flame that illuminates all the world. The flame is love: the love in his bosom who died on it. In the light of which we see how to possess all the things in heaven and earth after his similitude.

For he that suffered on it was the Son of God as you are, though he seemed only a mortal man. He had acquaintance and relations as you have, but he was a lover of men and angels. Was he not the Son of God and heir of the whole world? To this poor, bleeding, naked man did all the corn and wine and oil and gold and silver in the world minister in an invisible manner even as he was exposed lying and dying upon the cross.

Imitating Jesus

Here you learn all patience, meekness, self-denial, courage, prudence, zeal, love, charity, contempt of the world, penitence, contrition, modesty, fidelity, constancy, perseverance, contentation, holiness, and thanksgiving; with whatsoever else is requisite for a man, a Christian, or a king.

This man bleeding here was tutor to King Charles the Martyr, and great master to St. Paul, the convert who learned of him activity, and zeal unto all nations. Well therefore may we take up with this prospect and from hence behold all the things in heaven and earth. Here we learn to imitate Jesus in his love unto all.

CHAPTER 7
PRAYERS THANKING JESUS FOR ALL THE TREASURES HE HAS GIVEN US IN THE WORLD

What Return Can I Make?

Lord Jesus, what love shall I render unto you for your love unto me! Your eternal love! Oh what fervor, what ardor, what humiliation, what reverence, what joy, what adoration, what zeal, what thanksgiving! You who are perfect in beauty, you who are the king of eternal glory, you who reign in the highest heavens came down from heaven to die for me! And shall not I live unto you?

O my joy! O my sovereign friend! O my life and my all! I beseech you let those trickling drops of blood that ran down your flesh drop upon me. O let your love enflame me. Which is so deep and infinite that you did suffer the wrath of God for me, and purchase all nations and kingdoms to be my treasures.

O you who redeemed me from hell, and when you had overcome the sharpness of death opened the kingdom of heaven to all believers; what shall I do unto you? What shall I do for you, O you preserver of men? Live, love, and admire; and learn to become such unto you as you unto me.

O glorious soul, whose comprehensive understanding at once contains all kingdoms and ages! O glorious mind! Whose love extends to all creatures! O miraculous and eternal Godhead, now suffering on the cross for me. As Abraham saw your day and was glad, so did you see me and this day from all eternity, and seeing me was gracious and compassionate towards me.[26] (All transient things are permanent in God.) You set me before your face forever. O let me this day see you and be united to you in your holy sufferings. Let me learn, O God, such lessons from you as may make me wise and blessed as an angel of God!

Treasures of Your Goodness

Why, Lord Jesus, do you love men? Why are they all your treasures? What wonder is this, that you should so esteem them as to die for them?

Show me the reasons of your love that I may love them too.

O goodness ineffable! They are the treasures of your goodness—who so infinitely love them that you gave yourself for them. Your goodness delighted to be communicated to them whom you have saved.

O you who are more glorious in goodness, make me abundant in this goodness like unto you. That I may as deeply pity others' misery, and as ardently thirst for their happiness as you do.

Let the same mind be in me that is in Jesus Christ.[27] For he that is not led by the spirit of Christ is none of his.[28] Holy Jesus, I admire your love unto me also. O that I could see it through all those wounds! O that I could feel it in all those stripes! O that I could hear it in all those groans! O that I could taste it beneath the gall and vinegar! O that I could smell the savour of your sweet ointments even in this Golgotha, or place of a skull.[29]

I pray you teach me first your love unto me, and then unto mankind! But in your love unto mankind I am beloved.

You Created the World for Me

These wounds are in themselves orifices too small to let in my sight to the vast comprehensions of your eternal love. Those wounds engraven in your hands but shady impressions unless I see the glory of your soul, in which the fullness of the Godhead dwells bodily.[30] These bloody characters are too dim to let me read it in its luster and perfection, till I see your person and know your ways! O you that hangs upon this cross before mine eyes, whose face is bleeding and covered over with tears and filth and blows!

Angels adore the glory of your Godhead in the highest heavens. Who in every thought and in every work did glorious things for me from everlasting. What could I, O my Lord, desire more than such a world! Such heavens and such an earth! Such beasts and fowls and fishes made for me.

All these do homage unto me, and I have dominion over them from the beginning![31] The heavens and the earth minister unto me as if no man were greater, but I alone. I willingly acknowledge it to be your gift—your bounty unto me!

How many thousand ways do men also minister unto me! O what riches have you prepared out of nothing for me! All creatures labor for my sake, and I am made to enjoy all your creatures.

O what praises shall I return unto you, the wisdom of the Father and the brightness of the glory of his eternal goodness! Who did make all for me before you did redeem me.

The Palace You Made for Me

Had I been alive in Adam's stead, how should I have admired the glories of the world! What a confluence of thoughts and wonders and joys and thanksgivings would have replenished me in the sight of so magnificent a theatre, so bright a dwelling place; so great a temple, so stately a house replenished with all kind of treasure, raised out of nothing and created for me and for me alone.

Shall I now despise them?

When I consider the heavens which you have made, the moon and stars, which are the works of your fingers, what is man that you art mindful of him, or the son of man that you visit him! You have made him a little lower than the angels and crowned him with glory and honor.[32] O what love must that needs be, that prepared such a palace! Attended with what power! With what wisdom illuminated! Abounding with what zeal! And how glorious must the king be, that could out of nothing erect such a curious, so great, and so beautiful a fabric! It was glorious while new, and is as new as it was glorious.

The Treasures of My Body

But this is small.

What, O my Lord, could I desire to be which you have not made me! If you have expressed your love in furnishing the house, how gloriously does it shine in the possessor! My limbs and members when rightly prized are comparable to the fine gold, but that they exceed it. The topaz of Ethiopia and the gold of Ophir are not to be compared to them. What diamonds are equal to my eyes; what labyrinths to my ears; what gates of ivory or ruby leaves to the double portal of my lips and teeth? Is not sight a jewel? Is not hearing a treasure? Is not speech a glory?

O my Lord, pardon my ingratitude and pity my dullness who am not sensible of these gifts. The freedom of your bounty has deceived me. These things were too near to be considered. You presented me with your blessings, and I was not aware.

But now I give thanks and adore and praise you for your inestimable favors. I believe you love me, because you have endued me with those sacred and living treasures. Holy Father, henceforth I more desire to esteem them than palaces of gold! Yea, though they were given me by kings, I confess unto you that I am richer in them. O what joy, what delight and jubilee should there always be, would men prize the gifts of God according to their value!

Created in God's Image

But what creature could I desire to be which I am not made? There are angels and cherubim. I rejoice, O Lord, in their happiness, and that I am what I am by your grace and favor.

Suppose, O my soul, there were no creature made at all, and that God making you alone offered to make you what you would. What could you desire, or what would you wish or crave to be? Since God is the most glorious of all beings, and the most blessed, could you wish any more than to be his image?

O my soul, he has made you his image. Sing, O you angels, and laud his name, you cherubims. Let all the kingdoms of the earth be glad, and let all the host of heaven rejoice for he has made his image, the likeness of himself, his own similitude. What creature, what being, what thing more glorious could there be!

God from all eternity was infinitely blessed, and desired to make one infinitely blessed. He was infinite love, and being lovely in being so, would prepare for himself a most lovely object. Having studied from all eternity, he saw none more lovely than the image of his love, his own similitude.

O dignity unmeasurable! O exaltation passing knowledge! O joy unspeakable! Triumph, O my soul, and rejoice forever! I see that I am infinitely beloved. For infinite love has expressed and pleased itself in creating an infinite object. God is love and my soul is lovely! God is loving, and his image amiable.

O my soul, these are the foundations of an eternal friendship between God and you. He is infinitely prone to love and you are like him. He is infinitely lovely and you are like him. What can more agree than that which is infinitely lovely and that which is infinitely prone to love! Where both are so lovely, and so prone to love, joys and affections will be excited between them! What infinite treasures will they be to each other!

O my God, you have glorified yourself and your creature infinitely, in making your image! That is fitted for the throne of God! It is meet to be your companion! It is so sublime and wonderful and amiable, that all angels and men were created to admire it, as it was created to admire you, and to live in communion with you forever.

CHAPTER 8

PRAYERS THANKING JESUS FOR HIS LOVE & FOR HIMSELF

Millions of Friends

Being made alone, O my soul, you would be in your body like God in the world: an invisible mystery too great to be comprehended by all creatures. You would have all the goodness of God towards you to enjoy, in that your creation. Whatever is in him would be your treasure.

But had he determined to create no more, there had been no witnesses of your glory, no spectators of your communion with God, no other treasures beside God and you. One would think those were sufficient. But infinite goodness loves to abound and to overflow infinitely with infinite treasures. Love loves to do somewhat for its object more than to create it.

It is always more stately being surrounded with power, and more delightful being inaccessible in a multitude of treasures, and more honorable in the midst of admirers, and more glorious when it reigns over many attendants. Love therefore has prepared all these for itself and its object. And because it is always more great by how much the greater they are that minister unto it, it makes its attendants the most glorious that can be, and infinitely delights in giving them all with all its treasures to its beloved.

Had God created you alone he had not been so good as he is. He is good to innumerable millions now whom he creates besides. And he glorifies his eternal wisdom in making his goodness unto all them wholly yours, and wholly infinite unto each of them, yet wholly and solely yours in all. Friendship will manifest itself in doing all it can for its beloved.

Since therefore God will make some other creatures, what kind of creatures does your soul desire? Wish wisely you will receive a grant. Since love is so sweet, and you are by God's love so infinitely exalted, what can you desire but creatures like unto your creator? Behold therefore angels and men produced by his goodness and made to delight you.

God In Every Soul

O adorable Trinity! What have you done for me? You have made me the end of all things, and all the end of me. I in all and all in me. In every soul whom you have created, you have given me the similitude of yourself to enjoy!

Could my desires have aspired unto such treasures? Could my wisdom have devised such sublime enjoyments? Oh! You have done more for us than we could ask or think. I praise and admire and rejoice in you, who are infinitely infinite in all your doings.

Heavenly Mansions Around Us

But what laws, O my soul, would you desire, by which the lives of those creatures should be guided towards you? A friend commands all in his jurisdiction to love his friend, and therein supremely manifests his love.

God himself exalts you and causes you to reign in his soul. He exalts you by his laws and causes you to reign in all others. The world and souls are like his, your heavenly mansions. The lawgiver of heaven and earth employs all his authority for you. He promotes you in his eternal palace, and makes you his friend, and tells his nobles and all his subjects, "Whatsoever you do unto him you do unto me." Joseph was not so great in Pharaoh's court, nor Haman in the court of Ahasuerus, as you are in heaven.

He tenders you as the apple of his eye. He has set his heart upon you. You are the sole object of his eye, and the end of all his endeavours.

Our Natures Require Love

But what life would you lead? And by what laws would you yourself be guided? For none are so miserable as the lawless and disobedient. Laws are the rules of blessed living. You must therefore be guided by some laws.

What would you choose? Surely since your nature and God's are so excellent, the laws of blessedness and the laws of nature are the most pleasing.

God loved you with an infinite love, and became by doing so your infinite treasure; you are the end unto whom he lives. For all the lines of his works and counsels end in you and in your advancement. Will not you become to him an infinite treasure by loving him according to his desert? It is impossible but to love him that loves. Love is so amiable that it is irresistible. There is no defense against that arrow, nor any deliverance in that war, nor any safeguard from that charm.

Will you not live unto him? You must of necessity live unto something. And what so glorious as his infinite love? Since, therefore, laws are requisite to lead you, what laws can your soul desire than those that guide you in the most amiable paths to the highest end?

By love alone is God enjoyed, by love alone delighted in, by love alone approached or admired. His nature requires love; your nature requires love. The law of nature commands you to love him: the law of his nature and the law of yours.

Meeting God's Love in Everything

There is in love two strange perfections that make it infinite in goodness. It is infinitely diligent in doing good, and it infinitely delights in that goodness. It takes no pleasure comparable in anything to that it takes in exalting and blessing.

And therefore has it made you a comprehension infinite to see all ages, and an affection endless to love all kingdoms, and a power fathomless to enjoy all angels. And a thirst insatiable to desire and delight in them. And a never-wearied faculty all-sufficient to love, number, take in, prize, and esteem all the varieties of creatures and their excellencies in all worlds, that you may enjoy them in communion with him. It is all obligation that he requires it.

What life would you lead? Would you love God alone? God alone cannot be beloved. He cannot be loved with a finite love, because he is infinite. Were he beloved alone, his love would be limited. He must be loved in all with an unlimited love, even in all his doings, in all his friends, in all his creatures.

Everywhere in all things you must meet his love. And this the law of nature commands. And it is your glory that you are fitted for it. His love unto you is the law and measure of yours unto him; his love unto all others the law and obligation of yours unto all.

You Grow By Loving

His nature requires that you love all those whom he loves, and receive him in all those things wherein he gives himself unto you. Their nature loves to be beloved and being amiable require love, as well as delight in it. They require it both by desert and desire.

Your nature urges it. For without loving you are desolate and by loving you enjoy. Yea by loving you expand and enlarge yourself, and the more you love are the more glorious. You love all your friends' friends, and need not to fear any dearth of love or danger of insufficiency. For the more you love your friend, your sovereign friend, the more you love all his friends. Which shows the endless proneness of love to increase and never to decay. O my soul, you live in all those whom you love, and in them enjoy all their treasures.

Everyone is the End of All Things

Miraculous are the effects of divine wisdom. He loves everyone, makes everyone infinitely happy, and is infinitely happy in everyone. He gives all the world to me, he gives it to everyone in giving it to all, and gives it wholly to me in giving it to everyone for everyone's sake.

He is infinitely happy in everyone; as many times therefore as there are happy persons, he is infinitely happy. Everyone is infinitely happy in everyone; everyone therefore is as many times infinitely happy as there are happy persons. He is infinitely happy above all their happiness in comprehending all. And I, comprehending his and theirs, am oh, how happy!

Here is love! Here is a kingdom! Where all are knit in infinite unity. All are happy in each other. All are like Deities. Everyone the end of all things, everyone supreme, everyone a treasure and the joy of all, and everyone most infinitely delighted in being so.

All things are ever joys for everyone's sake and infinitely richer to everyone for the sake of all. The same thing is multiplied by being enjoyed. And he that is greatest is most my treasure. This is the effect of making images, and by all their love is every image infinitely exalted. Comprehending in his nature all angels, all cherubims, all seraphims, all worlds, all creatures, and God over all blessed forever.

Deceived in Paradise

Being to lead this life within, I was placed in paradise without with some advantages which the angels have not. And being designed to immortality and an endless life, was to abide with God from everlasting to everlasting in all his ways.

But I was deceived by my appetite and fell into sin. Ungratefully, I despised him that gave me my being. I offended in an apple against him that gave me the whole world. But you, O Saviour, are here upon the cross suffering for my sins.

What shall I render unto you for so great a mercy! All thanksgiving is too weak and all expression too feeble. I give you myself; my soul and body

I offer unto you. It is unworthy of you, but you love me. Wash me with your blood from all my sins. And fill me with your Holy Spirit that I may be like unto you. So shall I praise your name acceptably forevermore.

Amen.

Jesus, A Greater Treasure

And now, O Lord, heaven and earth are infinitely more valuable than they were before, being all bought with your precious blood. And you, O Jesus, are a treasure unto me far greater than all those. At what rate or measure shall I esteem you?

You have restored me again to the friendship of God, to the enjoyment of the world, to the hope of eternal glory, to the love of angels, cherubims, and men. To the enjoyment and obedience of your holy laws, which alone are sweeter to me than the honey and the honeycomb,[33] and more precious than thousands of gold and silver.[34]

You have restored me above all to the image of God. And you have redeemed all ages and kingdoms for me alone, who am commanded to love them as you do. O that I might be unto them as you are! O that I might be unto you as you are to me, as glorious and as rich in love! O that I might die for you! O that I might ever live unto you!

In every thought, in every action of my life, in every moment I bless you for renewing the old commandment upon new obligations among sinners: "As I have loved you, so do you also love one another."[35] O let your love be in me that your joy may be fulfilled in me forevermore.

The Greatness of Your Love, Jesus

Now, O Lord, I see the greatness of your love wherewith you died. And by your actions more than by your sufferings admire you.

But henceforth I will more admire you by your sufferings; for considering that such actions went before, what love must move you to come into the place of guilty sinners!

You Bring Good Out of Evil

Lord, I lament and abhor myself that I have been the occasion of these your sufferings. I had never known the dignity of my nature, had not you esteemed it. I had never seen or understood its glory, had not you assumed it. Be you pleased to unite me unto you in the bands of an individual love, that I may evermore live unto you and live in you. And by how much the more vile I have been, let my love be so much, O Lord, the more violent henceforth and fervent unto you.

O you who would never have permitted sin, had you not known how to bring good out of evil: Have pity upon me. Hear my prayer. O my God, since pity embalms love, let yours come enriched and be more precious to me, miserable sinner. Let the remembrance of all the glory wherein I was created make me more serious and humble, more deep and penitent, more pure and holy before you.

And since the world is sprinkled with your blood and adorned with all kingdoms and ages for me, which are heavenly treasures and vastly greater than heaven and earth, let me see your glory in the preparation of them and your goodness in their government. Open unto me the gate of righteousness, that I may enter in to the New Jerusalem.

CHAPTER 9
PRAYERS REQUESTING THAT I GROW IN JESUS' LOVE

Prayer for Lovingkindness

My Lord, you head of the holy catholic church, I admire and praise you for purchasing to yourself such a glorious bride and for uniting us all by the blood of your cross.

I beseech you, let my love unto all be regular like yours and pure and infinite. Make it divine and make it holy. I confess I can see (sic) but I cannot moderate nor love as I ought. I pray you, for your lovingkindness' sake, supply my want in this particular. And so make me to love all, that I may be a blessing to all and well pleasing to you in all.

Teach me wisdom how to expend my blood, estate, life, and time in your service for the good of all, and make all them that are round about me wise and holy as you are, that we might all be knit together in godly love and united in your service to your honor and glory.

Naturally Made to Love

My excellent friend, you see that there are treasures in heaven and earth fit to be enjoyed besides those of kings' courts and taverns. The joys of the temple are the greatest joys were they understood; they are the most magnificent, solemn, and divine. There are glorious entertainments in this miserable world, could we find them out.

What more delightful can be imagined than to see a Saviour at this distance, dying on the cross to redeem a man from hell, and to see oneself the beloved of God and all kingdoms, yea, the admired of ages and the heir of the whole world? Has not his blood united you and me; cannot we see and love and enjoy each other at a hundred miles distance? In him is the only sweet and divine enjoyment.

I desire but an amiable soul in any part of all eternity, and can love it unspeakably. And if love it, enjoy it. For love implies pleasure because it is ever pleased with what is beloved. Love God and Jesus Christ and angels and men, which you are made to do as naturally as the sun is made to shine, and the beauty of the Holy Ghost dwelling in you will make you my delight, the treasure of the holy angels. You will at last be seen by me and all others in all your thoughts and in all your motions.

In the meantime, delight only in the love of Jesus and direct all your love unto him. Adore him, rejoice in him, admire his love and praise him, secretly and in the congregation.

Enjoy his saints that are round about you. Make yourself amiable that you may be admitted to their enjoyment by meekness, temperance, modesty, humility, charity, chastity, devotion, cheerfulness, gratitude, joy, thanksgiving. Retire from them that you may be the more precious and come out unto them the more wise. So shall you make the place wherein you live a nest of sweet perfumes, and every soul that is round about you will be a bed of honor and sweet repose unto you.

Delighting in God's Saints

My goodness extends not to you, O Lord, but to your saints and to the excellent in the earth in whom is all my delight.[36] To delight in the saints of God is the way to heaven.

One would think it exceeding easy and reasonable to esteem those whom Jesus purchased with his precious blood. And if we do so, how can we help but inherit all things. All the saints of all ages and all kingdoms are his inheritance, his treasures, his jewels. Shall they not be yours since they are his whom you love so infinitely?

There is not a cup of cold water given to a disciple in the name of a disciple, but he accepts it as done to himself. Had you been with Mary Magdalen, would you not have anointed his feet and washed them in tears and wiped them with the hairs of your head? His poor servants, his contemptible and disguised members here upon earth, are his feet; yea more the apple of his eye; yea more for he gave his eyes and heart and hands and feet for them. O therefore universally in all places tender them, and at all times be ready and willing to minister unto them.

And that with infinite joy, knowing the excellency of your duty. For you are enjoying the world and communicating yourself like God unto them. You are laying up treasure in heaven and enlarging your soul, beautifying your life, and delighting the holy angels, offering up sacrifices unto God and perfuming the world; embracing Jesus Christ and caressing your Saviour, while you are dispensing charities among them. Every alms deed is a precious stone in the crown of glory.

Digging for Companions

But there are a sort of saints meet to be your companions in another manner, but that they be concealed. You must therefore make yourself exceeding virtuous that by the very splendour of your fame you may find them out. While the wicked are like heaps of rubbish, these few jewels lie buried in the ruins of mankind and must diligently be dug for.

You may know them by their lustre and by the very desire and esteem they have of you when you are virtuous. For as it is the glory of the sun that darkness cannot approach it, because it is always encompassed with its own beams; so it is the privilege of holy souls that they are always secure in their own light, which drives away devils and evil men, and is accessible by none but lovers of virtue.

Beginners and desirers will give you the opportunity of infusing yourself and your principles into them. Practicers and growers will mingle souls and be delightful companions. The sublime and perfect, in the lustre of their spirit, will show you the image of Almighty God and the joys of heaven. They will allure, protect, encourage, comfort, teach, honor, and delight you.

But you must be very good, for that is the way to find them. And very patient to endure some time, and very diligent to observe where they are.

Exchanging Souls

They will praise our Saviour with you and turn the world into heaven. And if you find those of noble and benevolent natures, discreet and magnanimous, liberal and cheerful, wise and holy as they ought to be, you will have in them treasures greater than all relations whatsoever. They will exchange souls with you, divide estates, communicate comforts, counsels, and honors, and in all tenderness, constancy, fidelity, and love be more yours than their own.

There are exceeding few such heavenly lovers as Jesus was, who imparted his own soul unto us. Yet some may doubtlessly be found. And half a dozen such as these wisely chosen will represent unto us the New Jerusalem, entertain us always with divine discourses, please us always with heavenly affections, delight us always with melody and praise, and ever make us near unto our Saviour.

Turn Vices Into Virtues

Yet you must arm yourself with expectations of their infirmities and resolve nobly to forgive them: not in a sordid and cowardly manner, by taking no notice of them, nor in a dim and lazy manner, by letting them alone, but in a divine and illustrious manner by chiding them meekly and vigorously rendering and showering down all kind of benefits. Cheerfully continuing to do good, and whatever you suffer by your piety and charity, confidence or love, to be like our Saviour, unwearied: who when he was abused and had often been evil-intreated among men, proceeded courageously through all treacheries and deceits to die for them. So shall you turn their very vices into virtues to you, and, as our Saviour did, make of a wreath of thorns a crown of glory.

But set the splendor of virtues before you, and when some fail, think with yourself, there are some sincere and excellent, and why should not I be the most virtuous?

Be Present in All Ages

With all their eyes behold our Saviour, with all their hearts adore him, with all their tongues and affections praise him. See how in all closets and in all temples, in all cities and in all fields, in all nations and in all generations, they are lifting up their hands and eyes unto his cross, and delight in all their adorations.

This will enlarge your soul and make you to dwell in all kingdoms and ages, strengthen your faith and enrich your affections, fill you with their joys and make you a lively partaker in communion with them. It will make you a possessor greater than the world.

Men do mightily wrong themselves when they refuse to be present in all ages, and neglect to see the beauty of all kingdoms, and despise the resentments of every soul, and busy themselves only with pots and cups and things at home or shops and trades and things in the street, but do not live to God manifesting himself in all the world, nor care to see (and be present with him in) all the glory of his eternal kingdom. By seeing the saints of all ages, we are present with them; by being present with them become too great for our own age and near to our Saviour.

CHAPTER 10
PRAYERS REQUESTING THAT I BECOME LIKE JESUS

Jesus Loves Everyone Alone

O Jesus, you king of saints whom all adore, and the holy imitate, I admire the perfection of your love in every soul! You love every one wholly as if him alone. Whose soul is so great an image of your eternal Father, that you came down from heaven to die for him and to purchase mankind that they might be his treasures.

I admire to see your cross in every understanding, your passion in every memory, your crown of thorns in every eye, and your bleeding, naked wounded body in every soul. Your death lives in every memory, your crucified person is embalmed in every affection, your pierced feet are bathed in everyone's tears, your blood all drops on every soul. You wholly communicate yourself to every soul in all kingdoms, and are wholly seen in every saint, and wholly fed upon by every Christian. It is my privilege that I can enter with you into every soul, and in every living temple of your manhood and your Godhead, behold again and enjoy your glory.

Becoming Mirrors of God's Brightness

O how do your affections extend like the sunbeams unto all stars in heaven and to all the kingdoms in the world. Yours at once enlighten both hemispheres. Quicken us with life, enable us to digest the nourishment of our souls, cause us to see the greatness of our nature, the love of God, and the joys of heaven. Melt us into tears, comfort and enflame us, and do all in a celestial manner that the sun can do in a terrene and earthly.

O let me so long eye you till I be turned into you, and look upon me till you are formed in me, that I may be a mirror of your brightness, a habitation of your love, and a temple of your glory. That all your saints might live in me and I in them, enjoying all their felicities, joys, and treasures.

Knowing Jesus with Hearts & Minds

O you sun of righteousness, eclipsed on the cross, overcast with sorrows, and crowned with the shadow of death: remove the veil of your flesh that I may see your glory. Those cheeks are shades, those limbs and members clouds that hide the glory of your mind, your knowledge, and your love from us. But were they removed, those inward excellencies would remain invisible. As therefore we see your flesh with our fleshly eyes and handle your wounds with our bodily senses, let us see your understanding with our understandings and read your love with our own. Let our souls have communion with your soul and let the eye of our mind enter into yours.

Who are you who bleeding here causes the ground to tremble and the locks to rend and the graves to open?[37] Has your death influence so high as the highest heavens? That the sun also mourns and is clothed in sables? Is your spirit present in the temple, that the veil rends in twain at your passion?[38]

O let me leave kings' courts to come unto you. I choose rather in a cave to serve you than on a throne to despise you. O my dying gracious Lord, I perceive the virtue of your passion everywhere. Let it, I beseech you, enter into my soul and rent my rocky, stony heart, and tear the veil of my flesh, that I may see into the Holy of Holies! O darken the sun of pride and vainglory. Yea, let the sun itself be dark in comparison of your love! And open the grave of my flesh, that my soul may arise to praise you.

Grant this for your mercy's sake. Amen!

With Jesus in His Sufferings

Is this he that was transfigured upon Mount Tabor? Pale, withered, extended, tortured, soiled with blood and sweat and dust, dried, parched! O sad, O dismal spectacle! All his joints are dissolved, all his blood is shed to the last drop, all his moisture is consumed! What is here but a heap of desolations, a deformed carcase, a disfigured countenance! A mass of miseries and silence, footsteps of innumerable sufferings!

Can this be a joy? Can this be an entertainment? Can this delight us?

O Jesus, the more vile I here behold you, the more I admire you. Into what low abysses did you descend, into what depths of misery do you now lie! Oh what confusions, what stripes and wounds, what desolations and deformities did you suffer for our sakes! In all the depths of your humiliation I here adore you! I prize and desire always to see those stripes and those deformities. It is sweeter to be with you in your sufferings than with princes on their thrones, and more do I rejoice with you in your misery than in all their solemnities.

I tremble also to see your condescensions, the great effects and expressions of your love! You were slain for me; and shall I leave your body in the field, O Lord? Shall I go away and be merry, while the love of my soul and my only lover is dead upon the cross. Groans here in the sight and apprehension of your love are beyond all melody, and the solemn sorrows of a loving soul, a faithful friend, a tender spouse, a deep and compassionate true lover, beyond all the entertainments in the world. Yours, O Jesus, will I ever be while I have any being.

Letting God's Goodness Shine in Us

This body is not the cloud, but the pillar assumed to manifest his love unto us.[39] In these shades does this sun break forth most oriently. In this death is his love painted in most lively colors. God never showed himself more a God than when he appeared man, never gained more glory than when he lost all glory, was never more sensible of our sad estate than when he was bereaved of all sense.

O let your goodness shine in me! I will love all, O Lord, by your grace assisting as you do. And in death itself will I find life, and in conquest victory. This Sampson by dying killed all his enemies and then carried the gates of hell and death away—when being dead, himself was borne to his grave. Teach me, O Lord, these mysterious ascencions. By descending into hell for the sake of others, let me ascend into the glory of the highest heavens. Let the fidelity and efficacy of my love appear in all my care and suffering for you.

Let Nothing Divide

O Jesus, Lord of Love and Prince of Life! who even being dead, are greater than all angels, cherubims. and men: let my love unto you be as strong as death and so deep that no waters may be able to drown it. O let it be ever endless and invincible! O that I could really so love you as rather to suffer with St. Anselm the pains of hell than to sin against you. O that no torments, no powers in heaven or earth, no stratagems, no allurements might divide me from you.

Let the length and breadth and height and depth of my love unto you be like yours unto me.[40] Let undrainable fountains and unmeasurable abysses be hidden in it. Let it be more vehement than flame, more abundant than the sea, more constant than the candle in Aaron's tabernacle that burned day and night.[41] Shall the sun shine for me, and be a light from the beginning of the world to this very day that never goes out, and shall my love cease or intermit, O Lord, to shine or burn? O let it be a perpetual fire on the altar of my heart, and let my soul itself be your living sacrifice.

Inheriting Heaven & Earth

It is an inestimable joy that I was raised out of nothing to see and enjoy this glorious world. It is a sacred gift whereby the children of men are made my treasures, but O you who are fairer than the children of men, how great and unconceivable is the joy of your love![42]

That I who was lately raised out of the dust have so great a friend; that I, who in this life am born to mean things according to the world, should be called to inherit such glorious things in the way of heaven. Such a Lord, so great a Lover, such heavenly mysteries, such doings and such sufferings, with all the benefit and pleasure of them in your intelligible kingdom. It amazes me; it transports and ravishes me.

I will leave my father's house and come unto you, for you are my Lord, and I will worship you—that all ages should appear so visibly before me and all your ways be so lively, powerful, and present with me; that the land of Canaan should be so near, and all the joys in heaven and earth be so sweet to comfort me! This, O Lord, declares your wisdom, and shows your power.

But O the riches of your infinite goodness in making my soul an interminable temple, out of which nothing can be, from which nothing is removed, to which nothing is afar off; but all things immediately near in a real, true, and lively manner. O the glory of that endless life that can at once extend to all eternity! Had the cross been twenty millions of ages further, it had still been equally near, nor is it possible to remove it, for it is with all distances in my understanding, and though it be removed many thousand-millions of ages more is as clearly seen and apprehended.

This soul for which you died, I desire to know more perfectly, O my Saviour, that I may praise you for it and believe it worthy, in its nature, to be an object of your love, though unworthy by reason of sin—and that I may use it in your service and keep it pure to your glory.

The Root of My Being

As my body without my soul is a carcase, so is my soul without your spirit, a chaos, a dark obscure heap of empty faculties: ignorant of itself, unsensible of your goodness, blind to your glory, dead in sins and trespasses. Having eyes I see not, having ears I hear not, having an heart I understand not the glory of your works and the glory of your kingdom.[43]

O you who are the root of my being and the captain of my salvation, look upon me.[44] Quicken me, O you life-giving and quickening seed. Visit me with your light and your truth; let them lead me to your Holy Hill[45] and make me to see the greatness of your love in all its excellencies, effects, emanations, gifts and operations; O my wisdom!

O my Righteousness, Sanctification, and Redemption—let your wisdom enlighten me; let your knowledge illuminate me; let your blood redeem me, wash me, and clean me; let your merits justify me, O you who are equal unto God and did suffer for me. Let your righteousness clothe me. Let your will imprint the form of itself upon mine; and let my will become conformable to yours, that your will and mine may be united and made one forevermore.

My Will & Jesus' Will

Your will, O Christ, and your spirit in essence are one. As therefore your human will is conformable to your divine, let my will be conformable to yours.

Your divine will is all wisdom, goodness, holiness, glory, and blessedness. It is all light and life and love. It extends to all things in heaven and earth. It illuminates all eternity; it beautifies the omnipresence of God with glory without dimensions. It is infinite in greatness and magnifies all that are united to it. Oh that my will, being made great by yours, might become divine, exalted, perfected!

O Jesus, without you I can do nothing. O you in whom the fullness of the Godhead dwells, I desire to learn of you, to become in spirit like unto you. I desire not to learn of my relations, acquaintance, tradesmen, merchants or earthly princes to be like unto them; but like unto you, the King of Glory, and to those who are your sons and friends in another world.

Grant therefore, O you of whom the whole family in heaven and earth is named, that being strengthened with might by your spirit in the inner man, I may be able to comprehend with all saints, what is the breadth and length and depth and height, and to know that love of Christ which passes knowledge, that I may be filled with all the fullness of God.[46]

Christ's Spirit in Me

O you who ascends up on high, and led captivity captive, and gave gifts unto men,[47] as after your ascension into heaven you did send your Holy Spirit down upon your apostles in the form of a rushing mighty wind and in the shape of cloven fiery tongues—send down the Holy Ghost upon me. Breathe upon me, inspire me, quicken me, illuminate me, enflame me, fill me with the Spirit of God, that I may overflow with praises and thanksgivings as they did. Fill me with the riches of your glory, that Christ may dwell in my heart by faith, that I being rooted and grounded in love may speak the wonderful works of God.[48] Let me be alive unto them: let me see them all, let me feel them all, let me enjoy them all, that I may admire the greatness of your love unto my soul, and rejoice in communion with you forevermore.

How happy, O Lord, am I who am called to a communion with God the Father, Son, and Holy Ghost in all their works and ways, in all their joys, in all their treasures, in all their glory! Who have such a Father, having in him the fountain of immortality, rest and glory, and the joy of seeing him creating all things for my sake! Such a Son, having in him the means of peace and felicity, and the joy of seeing him redeeming my soul by his sufferings on the cross, and doing all things that pertain to my salvation between the Father and me. Such a spirit and such a comforter dwelling in me to quicken, enlighten, and enable me, and to awaken all the powers of my soul that night and day the same mind may be in me that was in Christ Jesus!

The Treasure of Love

O you who has redeemed me to be a Son of God and called me from vanity to inherit all things, I praise you, that having loved me and given yourself for me, you command us saying, "As I have loved you, so do you also love one another."[49] Wherein you have commanded all men so to love me as to lay down their lives for my peace and welfare. Since love is the end for which heaven and earth was made, enable me to see and discern the sweetness of so great a treasure.

And since you have advanced me into the throne of God, in the bosom of all angels and men, commanding them by this precept to give me a union and communion with you in their dearest affection, in their highest esteem, and in the most near and inward room and seat in their hearts—give me the grace which Saint Paul prayed for, that I may be acceptable to the saints;[50] fill me with your Holy Spirit and make my soul and life beautiful; make me all wisdom, goodness, and love, that I may be worthy to be esteemed and accepted of them—that being delighted also with their felicity, I may be crowned with yours and with their glory.

Loving Everyone as My Friend

O Jesus, who having prepared all the joys in heaven and earth for me, and redeemed me to inherit your Father's treasures, has prepared for me the most glorious companions, in whose presence and society I may enjoy them—I bless you for the communion of saints and for your adorning the same with all manner of beauties, excellencies, perfections, and delights.

O what a glorious assembly is the Church of the first-born, how blessed and divine! What perfect lovers! How great and honorable! How wise! How sweet and delightful! Everyone being the end, everyone the king of heaven, everyone the Son of God in greatness and glory, everyone the entire and perfect friend of all the residue, everyone the light and ornament of your kingdom, everyone your peculiar friend, yet loving everyone as your peculiar friend and rejoicing in the pleasures and delights of everyone!

O my God, make me one of that happy assembly. And let me love everyone for whom Christ died, with a love as great and lively as his, that I may dwell in him, and he in me, and that we all may be made perfect in me, even as you, O Jesus, are in the Father, and the Father is in you;[51] that your love may be in us, and you in me forevermore.

Never Alone

Wisely, O Jesus, did you tell your disciples when you promised them the Comforter, that the world cannot receive the Spirit of Truth, because it sees him not, neither knows him. But you know him, for he dwells with you, and shall be in you.[52] O let the Spirit of Truth dwell with me, and then little matter for any other comforter.

When I see myself beloved of the Father, when I know the perfection of your love, when the Father and the Son love me, and both manifest themselves unto me; when they are near unto me and abide with me forever and ever, little harm can death do, or sickness and poverty. I can never be alone because the Father and Son are with me. No reproaches can discomfort me, no enemies can hurt me.

O let me know you, you Spirit of Truth, be you always with me and dwell within me. How is it possible, but you should be an infinite comforter who gives me a being as wide as eternity, a well-being as blessed as the Deity, a temple of glory in the omnipresence of God, and a light wherein to enjoy the New Jerusalem! An immovable inheritance and an everlasting kingdom that cannot be shaken!

You are he who shows me all the treasures in heaven and earth, who enables me to turn afflictions into pleasures, and to enjoy mine enemies. You enable me to love as I am beloved, and to be blessed in God. You seal me up unto the Day of Redemption, and give me a foretaste of heaven upon earth. You are my God and my exceeding joy, my comforter and my strength forevermore. You represent all things unto me, which the Father and the Son have done for me. You fill me with courage against all assaults and enable me to overcome in all temptations; you make me immovable by the very treasures and the joys which you show to me. O never leave me nor forsake me, but remain with me and be my comfort forever!

Sons of God

Wisely does St. John say, "We are the Sons of God; but the world knows us not because it knew him not."[53] He that knows not the Spirit of God, can never know a son of God, nor what it is to be his child.

He made us the sons of God in capacity by giving us a power to see eternity, to survey his treasures, to love his children, to know and to love as he does, to become righteous and holy as he is. The Holy Ghost makes us the Sons of God in act, when we are righteous as he is righteous, and holy as he is holy.

When we prize all the things in heaven and earth as he prizes him, and make a conscience of doing it as he does after his similitude; then are we actually present with them and blessed in them, being righteous and holy as he is. Then the spirit of God dwells in us, and then are we indeed the sons of God, a chosen generation, a royal priesthood, an holy nation, a peculiar people, zealous of good works, showing forth the praises of him who has called us out of darkness into his marvelous light.[54]

The Kingdom of God Within Us

Christ dwelling in our hearts by faith is an infinite mystery which may thus be understood: an object seen is in the faculty seeing it, and by that in the soul of the seer after the best of manners. Whereas there are eight manners of in-being, the in-being of an object in a faculty is the best of all. Dead things are in a room containing them in a vain manner, unless they are objectively in the soul of a seer. The pleasure of an enjoyer is the very end why things placed are in any place. The place and the thing placed in it, being both in the understanding of a spectator of them. Things dead in dead place effect nothing.

But in a living soul that sees their excellencies, they excite a pleasure answerable to their value, a wisdom to embrace them, a courage not to forsake them, a love of their donor, praises and thanksgivings, and a greatness and a joy equal to their goodness. And thus all ages are present in my soul, and all kingdoms, and God blessed forever. And thus Jesus Christ is seen in me and dwells in me, when I believe upon him. And thus all saints are in me and I in them. And thus all angels and the eternity and infinity of God are in me forevermore. I being the living temple and comprehensor of them.

Since therefore all other ways of in-being would be utterly vain, were it not for this: "And the kingdom of God," as our Saviour says, "is within you;"[55] let us ever meditate and think on him, that his conception, nativity, life, and death may be always within us. Let heaven and earth, men and angels, God and his creatures be always within us: that is, in our sight, in our sense, in our love and esteem; that in the light of the Holy Ghost we may see the glory of his eternal kingdom, and sing the song of Moses, and the song of the Lamb saying, "Great and marvelous are your works, Lord God Almighty, just and true are your ways, you King of Saints."[56]

III.
MY VISION OF THE WORLD
... WHERE ALL THE RICHES OF GOD'S KINGDOM APPEAR

CHAPTER 11
THE WORLD SERVES US

The World is a Promise of Eternal Joys

The services which the world does you are transcendent to all imagination. Did it only sustain your body and preserve your life and comfort your senses, you were bound to value it as much as those services were worth; but it discovers the being of God unto you. It opens his nature and shows you his wisdom, goodness, and power. It magnifies his love unto you. It serves angels and men for you. It entertains you with many lovely and glorious objects. It feeds you with joys and becomes a theme that furnishes you with perpetual praises and thanksgivings. It enflames you with the love of God and is the link of your union and communion with him.

It is the temple wherein you are exalted to glory and honor, and the visible porch or gate of eternity: a sure pledge of eternal joys to all them that walk before God and are perfect in it.

God's Gift to Every Infant

If you desire directions how to enjoy it, place yourself in it as if no one were created besides yourself, and consider all the services it does even to you alone. Prize those services with a joy answerable to the value of them; be truly thankful and as grateful for them as their merit deserves.

And remember always how great soever the world is, it is the beginning of gifts, the first thing which God bestows to every infant by the very right of his nativity. Which because men are blind, they cannot see and therefore know not that God is bountiful. From that first error, they proceed and multiply their mistaking all along. They know not themselves or their own glory; they understand not his commandments; they see not the sublimity of righteous actions; they know not the beauty of truth nor are acquainted with the glory of the Holy Scriptures.

The Greatness of Sin

Till you see that the world is yours, you cannot weigh the greatness of sin, nor the misery of your fall, nor prize your redeemer's love. One would think these should be motives sufficient to stir us up to the contemplation of God's works, wherein all the riches of his kingdom will appear.

For the greatness of sin proceeds from the greatness of his love whom we have offended, from the greatness of those obligations which were laid upon us, from the great blessedness and glory of the estate wherein we were placed—none of which can be seen till truth is seen, a great part of which is that the world is ours. So that indeed the knowledge of this is the very real light wherein all mysteries are evidenced to us.

The End for Which We Were Created

The misery of your fall arises naturally from the greatness of your sin. For to sin against infinite love is to make oneself infinitely deformed. To be infinitely deformed is to be infinitely odious in his eyes who once loved us with infinite love. To have sinned against all obligations and to have fallen from infinite glory and blessedness is infinite misery, but cannot be seen till the glory of the estate from which we are fallen is discerned.

To be infinitely odious in his eyes who infinitely loved us makes us unavoidably miserable because it bereaves us of the end for which we were created, which was to enjoy his love, and of the end also of all the creatures which were made only to manifest the same. For when we are bereaved of these, we live to no purpose, and having lost the end to which we were created, our life is cumbersome and irksome to us.

Remember Adam's Innocence

The counsel which our Saviour gives in the Revelation to the church of Ephesus is by all churches and by every soul diligently to be observed:

"Remember from whence you are fallen, and repent."[57] Which intimates our duty of remembering our happiness in the estate of innocence.

For without this we can never prize our redeemer's love. He that knows not to what he is redeemed cannot prize the work of redemption. The means cannot there be valued, where the end is despised.

Since therefore by the Second Adam, we are restored to that we lost in the first; unless we value that we lost in the first, we cannot truly rejoice in the second. But when we do, then all things receive an infinite esteem, and an augmentation infinitely infinite that follows after. Our Saviour's love, his incarnation, his life and death, his resurrection, his ascension into heaven, his intercession for us being then seen and infinitely prized in a glorious light, as also our deliverance from hell and our reconciliation unto God.

The World is Mine

The consideration also of this truth, that the world is mine, confirms my faith. God having placed the evidences of religion in the greatest and highest joys. For as long as I am ignorant that the world is mine, the love of God is defective to me.

How can I believe that he gave his Son to die for me, who having power to do otherwise gave me nothing but rags and cottages? But when I see once that he gave heaven and earth to me, and made me in his image to enjoy them in his similitude, I can easily believe that he gave his Son also for me—especially since he commanded all angels and men to love me as himself, and so highly honors me, that whatsoever is done unto me he accounts done unto him.

The Sun's Light Shines for You

Place yourself therefore in the midst of the world as if you were alone, and meditate upon all the services which it does unto you.

Suppose the sun were absent, and conceive the world to be a dungeon of darkness and death about you. You will then find his beams more delightful than the approach of angels, and loath the abomination of that sinful blindness whereby you see not the glory of so great and bright a creature, because the air is filled with its beams. Then you will think that all its light shines for you, and confess that God has manifested himself indeed in the preparation of so divine a creature.

You will abhor the madness of those who esteem a purse of gold more than it. Alas, what could a man do with a purse of gold in an everlasting dungeon? And shall we prize the sun less than it, which is the light and fountain of all our pleasures? You will then abhor the preposterous method of those, who in an evil sense are blinded with its beams, and to whom the presence of the light is the greatest darkness. For they who would repine at God without the sun, are unthankful, having it, and therefore only despise it because it is created.

All the Things the Sun Does for You

It raises corn to supply you with food. It melts waters to quench your thirst. It infuses sense into all your members. It illuminates the world to entertain you with prospects. It surrounds you with the beauty of hills and valleys.

It moves and labors night and day for your comfort and service. It sprinkles flowers upon the ground for your pleasure. And in all these things shows you the goodness and wisdom of a God that can make one thing so beautiful, delightful, and serviceable, having ordained the same to innumerable ends.

It concocts minerals, raises exhalations, begets clouds, sends down the dew and rain and snow that refreshes and repairs all the earth. And is far more glorious in its diurnal motion than if there were two suns to make on either side a perpetual day. The swiftness whereby it moves in twenty-four hours about so vast a universe manifests the power and care of a creator more than any station or quiet could do. And producing innumerable effects, it is more glorious than if millions of angels diversely did do them.

The Wisdom & Goodness of Night

Did the sun stand still that you might have a perpetual day, you would not know the sweetness of repose. The delightful vicissitudes of night and day, the early sweetness and spring of the morning, the perfume and beauty in the cool of the evening would all be swallowed up in meridian splendor, all which now entertains you with delights. The antipodes would be empty, perpetual darkness and horror there, and the works of God on the other side of the world in vain.

Better to Enjoy One Sun than Two

Were there two suns (that day might be alike in both places) standing still, there would be nothing but meridian splendor under them, and nothing but continual morning in other places. They would absume and dry up all the moisture of the earth, which now is repaired as fast as it decays. And perhaps when the nature of the sun is known, it is impossible there should be two. At least it is impossible they should be more excellent than this one, that we might magnify the Deity and rest satisfied in him for making the best of all possible works for our enjoyment.

The Wisdom of Finite Limits

Had the sun been made one infinite flame, it had been worse than it is, for there had been no living. It had filled all space and devoured all other things. So that it is far better being finite than if it were infinite.

Even as the sea within a finite shore

Is far the better 'cause it is no more.

Whence we may easily perceive that the divine wisdom has achieved things more than infinite in goodness and beauty as a sure token of their perfect excellency.

Enjoy What You Have First

Entering thus far into the nature of the sun, we may see a little heaven in the creatures. And yet we shall say less of the rest in particular, though every one in its place be as excellent as it, and this without these cannot be sustained.

Were all the earth filthy mires or devouring quicksands, firm land would be an unspeakable treasure. Were it all beaten gold, it would be of no value. It is a treasure therefore of far greater value to a noble spirit than if the globe of the earth were all gold. A noble spirit being only that which can survey it all and comprehend its uses.

The air is better being a living miracle as it now is than if it were crammed and filled with crowns and sceptres. The mountains are better than solid diamonds, and those things which scarcity makes jewels (when you enjoy these) are yours in their places.

Why should you not render thanks to God for them all? You are the Adam or the Eve that enjoy them. Why should you not exult and triumph in his love who has done such great things for you? Why should you not rejoice and sing his praises? Learn to enjoy what you have first, and covet more if you can afterwards.

Things in Their Proper Places

Could the seas serve you were you alone more than now they do? Why do you not render thanks for them? They serve you better than if you were in them: everything serving you best in its proper place. Alone you were lord over all, bound to admire his eternal love who raised you out of nothing into this glorious world which he created for you.

To see infinite wisdom, goodness, and power making the heavens and the earth, the seas, the air, the sun and stars! What wonder, what joy, what glory, what triumph, what delight should this afford! It is more yours than if you had been made alone.

Enjoying God's Goodness

The sun is but a little spark of his infinite love; the sea is but one drop of his goodness. But what flames of love ought that spark to kindle in your soul! What seas of affection ought to flow for that drop in your bosom!

The heavens are the canopy and the earth is the footstool of your throne,[58] who reign in communion with God, or at least are called so to do. How lively should his divine goodness appear unto you; how continually should it rest upon you; how deeply should it be impressed in you! Verily its impressions ought to be so deep as to be always remaining, always felt, always admired, always seen and rejoiced in.

You are never truly great till all the world is yours, and the goodness of your donor so much your joy, that you think upon it all day long. Which King David the Royal Man well understood, when he said, "My lips shall be filled with your praise and your honor all the day.[59] I will make mention of your lovingkindness in your holy temple."[60]

The World Serves You

The world serves you as in serving those cattle which you feed upon, so in serving those men that build and plough and plant and govern for you. It serves you in those that pray and adore and praise for you, that fill the world with beauty and virtue, that are made to love and honor you, to please and advance you with all the services that the art of man can devise.

So that you are alone in the world, though there are millions in it beside. You are alone to enjoy and rejoice in all, being the adequate object of his eternal love and the end of all. Thus the world serves to promote and advance you.

Hidden Pleasures

Those services are so great, that when you enter into them, they are ample fields and territories of joy though on the outside they seem so contemptible that they promise nothing. The magnified pleasures of this corrupted world are like the Egyptian temples in old time, that were *Magnifica in frontispicio Ridicula in penetrali*: 'They have a royal frontispiece, but are ridiculous when you come in.' These hidden pleasures, because they are great, common, and simple, are not understood.

CHAPTER 12

GOD CAN BE SEEN IN THE WORLD

Enjoying the Face of God

Besides these immediate pleasures here beneath, there are many sublime and celestial services which the world does do. It is a glorious mirror wherein you may see the verity of all religion: enjoy the remainders of paradise and talk with the Deity. Apply yourself vigorously to the enjoyment of it, for in it you shall see the face of God, and by enjoying it, be wholly converted to him.

Enjoying the World Like God Does

You shall be glorified, you shall live in communion with him, you shall ascend into the throne of the highest heavens. You shall be satisfied, you shall be made greater than the heavens, you shall be like him, when you enjoy the world as he does. You shall converse with his wisdom, goodness, and power above all worlds, and therefore shall know him. To know whom is a sublime thing, for it is life eternal.

All Things Flow from God

They that quarrel at the manner of God's revealing himself are troubled because he is invisible. Yet is it expedient that he should be so, for whatsoever is visible is a body; whatsoever is a body excludes other things out of the place where itself is. If God therefore being infinite were visible, he would make it impossible for anything to have a being.

Besides, bulk as such in itself is dead. Whatsoever is visible is so in like manner. That which inspires bulk with motion, life, and sense is invisible; and in itself distinct from the bulk which it inspires. Were God therefore pure bulk, he could neither move, nor will, nor desire anything; but being invisible, he leaves room for and effects all things. He fills nothing with a bodily presence, but includes all. He is pure life, knowledge, and desire, from which all things flow: pure wisdom, goodness, and love to which all things return.

God is Invisible

Hence we may know why God appears not in a visible manner is because he is invisible. Those who are angry with the Deity for not showing himself to their bodily eyes are not displeased with the manner of revelation, but that he is such a God as he is.

But though he is invisible, yet say they, he may assume a body and make himself visible therein. We ask them therefore what kind of body they desire, for if he should take upon himself a visible body, that body must represent some of his perfections. What perfections then would they have that body to express?

If his infinity, that body then must be infinite. Upon which the same absurdity would follow as before: for being infinite it would exclude all being beside out of place. If his eternity, that cannot by a body be represented. Neither is any sense able to judge of infinity or eternity. For if he should represent himself by an infinite wall, sight being too short might apprehend itself defective, and be assured that it could not apprehend the ends of that wall—but whether it had ends, which itself was not able to discern, it could not be satisfied.

Would you therefore have it to express some other of his perfections: as particularly that of his beauty? Beauty being a thing consisting of variety, that body could not be one simple being, but must be sweetly tempered of a manifold and delightful mixture of figures and colors, and be some such thing as Ezekiel saw in his vision.[61] For uniform beauty, the sun is the most delightful, yet is not that sun the most delightful thing that is possible. A body more beautiful than it may be made.

Suppose therefore the most beautiful that is possible were created.

What would follow? Being a silent and quiet object of the eye would be no more noted than if it had not a being. The most beautiful object, being always present, grows common and despised. Even as a picture is at first admired, but at length no more regarded than the bare wall. Since therefore the most beautiful thing that is possible, being always continued, would grow into contempt. How do we know, but the world is that body, which the Deity has assumed to manifest his beauty and by which he makes himself as visible as it is possible he should?

God Can Be Seen in the Material World

When Amasis the King of Egypt sent to the wise men of Greece to know, *Quid Pulcherrimum* ("What is the most beautiful?"), upon due and mature consideration they answered, "The world." The world certainly being so beautiful that nothing visible is capable of more. Were we to see it only once, the first appearance would amaze us. But being daily seen, we observe it not.

Ancient philosophers have thought God to be the soul of the world. Since therefore this visible world is the body of God—not his natural body, but which he has assumed—let us see how glorious his wisdom is in manifesting himself thereby. It has not only represented his infinity and eternity which we thought impossible to be represented by a body, but his beauty also, his wisdom, goodness, power, life, and glory; his righteousness, love, and blessedness: all which, as out of a plentiful treasury, may be taken and collected out of this world.

First, his infinity: for the dimensions of the world are unsearchable. An infinite wall is a poor thing to express his infinity. A narrow endless length is nothing: it might be, and if it were, were unprofitable. But the world is round and endlessly unsearchable every way. What astronomer, what mathematician, what philosopher did ever comprehend the measures of the world? The very earth alone, being round and globous, is unlimited. It has neither walls nor precipices, nor bounds, nor borders.

A man may lose himself in the midst of nations and kingdoms. And yet it is but a center compared to the universe. The distance of the sun, the altitude of the stars, the wideness of the heavens on every side, passes the reach of sight and search of the understanding. And whether it be infinite or no, we cannot tell.

The eternity of God is so apparent in it that the wisest of philosophers thought the world eternal. We come into it, leave it, as if it had neither beginning nor ending.

Concerning its beauty I need say nothing. No man can turn unto it, but must be ravished with its appearance. Only thus much, since these things are so beautiful, how much more beautiful is the author of them? Which was the note and observation of the wise man in the Book of Wisdom.[62] But the beauty of God is invisible. It is all wisdom, goodness, life and love, power, glory, blessedness etc.

How therefore shall these be expressed in a material world?

His wisdom is expressed in manifesting his infinity in such a commodious manner. He has made a penetrable body in which we may stand, to wit the air, and see the heavens and the regions of the earth at wonderful distances.

His goodness is manifest in making that beauty so delightful, and its varieties so profitable—the air to breathe in, the sea for moisture, the earth for fertility, the heavens for influences, the sun for productions, the stars and trees wherewith it is adorned for innumerable uses. Again his goodness is seen in the end to which he guides all this profitableness: in making it serviceable to supply our wants and delight our senses, to enflame us with his love and make us amiable before him and delighters in his blessedness.

God, having not only showed us his simple infinity in an endless wall, but in such an illustrious manner—by an infinite variety that he has drowned our understanding in a multitude of wonders—transported us with delights and enriched us with innumerable diversities of joys and pleasures. The very greatness of our felicity convinces us that there is a God.

God's Life Seen in the World's Motions

His power is evident by upholding it all. But how shall his life appear in that which is dead?

Life is the root of activity and motion. Did I see a man sitting in a chair, as long as he was quiet, I could not tell but his body was inanimate. But if he stirred, if he moved his legs or stretched forth his arms, if he breathed or twinkled with his eyes, I could easily tell he had a soul within him—motion being a far greater evidence of life than all lineaments whatsoever. Colors and features may be in a dead picture, but motion is always attended with life.

What shall I think, therefore, when the winds blow, the seas roar, the waters flow, the vapors ascend, the clouds fly, the drops of rain fall, the stars march forth in armies, the sun runs swiftly round about the world? Can all these things move so without a life or spring of motion? But the wheels in watches move, and so does the hand that points out the figures, this being a motion of dead things.

Therefore has God created living ones, that by lively motions and sensible desires, we might be sensible of a Deity. They breathe, they see, they feel, they grow, they flourish, they know, they love. O what a world of evidences! We are lost in abysses; we now are absorbed in wonders and swallowed up of demonstrations. Beasts, fowls, and fishes teaching and evidencing the glory of their creator. But these by an endless generation might succeed each other from everlasting.

Let us therefore survey their order and see by that whether we cannot discern their governor. The sun and moon and stars shine, and by shining minister influences to herbs and flowers. These grow and feed the cattle; the seas also and springs minister unto them, as they do unto fowls and fishes. All which are subservient unto man, a more noble creature endued with understanding to admire his creator. Who being king and lord of this world, is able to prize all in a reflexive manner, and render praises for all with joy, living blessedly in the fruition of them. None can question the being of a Deity but one that is ignorant of man's excellencies and the glory of his dominion over all the creatures.

Man Made in the Image of God

Above all, man discovers the glory of God, who being himself immortal, is the divinest creature. He has a dominion over all the rest, and God over him. By him, the fountain of all these things is the end of them, for he can return to their author deserved praises.

Senses cannot resemble that which they cannot apprehend, nor express that which they cannot resemble, but in a shady manner. But man is made in the image of God, and therefore is a mirror and representative of him, and therefore in himself he may see God, which is his glory and felicity.

His thoughts and desires can run out to everlasting. His love can extend to all objects. His understanding is an endless light and can infinitely be present in all places, and see and examine all beings: survey the reasons, surmount the greatness, exceed the strength, contemplate the beauty, enjoy the benefit, and reign over all it sees and enjoys like the eternal Godhead. Here is an invisible power, an indivisible omnipresence, a spiritual supremacy, an inward, hidden, unknown being greater than all, a sublime and sovereign creature meet to live in communion with God in the fruition of them.

God Appears to Our Understanding

That you are a man should fill you with joys and make you to overflow with praises. The privilege of your nature being infinitely infinite. And that the world serves you in this fathomless manner, exhibiting the Deity, and ministering to your blessedness, ought daily to transport you with a blessed vision into ravishments and ecstasies.

What knowledge could you have had of God by an unprofitable wall though endless and infinite? For though as things now are, nothing can be, but it exhibits a Deity; as the Apostle says, "By things that are seen the invisible things of God are manifested, even his power and Godhead,"[63] because everything is a demonstration of his goodness and power; by its existence and the end to which it is guided. Yet an endless wall could never manifest his being, were it present with you alone, for it would deny that infinity by its unprofitableness, which it shows by its endlessness.

The true exemplar of God's infinity is that of your understanding, which is a lively pattern and idea of it. It excludes nothing and contains all things, being a power that permits all objects to be and is able to enjoy them. Here is a profitable endlessness of infinite value, because without it infinite joys and blessings would be lost, which by it are enjoyed.

How great does God appear, in wisely preparing such an understanding to enjoy his creatures; such an endless, invisible, and mysterious receiver! And how blessed and divine are you, to whom God has not only simply appeared, but whom he has exalted as an immortal king among all his creatures!

CHAPTER 13

LET GOD'S LOVE RESTORE YOUR PERSON TO GREATER BEAUTY

The Infinite Benefits & Rightness of Love

You are able to see his righteousness and blessedness and glory, which are invisible. Yea, which is infinitely more, to resemble and attain them, to express them in yourself, enjoying them and the similitude of them.

No beast can see what righteousness is, nor is any brute capable of imitating it. You are, being admitted into the fellowship and order of angels. Which have neither eyes nor ears, and yet see and understand things which are infinitely higher than the sphere of senses.

You are able to discern that in all these things he is love to you; and that love is a fountain of infinite benefits, and does all that is possible for its beloved object. It endlessly desires to delight itself, and its delight is to magnify its beloved.

You are able to see the righteousness of love in this. For in doing the best of all possible things, it is right wise to itself and to all other beings. Right wise to itself in glorifying itself in the best of manners, and to all other things in making them most excellent. Right wise to itself in preparing for itself the best of treasures, and to its object in like manner in making its beloved the most blessed. Right wise unto itself in satisfying itself in its infinite desire of becoming delightful to its object, in preparing for itself infinite pleasures, and in making for itself the most delightful object that can possibly be made. Right wise unto you in making you that object, and providing all the treasures of itself for you, and making itself infinitely joyous and delightful to you.

Nothing is so righteous or right wise as love. For by making itself glorious it becomes infinite, and by loving its object infinitely it enables itself to delight infinitely in its object's happiness, and wisely prepares infinite treasures—right wisely thereby at once enriching itself and its object, so that you are able evidently to discern that God is love, and therein to contemplate all his perfections.

God's Works: The Expression of His Love

You are able therein to see the infinite glory of your high estate. For if God is love, and love be so restless a principle in exalting its object and so secure that it always promotes and glorifies and exalts itself thereby, where will there be any bounds in your exaltation? How dreadful, how amiable, how blessed, how great, how unsearchable, how incomprehensible must you be in your true real inward happiness!

The object of love is infinitely exalted. Love is infinitely delightful to its object: God by all his works manifests himself to be love, and you being the end of them are evidently its object. Go where you will, here alone shall you find your happiness. Contemplate therefore the works of God, for they serve you not only in manifesting him, but in making you to know yourself and your blessedness.

God's Works: A Gate to Seeing God's Kingdom

As love is righteous in glorifying itself and making its object blessed, so is it in all its dealings and dispensations towards it. Having made it amiable, it cannot but love it, which it is righteous in doing, for to love what is lovely is a righteous thing. To make it infinitely amiable is a righteous thing to infinite love, and to love it infinitely, being infinitely amiable. For thereby infinite love does right to itself and its measure; yea, to itself and its object.

To tender what is amiable is a righteous thing; to hurt it is evil. Love therefore is infinitely righteous in being infinitely tender of its object's welfare, and in hating infinitely the sin of hurting it. It is righteous in commanding others to promote it, and in punishing those that injure or offend it.

And thus have you a gate, in the prospect even of this world, whereby you may see into God's kingdom. For by his works you see that God is love, and by his love see the nature of all righteousness opened and unfolded with the ground and foundations of rewards and punishments.

God's Works: His Gifts That We Must Appreciate

But God being infinite is infinitely righteous. His love therefore is righteous to itself and all its works as well as its object. To itself in requiring that it be infinitely esteemed, of which it is infinitely desirous.

The contemners of it therefore it infinitely punishes. To its works not only in making them the best that may be, but in requiring an exact and due esteem from the enjoyers of them. Is not love jealous of the honor of its gifts? Does not a contempt of its presents rebound upon itself?

The world therefore serves you abundantly in teaching you your duty. They daily cry in a living manner with a silent and yet most loud voice, "We are all his gifts. We are tokens and presents of his love. You must therefore esteem us according to the beauty and worth that is in us, and the love from whence we came." Which to do is certainly the most blessed thing in all worlds, as not to do it is most wicked and most miserable.

Our Obligation to Love

Love further manifests itself in joining righteousness and blessedness together, for wherein can love appear more than in making our duty most blessed. Which here is done by making obedience the fruition of one's blessedness.

God cannot therefore but be infinitely provoked when we break his laws. Not only because love is jealous and cruel as the grave,[64] but because also our duty being so amiable, which it imposes on us with infinite obligations, they are all despised: his love itself, our most beautiful duty and all its obligations. So that his wrath must be very heavy and his indignation infinite.

Reconciled to Your Person, Not Your Ugly Sin

Yet love can forbear and love can forgive, though it can never be reconciled to an unlovely object. And hence it is that though you have so little considered the works of God and prized his love, yet you are permitted to live, and live at ease, and enjoy your pleasure. But love can never be reconciled to an unlovely object, and you are infinitely unlovely by despising God and his love so long. Yea, one act only of despite done to the smallest creature made you infinitely deformed.

What shall become of you therefore since God cannot be reconciled to an ugly object? Verily you are in danger of perishing eternally. He cannot indeed be reconciled to an ugly object as it is ugly, but as it is capable of being otherwise he may. He can never therefore be reconciled to your sin, because sin itself is incapable of being altered; but he may be reconciled to your person because that may be restored, and, which is an infinite wonder, to greater beauty and splendor than before.

Severing the Sin From the Sinner

By how much the greater his love was, by so much the greater may his sorrow be at the loss of his object, and by so much the greater his desire also of its restoration.

His love therefore being infinite, may do infinite things for an object infinitely valued. Being infinite in wisdom, it is able also to devise a way inscrutable to us, whereby to sever the sin from the sinner, and to satisfy its righteousness in punishing the transgression, yet satisfy itself in saving the transgressor. And to purge away the dross and incorporated filth and leprosy of sin, restoring the soul to its primitive beauty, health, and glory.

But then it does this at an infinite expense, wherein also it is more delighted, and especially magnified, for it gives another equally dear unto itself to suffer in its stead. And thus we come again by the works of God to our Lord Jesus Christ.

Angels Not Bound to Die for Men

Whoever suffers innocently and justly in another's stead must become a surety by his voluntary act. And this an angel or a cherubim might have done. He might also perhaps have suffered an infinite punishment in the removal of that love of God which he infinitely prized, and perhaps also he might have paid an obedience which he owed not.

For the angels are bound to love God with all their might, and men as themselves, while they are innocent, and to live by loving them in their blessedness and glory. Yet they are not bound by virtue of this law to die for men, being wicked and deformed; and therefore in undertaking this might have undertaken more than was their duty, and perhaps loving God infinitely (had they seen his love to man), they would.

Yea, perhaps also they might have suffered in our nature; and been able to have sustained infinite wrath; which are all the conditions usually reckoned up and numbered by Divines, as requisite in a mediator and redeemer of others. For they might have been hypostatically united to our nature, and though they were creatures, yet almighty power can sustain a creature under as great a punishment as almighty power can inflict. Almighty power upholding it being like the nether millstone, and almighty power punishing like the upper millstone, between which two it is infinitely tormented.

We must therefore search higher into the causes of our Saviour's prelation above them.

Jesus' Suffering for Man

One great cause why no angel was admitted to this office was because it was an honor infinitely too great and sublime for them, God accounting none but his own Son worthy of that dignity. Wherefore, it is written, "No man takes this honor to himself, but he that is called of God, as was Aaron."[65]

Neither did Jesus (though he were the Son of God) make himself a High Priest, but he that said unto him, "You are a priest forever after the order of Melchisedec."[66] Nor yet was it forced or imposed upon him, but he voluntarily undertook it. For which cause God has highly exalted him, and given him a name which is above every name in heaven and earth, because being in the form of God, he thought it not robbery to be equal with God, yet took upon him the form of a servant, and being found in the fashion of a man would humble himself to the death of the cross for our sakes.[67]

Where we learn several strange and admirable things: first, how high an honor it is to suffer for God in this world; secondly, in what an infinite dignity man is exalted, for whom God counted none worthy to suffer but his own Son; and thirdly, the equity of God's proceeding in chastising another for our sins (against the Socinians who, being blind in this mystery, are the enemies of our Saviour's Deity in this world). For had he imposed this task upon one that was unwilling, it had been injustice. Had he imposed it upon one that was unable to perform it, it had been folly. Had he imposed it upon anyone to his harm, cruelty. But laying it upon one that was willing and able, to his highest benefit, it was righteousness, wisdom, and glory. All mercy, goodness, and love on every side.

Objects of Infinite Love

How vile are they, and blind and ignorant, that will not see everyone to be the heir of the world, for whose sake all this was done!

"He that spared not his own Son but gave him up for us all, how shall he not with him also freely give us all things?"[68]

Is not he an object of infinite love for whom our Saviour died? Shall not all things in heaven and earth serve him in splendor and glory, for whom the Son of God came down to minister in agonies and sufferings? O here contemplate the glory of man and his high exaltation in the throne of God. Here consider how you are beloved, and be transported with excess of joy at this wonderful mystery.

Leave the trash and vanities of the world to live here in communion with the blessed Trinity. Imitate St. Paul who counted all things but dross and dung for the excellency of the knowledge of God in Christ.[69] And thus the works of God serve you in teaching you the knowledge of our Lord and Saviour.

Dignity of Man

Another reason for which our redemption was denied to angels and reserved only to be wrought by our Saviour is the dignity of man; for the redemption of their soul is precious and it ceases forever. None of them can by any means redeem him, nor give to God a ransom for him.[70]

Having sinned, he must be clothed in the righteousness of God or perish forever. All the angels and cherubims in heaven, though their righteousness should be imputed to him, could not justify him. No created righteousness is able to cover him, the exceeding glory of his primitive estate being so great that it made his sin infinitely infinite.

Infinite Punishments & Love

Yet further, another reason why this office was delegated to none of them was this: He that died for us must by his own merits save us. Being therefore our Saviour was to merit for us by his own actions, it was necessary that he should be such a one, who, by his own power, could sustain infinite punishments and offer them up to God on our behalf with infinite love as a voluntary obedience. Which only Christ was able to do out of the treasury of his own fullness. For the divine essence in him could overcome infinite punishments and infinitely love the inflicter of them without any repining, despondency, or hatred, returned for the same.

Where it is curious to observe how fully our Saviour satisfied for us. We hated God when he loved us. Our Saviour not only loved God, while God loved him, but loved him also with infinite love even while he expressed hatred against him.

Eternal Sacrifice

Finally, another reason was the dignity of our Saviour's person, who, being infinitely more excellent than all angels, was, in his condescensions, infinitely more acceptable. Which excellency both of his person and condescension is not a little magnified by his eternity. By his sufferings he brought in eternal righteousness. That he should stoop down for our sakes was infinitely meritorious.

And since the will before God is the highest deed, accepting this from all eternity, it is as if from all eternity he had suffered for us. His love to God and man in this act was infinite and eternal. And therefore is it said that he, through the eternal spirit, offered up himself a sacrifice to God for us.[71] His eternal spirit from everlasting offered up itself when he said, "Lo, I come. In the volume of the Book is it written of me: to do your will, O God."[72] And he offered up himself through the eternal spirit in time when he was slain upon the cross.

Now no creature can offer up itself eternally, because it was not from everlasting. Nor can anything work eternal righteousness for us but God alone.

Love's Suffering

How then should we be saved? Since eternal righteousness must be paid for our temporal iniquity. Since one must suffer by his own strength on our behalf, and out of his own fullness defray our debt of infinite charity, and that in the midst of sufferings; which no angel or seraphin is able. Since he must pay an obedience which he did not owe, both in loving men when themselves were hateful and in loving God when he was hated of him. Since none but God could do this, and it was inconvenient for God to do it, whither shall we fly for refuge?

Verily, we are in a great strait; but in the midst of these exigencies, love prepares for itself an offering. One mighty to save, concerning whom it is written, "This day have I begotten you."[73]

CHAPTER 14

SEE GOD'S LOVE IN THE TRINITY

Love Begetting Love

God by loving begot his Son. For God is love, and by loving he begot his love. He is of himself, and by loving he is what he is, infinite love. God is not a mixed and compounded being, so that his love is one thing and himself another; but the most pure and simple of all beings, all act, and pure love in the abstract.

Being love therefore itself, by loving he begot his love. Had he not loved, he had not been what he now is: the God of love, the most righteous of all beings, in being infinitely righteous to himself and all. But, by loving, he is infinitely righteous to himself and all.

For he is of himself, infinitely blessed and most glorious; and all his creatures are of him, in whom they are infinitely delighted and blessed and glorious.

A Love Trinity

In all love there is a love begetting and a love begotten and a love proceeding. Which, though they are one in essence, subsist nevertheless in three several manners.

For love is benevolent affection to another, which is of itself, and by itself relates to its object. It flows from itself and rests in its object. Love proceeds of necessity from itself, for unless it be of itself it is not love. Constraint is destructive and opposite to its nature.

The love from which it flows is the fountain of love. The love which streams from it is the communication of love, or love communicated. The love which rests in the object is the love which streams to it. So that in all love, the trinity is clear.

By secret passages without stirring it proceeds to its object, and is as powerfully present as if it did not proceed at all. The love that lies in the bosom of the lover, being the love that is perceived in the spirit of the beloved: that is, the same in substance, though in the manner of substance or subsistence different. Love in the bosom is the parent of love, love in the stream is the effect of love, love seen or dwelling in the object proceeds from both.

Yet are all these one and the self-same love, though three loves.

Love in the Fountain & In the Stream

Love in the fountain and love in the stream are both the same. And therefore are they both equal in time and glory. For love communicates itself, and therefore love in the fountain is the very love communicated to its object.

Love in the fountain is love in the stream, and love in the stream equally glorious with love in the fountain. Though it streams to its object it abides in the lover, and is the love of the lover.

Lover Existing in Another Person

Where love is the lover, love streaming from the lover is the lover; the lover streaming from himself and existing in another person.

Jesus: The Wisdom & Love of the Father

This person is the Son of God; who, as he is the wisdom of the Father, so is he the love of the Father. For the love of the Father is the wisdom of the Father.

And this person did God, by loving us, beget, that he might be the means of all our glory.

Jesus And His Father

This person differs in nothing from the Father, but only in this: that he is begotten of him. He is eternal with the Father, as glorious and as intelligent. He is of the same mind in everything in all worlds: loves the same objects in as infinite a measure.

He is the means by which the Father loves, acts, creates, redeems, governs, and perfects all things. And the means also by which we see and love the Father: our strength and our eternity. He is the mediator between God and his creatures. God therefore being willing to redeem us by his own blood,[74] by him redeemed us, and in his person died for us.

Love is the Spirit of God

How wonderful is it that God, by being love, should prepare a redeemer to die for us? But how much more wonderful, that by this means himself should be, and be God by being love!

By this means also he refines our nature and enables us to purge out the poison and the filthy plague of sin. For love is so amiable and desirable to the soul that it cannot be resisted. Love is the spirit of God. In himself it is the Father, or else the Son, for the Father is in the Son, and the Son is in the Father. In us it is the Holy Ghost.

The love of God being seen, being God in us: purifying, illuminating, strengthening, and comforting the soul of the seer. For God, by spewing, communicates himself to men and angels. And when he dwells in the soul, dwells in the sight. And when he dwells in the sight, achieving all that love can do for such a soul.

And thus the world serves you as it is a mirror wherein you contemplate the blessed Trinity. For it plainly shows that God is love, and in his being love, you see the unity of the blessed trinity, and a glorious trinity in the blessed unity.

Love is the End of Itself

In all love there is some producer, some means, and some end; all these being internal in the thing itself. Love loving is the producer, and that is the Father. Love produced is the means, and that is the Son. For love is the means by which a lover loves. The end of these means is love, for it is love by loving, and that is the Holy Ghost. The end and the producer being both the same by the means attained. For by loving, love attains itself and being. The producer is attained by loving, and is the end of himself.

That love is the end of itself, and that God loves that he might be love, is as evident to him that considers spiritual things, as the sun. Because it is impossible there should be a higher end or a better proposed. What can be more desirable than the most delightful operation; what more eligible, than the most glorious being; what further can be proposed than the most blessed and perfect life?

Since God therefore chooses the most perfect life, what can be more perfect than that life and that being which is at once the fountain and the end of all things? There being in it the perpetual joy of giving and receiving infinite treasures. To be the fountain of joys and blessings is delightful. And by being love, God is the fountain of all worlds. To receive all and to be the end of all is equally delightful, and, by being love, God receives and is the end of all. For all the benefits that are done unto all, by loving all, himself receives. What good could heaven and earth do him were it not for his love to the children of men? By being what he is, which is love unto all, he enjoys all.

The Delightful Life of Love

What life can be more pleasant than that which is delighted in itself and in all objects; in which also all objects infinitely delight? What life can be more pleasant than that which is blessed in all and glorious before all? Now this life is the life of love.

For this end therefore did he desire to love: that he might be love. Infinitely delightful to all objects, infinitely delighted in all, and infinitely pleased in himself for being infinitely delightful to all and delighted in all. All this he attains by love.

For love is the most delightful of all employments. All the objects of love are delightful to it, and love is delightful to all its objects. Well then may love be the end of loving, which is so complete. It being a thing so delightful, that God infinitely rejoices in himself for being love.

And thus you see how God is the end of himself. He does what he does, that he may be what he is: wise and glorious and bountiful and blessed in being perfect love.

Souls Are Made to Love

Love is so divine and perfect a thing, that it is worthy to be the very end and being of the Deity. It is his goodness, and it is his glory. We therefore so vastly delight in love, because all these excellencies and all other whatsoever lie within it.

By loving a soul does propagate and beget itself. By loving it does dilate and magnify itself. By loving it does enlarge and delight itself. By loving also it delights others, as by loving it honors and enriches itself. But above all, by loving it does attain itself.

Love also being the end of souls, which are never perfect till they are in act what they are in power. They were made to love, and are dark and vain and comfortless till they do it. Till they love they are idle or misemployed. Till they love they are desolate: without their objects, and narrow and little and dishonorable. But when they shine by love upon all objects, they are accompanied with them and enlightened by them. Till we become therefore all act as God is, we can never rest, nor ever be satisfied.

Enjoying God's Goodness to the World

Love is so noble that it enjoys others' enjoyments, delights in giving all unto its object, and in seeing all given to its object. So that whosoever loves all mankind, he enjoys all the goodness of God to the whole world, and endeavors the benefit of kingdoms and ages with all whom he is present by love, which is the best manner of presence that is possible.

God Is Present by Love Alone

God is present by love alone. By love alone he is great and glorious. By love alone he lives and feels in other persons. By love alone he enjoys all the creatures; by love alone he is pleasing to himself; by love alone he is rich and blessed.

O why do not you by love alone seek to achieve all these, by love alone attain another self, by love alone live in others, by love attain your glory? The soul is shriveled up and buried in a grave that does not love. But that which does love wisely and truly is the joy and end of all the world, the king of heaven and the friend of God, the shining light and temple of eternity, the brother of Christ Jesus and one spirit with the Holy Ghost.

CHAPTER 15

EXTEND YOUR LOVE TO ALL OBJECTS

Love: A Candle in the Lantern of Our Bodies

Love is a far more glorious being than flesh and bones. If you will, it is endless, and infinitely more sweet than your body can be to you and others. Your body is confined and is a dull lump of heavy clay by which you are retarded, rather than moves. It was given you to be a lantern only to the candle of love that shines in your soul. By it you see and feel and eat and drink, but the end of all is that you might be as God is: a joy and blessing by being love.

Your love is unlimited. Your love can extend to all objects. Your love can see God and accompany his love throughout all eternity. Your love is infinitely profitable to yourself and others. To yourself, for thereby may you receive infinite good things. To others, for thereby you are prone to do infinite good to all.

Your body can receive but few pleasures. Your love can feed upon all: take into itself all worlds, and all eternities above all worlds, and all the joys of God before and after. Your flesh and bones can do but little good, nor that little unless as by love it is inspired and directed. A poor carcase your body is; but love is delightful and profitable to thousands.

O live therefore by the more noble part. Be like him who baptizes with fire. Feel your spirit, awaken your soul, be an enlarged seraphim, an infinite good, or like unto him.

Living Infinitely by Loving God

The true way we may go unto his throne, and can never exceed, nor be too high. All hyperboles are but little pigmies and diminutive expressions, in comparison of the truth. All that Adam could propose to himself, or hope for, was laid up in store for him in a better way than he could ask or think. But in seeking for it a false way, he lost all: what he had in hope and what he had in fruition.

To be as God, we are prompted to desire by the instinct of nature. And that we shall be by loving all that he does. But by loving him, what O what shall we be? By loving him according to the greatness of his love unto us, according to his amiableness as we ought, and according to the obligations that lie upon us, we shall be no man can devise what. We shall love him infinitely more than ourselves, and therefore live infinitely more in him than in ourselves, and be infinitely more delighted with his eternal blessedness than our own. We shall infinitely more delight in him than in ourselves. All worlds, all angels, all men, all kingdoms, all creatures will be more ours in him than in ourselves—so will his essence and eternal Godhead. Oh love, what have you done!

God is Infinitely More Blessed

And he will so love us, when all this beauty of love is within us, that though we by our love to him seem more blessed in his blessedness than he, he is infinitely more blessed than we even in our blessedness—we being so united to each other by living in each other, that nothing can divide us forevermore.

The Ironies of Love

Love is infinitely delightful to its object, and the more violent the more glorious. It is infinitely high, nothing can hurt it. And infinitely great in all extremes of beauty and excellency. Excess is its true moderation, activity its rest, and burning fervency its only refreshment.

Nothing is more glorious, yet nothing more humble. Nothing more precious, yet nothing more cheap. Nothing more familiar, yet nothing so inaccessible. Nothing more nice, yet nothing more laborious. Nothing more liberal, yet nothing more covetous.

It does all things for its object's sake, yet it is the most self-ended thing in the whole world; for of all things in nature it can least endure to be displeased. Since therefore it contains so many miracles, it may well contain this one more—that it makes every one greatest, and among lovers every one is supreme and sovereign.

Crowning My Friends with Glory and Happiness

God, by love, wholly ministers to others, and yet wholly ministers to himself, love having this wonder in it also: that among innumerable millions, it makes everyone the sole and single end of all things. It attains all unattainables and achieves impossibilities—that is, seeming impossibilities to our inexperience, and real impossibilities to any other means or endeavors. For indeed it makes every one more than the end of all things, and infinitely more than the sole supreme and sovereign of all.

For it makes him so first in himself and then in all. For while all things in heaven and earth fall out after my desire, I am the end and sovereign of all. Which conspiring always to crown my friends with glory and happiness, and pleasing all in the same manner whom I love as myself, I am in every one of them the end of all things again, being as much concerned in their happiness as my own.

Love: How a Soul Propagates Itself

By loving, a soul does propagate and beget itself, because, before it loved, it lived only in itself—after it loved, and while it loves, it lives in its object. Nay, it did not so much as live in itself before it loved.

For as the sun would be unseen and buried in itself, did it not scatter and spread abroad its beams, by which alone it becomes glorious, so the soul without extending and living in its object, is dead within itself—an idle chaos of blind and confused powers—for which when it loves, it gains three subsistencies in itself by the act of loving: a glorious spirit that abides within, a glorious spirit that flows in the stream, a glorious spirit that resides in the object. Insomuch that now it can enjoy a sweet communion with itself: in contemplating what it is in itself and to its object.

Our Strong Desire to Be Good to Others

Love is so vastly delightful in the lover because it is the communication of his goodness. For the natural end of goodness is to be enjoyed: it desires to be another's happiness. Which goodness of God is so deeply implanted in our natures that we never enjoy ourselves but when we are the joy of others.

Of all our desires, the strongest is to be good to others. We delight in receiving, more in giving. We love to be rich, but then it is that we thereby might be more greatly delightful. Thus we see the seeds of eternity sparkling in our natures.

Love: The Only Throne That Exalts Us

Love is so vastly delightful to him that is beloved because it is the fountain of all affections, services, and endeavors, a spring of honor and liberality, and a secure pledge of future benefits. It is the sole title by which we reign in another's bosom and the only throne by which we are exalted. The body and soul of him that loves is his that is beloved. What then can love deny?

All greatness, power, and dominion befalls him that is beloved, in the soul that loves him. So that while all the glorious creatures in all worlds love you, you reign in all souls, are the image of God, and exalted like God in every bosom.

The End of Riches

Though no riches follow, yet we are all naturally delighted with love—both for what we receive and for what we give. When we are beloved, we receive the quintessence and glory of another's soul, the end of heaven and earth, the cream and flower of all perfections, the tribute of God Almighty, peace and welfare, pleasure and honor, help and safety, all in readiness. And something infinitely more and which we are not able to express.

When we are beloved, we attain the end of riches in an immediate manner, and having the end need not regard the means. For the end of riches is that we may be beloved.

We receive power to see ourselves amiable in another's soul, and to delight and please another person. For it is impossible to delight a lukewarm person or an alienated affection with giving crowns and scepters, so as we may a person that violently loves us with our very presence and affections.

Power to Please God

By this we may discern what strange power God has given to us by loving us infinitely. He gives us a power more to please him, than if we were able to create worlds and present them unto him.

Living in All

How happy we are that we may live in all as well as one; and how all-sufficient love is, we may see by this: the more we live in all, the more we live in one. For while he sees us to live in all, we are a more great and glorious object unto him; the more we are beloved of all, the more we are admired by him; the more we are the joy of all, the more blessed we are to him. The more blessed we are to him, the greater is our blessedness.

We are all naturally ambitious of being magnified in others, and of seeming great in others. Which inclination was implanted in us that our happiness might be enlarged by the multitude of spectators.

Love: How the World is Enjoyed

Love is the true means by which the world is enjoyed: our love to others and others' love to us. We ought therefore above all things to get acquainted with the nature of love. For love is the root and foundation of nature. Love is the soul of life and crown of rewards.

If we cannot be satisfied in the nature of love, we can never be satisfied at all. The very end for which God made the world was that he might manifest his love. Unless therefore we can be satisfied with his love so manifested, we can never be satisfied.

There are many glorious excellencies in the material world, but without love they are all abortive. We might spend ages in contemplating the nature of the sun, and entertain ourselves many years with the beauty of the stars and services of the sea. But the soul of man is above all these—it comprehends all ages in a moment, and, unless it perceive something more excellent, is very desolate. All worlds being but a silent wilderness without some living thing more sweet and blessed after which it aspires.

Love in the fountain and love in the end is the glory of the world and the soul of joy—which it infinitely prefers above all worlds, and delights in, and loves to contemplate more than all visible beings that are possible. So that you must be sure to see causes wherefore infinitely to be delighted with the love of God, if ever you would be happy.

Contemplate the Glory of Love and Being Loved

See causes also wherefore to be delighted in your love to men and in the love of men to you. For the world serves you to this end, that you might love them and be beloved of them. And unless you are pleased with the end for which the world serves you, you can never be pleased with the means leading to that end.

Above all things therefore, contemplate the glory of loving men, and of being beloved of them. For this end our Saviour died and for this end he came into the world: that you might be restored from hatred, which is the greatest misery—from the hatred of God and men which was due for sin, and from the misery of hating God and men; for to hate and be hated is the greatest misery. The necessity of hating God and men being the greatest bondage that hell can impose.

The World Becomes Ours Through Love

When you love men, the world quickly becomes yours, and yourself become a greater treasure than the world is. For all their persons are your treasures and all the things in heaven and earth that serve them are yours. For those are the riches of love, which minister to its object.

Our Proneness to Love

You are as prone to love as the sun is to shine, it being the most delightful and natural employment of the soul of man: without which you are dark and miserable. Consider therefore the extent of love, its vigor and excellency. For certainly he that delights not in love makes vain the universe, and is of necessity to himself the greatest burden.

The whole world ministers to you as the theatre of your love. It sustains you and all objects that you may continue to love them. Without which it were better for you to have no being. Life without objects is sensible emptiness, and that is a greater misery than death or nothing. Objects without love are a delusion of life. The objects of love are its greatest treasures, and without love it is impossible they should be treasures. For the objects which we love are the pleasing objects and delightful things. And whatsoever is not pleasing and delightful to you can be no treasure: nay it is distasteful and worse than nothing, since we had rather it should have no being.

Doting on One Person

That violence wherewith sometimes a man dotes upon one creature is but a little spark of that love, even towards all, which lurks in his nature. We are made to love, both to satisfy the necessity of our active nature and to answer the beauties in every creature.

By love our souls are married and soldered to the creatures and it is our duty like God to be united to them all. We must love them infinitely, but in God and for God and God in them: namely all his excellencies manifested in them.

When we dote upon the perfections and beauties of some one creature, we do not love that too much, but other things too little. Never was anything in this world loved too much, but many things have been loved in a false way, and all in too short a measure.

You Can't Love Too Much

Suppose a river, or a drop of water, an apple or a sand, an ear of corn, or an herb: God knows infinite exellencies in it more than we. He sees how it relates to angels and men, how it proceeds from the most perfect lover to the most perfectly beloved, how it represents all his attributes, how it conduces in its place by the best of means to the best of ends: and for this cause it cannot be beloved too much. God the author and God the end is to be beloved in it; angels and men are to be beloved in it; and it is highly to be esteemed for all their sakes.

O what a treasure is every sand when truly understood! Who can love anything that God made too much? What a world would this be, were everything beloved as it ought to be!

Ten Thousand Beauties in Every Woman

Suppose a curious and fair woman. Some have seen the beauties of heaven in such a person. It is a vain thing to say they loved too much. I dare say there are ten thousand beauties in that creature which they have not seen. They loved it not too much, but upon false causes. Nor so much upon false ones, as only upon some little ones.

They love a creature for sparkling eyes and curled hair, lily breasts and ruddy cheeks, which they should love moreover for being God's image, queen of the universe, beloved by angels, redeemed by Jesus Christ, an heiress of heaven, and temple of the Holy Ghost: a mine and fountain of all virtues, a treasury of graces, and a child of God. But these excellencies are unknown.

They love her perhaps, but do not love God more, nor men as much, nor heaven and earth at all. And so, being defective to other things, perish by a seeming excess to that. We should be all life and mettle and vigor and love to everything—and that would poise us. I dare confidently say that every person in the whole world ought to be beloved as much as this: and she if there be any cause of difference more than she is.

But God being beloved infinitely more, will be infinitely more our joy, and our heart will be more with him, so that no man can be in danger by loving others too much, that loves God as he ought.

Managing Our Love

The sun and stars please me in ministering to you. They please me in ministering to a thousand others as well as you.

And you please me because you can live and love in the image of God: not in a blind and brutish manner as beasts do—by a mere appetite and rude propensity—but with a regulated, well-ordered love, upon clear caus-es, and with a rational affection guided to divine and celestial ends. Which is to love with a divine and holy love, glorious and blessed.

We are all prone to love, but the art lies in managing our love: to make it truly amiable and proportionable. To love for God's sake and to this end: that we may be well-pleasing unto him. To love with a design to imitate him, and to satisfy the principles of intelligent nature, and to become hon-orable, is to love in a blessed and holy manner.

CHAPTER 16
GO OUT OF YOURSELF WITH THE POWER OF YOUR SOUL

Spiritually Multiplying Ourselves

In one soul we may be entertained and taken up with innumerable beauties. But in the soul of man there are innumerable infinities. One soul, in the immensity of its intelligence, is greater and more excellent than the whole world. The ocean is but the drop of a bucket to it, the heavens but a center, the sun obscurity, and all ages but as one day. It being by its understanding a temple of eternity, and God's omnipresence, between which and the whole world there is no proportion. Its love is a dominion greater than that which Adam had in paradise, and yet the fruition of it is but solitary.

We need spectators and other diversities of friends and lovers, in whose souls we might likewise dwell, and with whose beauties we might be crowned and entertained. In all whom we can dwell exactly, and be present with them fully. Lest therefore the other depths and faculties of our souls should be desolate and idle, they also are created to entertain us. And as in many mirrors we are so many other selves, so are we spiritually multiplied when we meet ourselves more sweetly, and live again in other persons.

An Infinite Wonder: Millions of Souls

Creatures are multiplied that our treasures may be multiplied, and their places enlarged that the territories of our joys might be enlarged—with all which our souls may be present in immediate manner.

For since the sun, which is a poor little dead thing, can at once shine upon many kingdoms and be wholly present, not only in many cities and realms upon earth, but in all the stars in the firmament of heaven; surely the soul which is a far more perfect sun, nearer unto God in excellency and nature, can do far more.

But that which of all wonders is the most deep and incredible is that a soul, whereas one would think it could measure but one soul which is as large as it, can exceed that, and measure all souls wholly and fully. This is an infinite wonder indeed. For admit that the powers of one soul were fathomless and infinite: are not the powers so also of another?

One would think therefore that one soul should be lost in another, and that two souls should be exactly adequate. Yet indeed my soul can examine and search all the chambers and endless operations of another, being prepared to see innumerable millions.

Seeing & Accompanying the Endless Perfections in Every Soul

Here is a glorious creature! But that which makes the wonder infinitely infinite is this: that one soul, which is the object of mine, can see all souls and all the secret chambers and endless perfections in every soul: yea, and all souls with all their objects in every soul. Yet mine can accompany all these in one soul and without deficiency exceed that soul and accompany all these in every other soul—which shows the work of God to be deep and infinite.

By Desire, The Soul Extends Itself

Here upon earth perhaps, where our estate is imperfect, this is impossible; but in heaven, where the soul is all act, it is necessary—for the soul is there all that it can be. Here it is to rejoice in what it may be.

Till therefore the mists of error and clouds of ignorance, that confine this sun, be removed, it must be present in all kingdoms and ages virtually, as the sun is by night—if not by clear sight and love, at least by its desire. Which are its influences and its beams, working in a latent and obscure manner on earth, above in a strong and clear.

Maintaining All People in All Kingdoms as Our Joys

The world serves you therefore in maintaining all people in all kingdoms, which are the Father's treasures and your as yet invisible joys, that their multitudes at last may come to heaven, and make those innumerable thousands whose hosts and employments will be your joy. Whose order, beauty, melody, and glory will be your eternal delights. And of whom you have many a sweet description in the Revelation.

These are they of whom it is said:
"After this I beheld, and lo, a great multitude which no man could number, of all nations and kindred and people and tongues, stood before the throne and before the Lamb, clothed with white robes and palms in their hands, and they cried with a loud voice, saying, 'Salvation to our God which sits upon the Throne, and to the Lamb.' "[75]

Of which it is said,
"They fell down before the Lamb, having every one of them harps and golden vials full of odors which are the prayers of the saints, and they sang a new song saying, 'You are worthy to take the book, and to open the seals thereof: for you were slain, and have redeemed us to God by your blood, out of every kindred and tongue and people and nation, and have made us unto our God kings and priests."[76]

Of whom it is said,
"I saw a sea of glass, and they that had gotten the victory over the beast standing on it, and they sing the song of Moses, the servant of God, and the song of the Lamb, saying, 'Great and marvelous are your works, Lord God Almighty. Just and true are your ways, you King of Saints. Who shall not fear you, O Lord, and glorify your

name. For you only are holy; for all nations shall come
and worship before you, because your judgments are
made manifest.' "[77]

Our Souls' Actions in the Kingdom of Heaven

That all the powers of your soul shall be turned into act in the kingdom
of heaven is manifest by what Saint John writes in the Isle of Patmos:

> "And I beheld and I heard the voice of many angels round about the
> throne, and the beasts and the elders, and the number of them was
> ten thousand times ten thousand, and thousands of thousands:
> Saying with a loud voice, 'Worthy is the Lamb that was slain, to
> receive power and riches and wisdom and strength and honor and
> glory and blessing.' And every creature which is in heaven and on
> earth and under the earth, and such as are in the sea, and all
> that are in them, heard I saying, 'Blessing and honor and glory
> and power be unto him that sits upon the throne and unto the
> Lamb forever and ever.' "[78]

Going Out of Yourself

These things shall never be seen with your bodily eyes, but in a more
perfect manner: you shall be present with them in your understanding. You
shall be in them to the very center and they in you. As light is in a piece of
crystal, so shall you be with every part and excellency of them.

An act of the understanding is the presence of the soul, which being no
body but a living act, is a pure spirit and mysteriously fathomless in its true
dimensions. By an act of the understanding therefore be present now with
all the creatures among which you live, and hear them in their beings and

operations praising God in a heavenly manner—some of them vocally, others in their ministry, all of them naturally and continually.

We infinitely wrong ourselves by laziness and confinement. All creatures in all nations and tongues and people praise God infinitely, and the more, for being your sole and perfect treasures. You are never what you ought till you go out of yourself and walk among them.

Seeking Riches in All Places

Were all your riches here in some little place, all other places would be empty. It is necessary therefore, for your contentment and true satisfaction, that your riches be dispersed everywhere.

What is more delightful: to have some few private riches in one place, and all other places void, or to have all places everywhere filled with our proper treasures? Certainly to have treasures in all places. For by that means we are entertained everywhere with pleasures, are everywhere at home honored and delighted, everywhere enlarged and in our own possessions.

But to have a few riches in some narrow bounds, though we should suppose a kingdom full, would be to have our delights limited, and infinite spaces dark and empty, wherein we might wander without satisfaction. So that God must of necessity to satisfy his love give us infinite treasures. And we of necessity seek for our riches in all places.

How Objects Make Our Soul Known

The heavens and the earth serve you, not only in showing unto you your Father's glory, as all things without you are your riches and enjoyments, but as within you also they magnify, beautify, and illuminate your soul. For as the sunbeams illuminate the air and all objects, yet are themselves also illuminated by them, so fares it with the powers of your soul.

The rays of the sun carry light in them as they pass through the air, but go on in vain till they meet an object—and there they are expressed. They illuminate a mirror, and are illuminated by it.

For a looking glass without them would be in the dark, and they without the glass unperceived. There they revive and overtake themselves, and represent the effigies from whence they came—both of the sun and heavens, and trees and mountains—if the glass be seated conveniently to receive them. Which, were it not that the glass were present there, one would have thought even the ideas of them absent from the place.

Even so your soul in its rays and powers is unknown, and no man would believe it present everywhere, were there no objects there to be discerned. Your thoughts and inclinations pass on and are unperceived, but by their objects are discerned to be present—being illuminated by them. For they are present with them and active about them. They receive and feel themselves, and by those objects live in employment, being turned into the figure and idea of them.

For as light varies upon all objects whither it comes, and returns with the form and figure of them, so is the soul transformed into the being of its object. Like light from the sun, its first effigy is simple life, the pure resemblance of its primitive fountain; but on the object which it meets it is quickly changed, and by understanding becomes all things.

Both Enjoying Everything for Ourselves & Sharing All of It With Others

Objective treasures are always delightful, and, though we travail endlessly to see them all our own, are infinitely pleasant and, the further we go, the more delightful. If they are all ours wholly and solely, and yet nevertheless everyone's too, it is the most delightful accident that is imaginable—for thereby two contrary humors are at once delighted, and two inclinations, that are both in our natures yet seem contradictory, are at once satisfied.

The one is the avaricious humor and love of propriety, whereby we refer all unto ourselves and naturally desire to have all alone in our private possession, and to be the alone and single end of all things. This we perceive ourselves because all, universally and everywhere, is ours.

The other is the communicative humor that is in us, whereby we desire to have companions in our enjoyments to tell our joys and to spread abroad our delights and to be ourselves the joy and delight of other persons. For thousands enjoy all as well as we, and are the end of all; and God communicates all to them as well as us. And yet to us alone because he communicates them to us, and makes them our rich and glorious companions: to whom we may tell our joys and be blessed again.

How much ought we to praise God for satisfying two such insatiable humors that are contrary to each other! One would think it impossible that both should be pleased, and yet his divine wisdom has made them helpful and perfective to each other.

Filling All Time & Spaces With Our Love

Infinite love cannot be expressed in finite room, but must have infinite places wherein to utter and show itself. It must therefore fill all eternity and the omnipresence of God with joys and treasures for my fruition. And yet it must be expressed in a finite room by making me able in a center to enjoy them. It must be infinitely expressed in the smallest moment by making me able in every moment to see them all.

It is both ways infinite, for my soul is an infinite sphere in a center. By this way you know that you are infinitely beloved: God has made your spirit a center in eternity comprehending all, and filled all about you in an endless manner with infinite riches which shine before you and surround you with divine and heavenly enjoyments.

Infinity is Primary, Limit Secondary

Few will believe the soul to be infinite, yet infinity is the first thing which is naturally known. Bounds and limits are discerned only in a secondary manner.

Suppose a man were born deaf and blind. By the very feeling of his soul, he apprehends infinity about him—infinite space, infinite darkness. He thinks not of walls and limits till he feels them and is stopped by them.

That things are finite therefore, we learn by our senses. But infinity we know and feel by our souls, and feel it so naturally, as if it were the very essence and being of the soul. The truth of it is, it is individually in the soul: for God is there, and more near to us than we are to ourselves. So that we cannot feel our souls, but we must feel him in that first of properties: infinite space. And this we know so naturally, that it is the only *primo et necessario cognitum in rerum naturâ*: 'of all things the only first and most necessarily known.'

For we can unsuppose heaven and earth, and annihilate the world in our imagination—but the place where they stood will remain behind, and we cannot unsuppose or annihilate that, do what we can. Which without us is the chamber of our infinite treasures, and within us the repository and recipient of them.

God Exerting All His Power to Show His Goodness

What shall we render unto God for this infinite space in our understandings? Since, in giving us this, he has laid the foundation of infinite blessedness, manifested infinite love, and made us in capacity infinite creatures—in this he has glorified and gratified infinite goodness, exerted infinite power, and made himself thereby infinitely delightful and infinitely great, in being Lord and upholder of such infinite creatures.

For being wholly everywhere, his omnipresence was wholly in every center, and he could do no more than that would bear: communicate himself wholly in every center. His nature and essence being the foundation of his power and of our happiness, of his glory and our greatness, of his goodness and our satisfaction. For we could never believe that he loved us infinitely unless he exerted all his power. For *kata Dunamin* is one of the principal properties of love, as well as *ekeinou eneka*—'to the utmost of its power,' as well as 'for his sake.'

Our Cowardly & Lazy Expectations of God

He therefore has not only made us infinite treasures only in extent, and souls infinite to see and enjoy them, which is to measure and run parallel with them—but in depth also they are everywhere infinite, being infinite in excellency. And the soul is a miraculous abyss of infinite abysses, an undrainable ocean, an unexhausted fountain of endless oceans, when it will exert itself to fill and fathom them.

For if it were otherwise, man is a creature of such noble principles and severe expectations, that could he perceive the least defect to be in the Deity, it would infinitely displease him—the smallest distaste, spreading like a cloud from a hand over all the heavens.[79] Neither will any pretence serve the turn to cover our cowardice, which we call modesty, in not daring to say or expect this of the Deity. Unless we expect this with infinite ardency, we are a lazy kind of creatures, good for nothing.

'Tis man's holiness and glory to desire absolute perfection in God with a jealousy and care infinitely cruel. For when we so desire it, that without this we should be infinitely displeased and altogether lost and desperate forever, finding God to have exceeded all our desires, it becomes the foundation of infinite love. In the fruition of the fruits of which, we are to live in communion with him for evermore.

Space perfects its stature
Affections its colors
Objects its lineaments
Actions its graces.

The World Serves Our Souls with Ideas

Your soul being naturally very dark and deformed and empty when extended through infinite but empty space, the world serves you in beautifying and filling it with amiable ideas—for the perfecting of its stature in the eye of God.

For the thorough understanding of which you must know, that God is a being whose power from all eternity was prevented with act. And that he is one infinite act of knowledge and wisdom, which is infinitely beautified with many consequences of love, etc. Being one act of eternal knowledge, he knows all which he is able to know, all objects in all worlds being seen in his understanding. His greatness is the presence of his soul with all objects in infinite spaces, and his brightness the light of eternal wisdom.

His essence also is the light of things. For he is all eye and all ear. Being therefore perfect, and the mirror of all perfection, he has commanded us to be perfect as he is perfect. And we are to grow up into him till we are filled with the fullness of his Godhead.[80] We are to be conformed to the image of his glory till we become the resemblance of his great exemplar.

Which we then are, when our power is converted into act and covered with it, we being an act of knowledge and wisdom as he is. When our souls are present with all objects and beautified with the ideas and figures of them all. For then shall we be *MENTES* as he is *MENS*. We being of the same mind with him who is an infinite eternal mind. As both Plato and Cato with the Apostle, term him.

Si Deus est Animus sit pura Mente Colendus.
If God, as verses say, a spirit be
We must in spirit like the Deity
Become: we must the image of his mind
And union with it, in our spirit find.[81]

Heaven and earth, angels and men, God and all things must be contained in our souls, that we may become glorious personages and like unto him in all our actions.

Our Love is Valuable & Prized

You know that love receives a grandeur of value and esteem from the greatness of the person from whom it proceeds. The love of a king is naturally more delightful than the love of a beggar: the love of God more excellent than the love of a king. The love of a beautiful person is more pleasing than that of one deformed. The love of a wise man is far more precious than the love of a fool.

When you are so great a creature as to fill ages and kingdoms with the beauty of your soul, and to reign over them like the wisdom of the Father filling eternity with light and glory, your love shall be acceptable and sweet and precious. The world therefore serves you, not only in furnishing you with riches and making you beautiful and great and wise when it is rightly used: but in doing that which does infinitely concern you, in making your love precious.

For above all things in all worlds you naturally desire most violently that your love should be prized. And the reason is: because that being the best thing you can do or give, all is worthless that you can do besides; and you have no more power left to be good, or to please, or to do anything, when once your love is despised.

Preparing Ourselves to Speak to God

Since therefore love does all it is able to make itself accepted, both in increasing its own vehemence and in adorning the person of the lover, as well as in offering up the most choice and perfect gifts, with what care ought you to express your love in beautifying yourself with this wisdom, and in making your person acceptable? Especially since your person is the greatest gift your love can offer up to God Almighty.

Clothe yourself with light as with a garment[82] when you come before him: put on the greatness of heaven and earth, adorn yourself with the excellencies of God himself. When you prepare yourself to speak to him, be all the knowledge and light you are able, as great, as clear, and as perfect as is possible. So at length shall you appear before God in Zion,[83] and as God, converse with God forevermore.

Our Souls Should Contain Heaven & Earth

God has made it easy to convert our soul into a thought containing heaven and earth, not that it should be contemptible because it is easy, but done because it is divine. Which thought is as easily abolished, that by a perpetual influx of life it may be maintained. If he would but suspend his power, no doubt but heaven and earth would straight be abolished, which he upholds in himself as easily and as continually as we do the idea of them in our own mind.

Since therefore all things depending so continually upon his care and love, the perpetual influx of his almighty power is infinitely precious and his life exercised incessantly in the manifestation of eternal love. In that every moment throughout all generations he continues without failing to uphold all things for us, we likewise ought to show our infinite love by upholding heaven and earth, time and eternity, God and all things in our souls, without wavering or intermission—by the perpetual influx of our life.

To which we are by the goodness of all things infinitely obliged. Once to cease is to draw upon ourselves infinite darkness, after we have begun to be so illuminated—for it shows a forgetfulness and defect in love, and it is an infinite wonder that we are afterward restored.

God's Mercy

Being that we are here upon earth turmoiled with cares, and often shaken with winds and by disturbances distracted, it is the infinite mercy of God that we are permitted to breathe and be diverted. For all the things in heaven and earth attend upon us while we ought to answer and observe them by upholding their beauty within.

But we are spared and God winks at our defect, all the world attending us while we are about some little trifling business. But in the estate of glory, the least intermission would be an eternal apostasy. But there by reason of our infinite union with God, it is impossible.

The Value of the World in Our Thoughts

We could easily show that the idea of heaven and earth in the soul of man is more precious with God than the things themselves, and more excellent in nature. Which because it will surprise you a little, I will.

What would heaven and earth be worth, were there no spectator, no enjoyer? As much therefore as the end is better than the means, the thought of the world whereby it is enjoyed is better than the world.

So is the idea of it in the soul of man better than the world in the esteem of God: it being the end of the world, without which heaven and earth would be in vain. It is better to you because by it you receive the world, and it is the tribute you pay. It more immediately beautifies and perfects your nature. How deformed would you be should all the world stand about you and you be idle. Were you able to create other worlds, God had rather you should think on this. For thereby you are united to him.

The sun in your eye is as much to you as the sun in the heavens. For by this the other is enjoyed. It would shine on all rivers, trees, and beasts in vain to you could you not think upon it. The sun in your understanding illuminates your soul; the sun in the heavens enlightens the hemisphere.

The world within you is an offering returned, which is infinitely more acceptable to God Almighty since it came from him, that it might return unto him. Wherein the mystery is great. For God has made you able to create worlds in your own mind which are more precious unto him than those which he created; and to give and offer up the world unto him, which is very delightful in flowing from him, but much more in returning to him.

Besides all which in its own nature also, a thought of the world, or the world in a thought, is more excellent than the world because it is spiritual and nearer unto God. The material world is dead and feels nothing, but this spiritual world, though it be invisible, has all dimensions, and is a divine and living being, the voluntary act of an obedient soul.

CHAPTER 17

REST & DELIGHT IN THE GREATNESS OF YOUR TRUE SELF

Continuing to Uphold Our Thoughts of Heaven

Once more, that I might close up this point with an infinite wonder: As among divines, it is said,

> That every moment's preservation is a new creation—and therefore blessings continued must not be despised, but be more and more esteemed—because every moment's preservation is another obligation.

Even so in the continual series of thoughts whereby we continue to uphold the frame of heaven and earth in the soul towards God, every thought is another world to the Deity as acceptable as the first. Yea, the continuance puts an infinite worth and luster on them.

For to be desultory and inconstant is the part of a fickle and careless soul, and makes the imagination of it worthless and despised. But to continue serious in upholding these thoughts for God's sake, is the part of a faithful and loving soul: which as it thereby continues great and honorable with God, so is it thereby divine and holy, and every act of it of infinite importance, and the continuance of its life transcendently esteemed.

So that though you can build or demolish such worlds as often as you please, yet it infinitely concerns you faithfully to continue them and wisely to repair them. For though to make them suddenly be to a wise man very easy, yet to uphold them always is very difficult—a work of unspeakable diligence and an argument of infinite love.

The Unlimited Extent of Your Soul

As it becomes you to retain a glorious sense of the world, because the earth and the heavens and the heaven of heavens are the magnificent and glorious territories of God's kingdom, so are you to remember always the unsearchable extent and unlimited greatness of your own soul—the length and breadth and depth and height of your own understanding.[84] Because it is the house of God, a living temple,[85] and a glorious throne of the Blessed Trinity: far more magnificent and great than the heavens; yea a person that in union and communion with God is to see eternity, to fill his omnipresence, to possess his greatness, to admire his love, to receive his gifts, to enjoy the world, and to live in his image.

Let all your actions proceed from a sense of this greatness. Let all your affections extend to this endless wideness. Let all your prayers be animated by this spirit and let all your praises arise and ascend from this fountain. For you are never your true self till you live by your soul more than by your body, and you never live by your soul till you feel its incomparable excellency, and rest satisfied and delighted in the unsearchable greatness of its comprehension.

Every Man Loving & Honoring You

The world does serve you, not only as it is the place and receptacle of all your joys, but as it is a great obligation laid upon all mankind and upon every person in all ages to love you as himself; as it also magnifies all your companions, and shows your heavenly Father's glory. Yea, as it exalts you in the eyes of the illuminate, and makes you to be honored and reverenced by the holy.

For there is not a man in the whole world that knows God or himself, but he must honor you. Not only as an angel or a cherubim, but as one redeemed by the blood of Christ, beloved by all angels, cherubims, and men, an heir of the world, and as much greater than the universe as he that possesses the house is greater than the house.

O what a holy and blessed life would men lead, what joys and treasures would they be to each other, in what a sphere of excellency would every man move, how sublime and glorious would their estate be, how full of peace and quiet would the world be, yea of joy and honor, order and beauty, did men perceive this of themselves and had they this esteem for one another!

Praises are Transformed & Returning Benefits

As the world serves you by showing the greatness of God's love to you, so does it serve you as fuel to foment and increase your praises. Men's lips are closed because their eyes are blinded; their tongues are dumb because their ears are deaf; and there is no life in their mouths because death is in their hearts. But did they all see their creator's glory, which appears chiefly in the greatness of his bounty; did they all know the blessedness of their estate, O what a place full of joys, what an amiable region and territory of praises would the world become; yea, what a sphere of light and glory!

As no man can breathe out more air than he draws in, so no man can offer up more praises than he receives benefits to return in praises. For praises are transformed and returning benefits.

And therefore does God so greatly desire the knowledge of him, because God when he is known is all love. And the praises which he desires are the reflection of his beams which will not return till they are apprehended. The world therefore is not only the temple of these praises, and the altar whereon they are offered, but the fuel also that enkindles them, and the very matter that composes them. Which so much the more serves you, because it enkindles a desire in you that God should be praised, and moves you to take delight in all that praise him. So that as it incites yours, it gives you an interest in others' praises, and is a valley of vision[86] wherein you see the blessed sight of all men's praises ascending, and of all God's blessings coming down upon them.

Prizing Jesus' Love

The world serves you as it teaches you more abundantly to prize the love of Jesus Christ. For since the inheritance is so great to which you are restored, and no less than the whole world is the benefit of your Saviour's love, how much are you to admire that person that redeemed you from the lowest hell to the fruition of it?

Your forfeiture was unmeasurable and your sin infinite, your despair insupportable and your danger eternal. How happy are you therefore, that you have so great a Lord, whose love rescued you from the extremest misery! Had you seen Adam turned into hell, and going out of this fair mansion which the Lord had given him into everlasting torments or eternal darkness, you would have thought the world a glorious place which was created for him, and the light of Eden would have appeared in greater luster than it did before, and his love by whom he was recovered the greatest jewel.

It is a heavenly thing to understand his love and to see it well. Had Adam had no esteem for the place to which he was restored, he had not valued the benefit of his restitution. But now looking upon it with those eyes wherewith noble men look upon their territories and palaces when they are going to die—his mercy who died for him, that he after his condemnation might return again into his dear enjoyments, makes him by whom they were purchased the best and greatest of all enjoyments.

Darius, when he had conquered Babylon by the art of Zopyrus—who cut off his nose and ears and lips, that making the Babylonians to confide in him, he might deliver up the city into the King's hands—admiring the fidelity and love of Zopyrus, protested that he had rather have one Zopyrus whole than ten Babylons. Even so we, were our spirits divine and noble and genuine, should by the greatness of the benefit be excited above ourselves, and to exceed the gift, in the love of our Saviour. Being afterwards asked, upon the sight of a pomegranate slit in the midst, what thing he would above all other desire, might he have as many of them as there were seeds in that pomegranate, answered, 'Tot Zopyrorum': 'As many Zopyruses.' One Saviour is worth innumerable worlds.

Seeds of Grace & Seeds of Glory

The world is a pomegranate indeed, which God has put into man's heart, as Solomon observes in the Ecclesiastes, because it contains the seeds of grace and the seeds of glory. All virtues lie in the world, as seeds in a pomegranate: I mean in the fruition of it, out of which when it is sown in man's heart they naturally arise. The fidelity of Zopyrus and the love of Darius are included in it.

For when we consider how great a Lord gave us so great a dominion, we shall think it abominable to be treacherous and unfaithful in the midst of his dominions. When we consider we cannot choose but sin, if we sin at all, being surrounded with his gifts, and that the land we tread on is of his munificence: how can we err against him who gave it to us? Can we forsake him whose gifts we cannot leave? The whole world is better than Babylon; and at greater expense than Zopyrus' lips was it purchased for us.

God's Kingdom Lifts Us Above Sin

This visible world is wonderfully to be delighted in and highly to be esteemed because it is the theatre of God's righteous kingdom. Who as himself was righteous, because he made it freely, so he made it that we might freely be righteous too.

For in the kingdom of glory, it is impossible to fall. No man can sin that clearly sees the beauty of God's face because no man can sin against his own happiness; that is, none can, when he sees it clearly, willingly, and wittingly, forsake it—tempter, temptation, loss, and danger being all seen. But here we see his face in a glass, and more dimly behold our happiness as in a mirror;[87] by faith therefore we are to live, and to sharpen our eye that we may see his glory. We are to be studious and intent in our desires and endeavors.

For we may sin or we may be holy. Holiness therefore and righteousness naturally flow out of our fruition of the world, for who can vilify and debase himself by any sin, while he actually considers he is the heir of it? It exalts a man to a sublime and honorable life. It lifts him above lusts and makes him angelical.

The World Makes Vices & Virtues Visible

It makes him sensible of the reality of happiness.

It feeds him with contentment, and fills him with gratitude.

It delivers him from the love of money, which is the root of all evil.[88]

It causes him to reign over the perverse customs and opinions that are in the world.

It opens his eyes and makes him to see man's blindness and errors.

It satiates his covetousness, feeds his curiosity, and pleases his ambition. It makes him too great for preferments and allurements.

It causes him to delight in retirement, and to be in love with prayer and communion with God. It lifts him up above men's scandals and censures. It makes him zealous of the salvation of all.

It fills him with courage on the behalf of God. It makes him to rejoice in a present, visible, immovable treasure to which the rest of the world is blind, and strengthens his faith and hope of the invisible.

Yea it makes him wise, and many invisible joys does he see in this. Glory and dominion are invisible joys. And so is that great interest a man has to all kingdoms and ages, which a true possessor of the world is more sensible of than of his houses and lands.

It makes him meek in pardoning all injuries because he is above the reach of all his enemies, and infinitely secure in the midst of his fruitions.

How great a thing is the enjoyment of the world; how highly to be esteemed and how zealously to be thirsted after, that eminently contains all these! Verily it is a thing so divine and heavenly that it makes vices and virtues almost visible to our very eyes.

The Sources of Happiness

Varro cites 288 opinions of philosophers concerning happiness. They were so blind in the knowledge of it, and so different in their apprehensions. All which opinions fall in here, as all rivers fall into the sea, and agree together.

Some placed happiness in riches and some in honor; some in pleasure and some in the contempt of all riches, honor, and pleasure; some in wisdom and some in firm stability of mind; some in empire and some in love. Some in bare and naked contentment, some in contemplation, and some in action; some in rest and some in sufferings; and some in victory and triumph.

All which occur here, for here is victory and triumph over our lusts, that we might live the life of clear reason, in the fruition of all riches, honors, and pleasures—which are by wisdom to be seen and by love to be enjoyed in the highest empire, with great contentation, in solitude alone, in communion with all, by action and contemplation, attaining it by sufferings, and resting in the possession with perfect victory and triumph over the world and evil men, or sin, death and hell, in spite of all the oppositions of men and devils.

Neither angels, nor principalities, nor power, nor height nor depth, nor things present nor things to come, being able to separate us from the love of God which is in Christ Jesus our Lord.[89]

How Happiness is Attained

Felicity is a thing coveted of all. The whole world is taken with the beauty of it, and he is no man but a stock or stone that does not desire it. Nevertheless, great offence has been done by the philosophers and scandal given through their blindness—many of them, in making felicity to consist in negatives.

They tell us it does not consist in riches, it does not consist in honors, it does not consist in pleasures. Wherein then, says a miserable man, does it consist?

Why in contentment, in self-sufficiency, in virtues, in the right government of our passions, etc. Were it not better to show the amiableness of virtues and the benefit of the right government of our passions, the objects of contentment and the grounds of self sufficiency, by the truest means? Which these never do.

Ought they not to distinguish between true and false riches as our Saviour does, between real and feigned honors, between clear and pure pleasures and those which are muddy and unwholesome? The honor that comes from above, the true treasures, those rivers of pleasure that flow at his right hand forevermore, are by all to be sought and by all to be desired. For it is the affront of nature—a making vain the powers, and a baffling the expectations of the soul—to deny it all objects, and a confining it to the grave, and a condemning of it to death, to tie it to the inward, unnatural, mistaken self-sufficiency and contentment they talk of.

By the true government of our passions, we disentangle them from impediments, and fit and guide them to their proper objects. The amiableness of virtue consists in this: that by it, all happiness is either attained or enjoyed. Contentment and rest arise from a full perception of infinite treasures.

So that whosoever will profit in the mystery of felicity, must see the objects of his happiness and the manner how they are to be enjoyed, and discern also the powers of his soul by which he is to enjoy them, and perhaps the rules that shall guide him in the way of enjoyment. All which you have here—God, the world, yourself, all things—in time and eternity being the objects of your felicity, God the giver and you the receiver.

IV.
THE STORY OF MY PERSONAL JOURNEY

CHAPTER 18

MY CHILDHOOD & ADOLESCENCE

Praying for the Divine Light Wherewith I Was Born

Will you see the infancy of this sublime and celestial greatness?

Those pure and virgin apprehensions I had from the womb, and that divine light wherewith I was born, are the best unto this day, wherein I can see the universe. By the gift of God, they attended me into the world, and by his special favor I remember them till now.

Verily they seem the greatest gifts his wisdom could bestow, for without them all other gifts had been dead and vain. They are unattainable by book, and therefore I will teach them by experience. Pray for them earnestly, for they will make you angelical and wholly celestial. Certainly Adam in Paradise had not more sweet and curious apprehensions of the world than I when I was a child.

Surrounded with Innumerable Joys

All appeared new and strange at first, inexpressibly rare and delightful and beautiful. I was a little stranger, which at my entrance into the world was saluted and surrounded with innumerable joys.

My knowledge was divine. I knew by intuition those things which, since my apostasy, I collected again by the highest reason. My very ignorance was advantageous. I seemed as one brought into the estate of innocence. All things were spotless and pure and glorious; yea, and infinitely mine, and joyful and precious. I knew not that there were any sins or complaints or laws. I dreamed not of poverties, contentions, or vices. All tears and quarrels were hidden from mine eyes. Everything was at rest, free and immortal. I knew nothing of sickness or death or rents or exaction, either for tribute or bread.

In the absence of these, I was entertained like an angel with the works of God in their splendor and glory. I saw all in the peace of Eden—heaven and earth did sing my Creator's praises, and could not make more melody to Adam than to me. All time was eternity, and a perpetual Sabbath. Is it not strange that an infant should be heir of the whole world, and see those mysteries which the books of the learned never unfold?

All Things Were Mine Before I was Corrupted

The corn was orient and immortal wheat, which never should be reaped nor was ever sown. I thought it had stood from everlasting to everlasting. The dust and stones of the street were as precious as gold. The gates were at first the end of the world. The green trees, when I saw them first through one of the gates, transported and ravished me; their sweetness and unusual beauty made my heart to leap, and almost mad with ecstasy, they were such strange and wonderful things.

The men! O what venerable and reverend creatures did the aged seem! Immortal cherubims! And young men glittering and sparkling angels, and maids strange seraphic pieces of life and beauty! Boys and girls tumbling in the street and playing, were moving jewels. I knew not that they were born or should die, but all things abided eternally as they were in their proper places.

Eternity was manifest in the light of the day, and something infinite behind everything appeared, which talked with my expectation and moved my desire. The city seemed to stand in Eden, or to be built in heaven.

The streets were mine, the temple was mine, the people were mine, their clothes and gold and silver were mine, as much as their sparkling eyes, fair skins, and ruddy faces. The skies were mine, and so were the sun and moon and stars, and all the world was mine; and I the only spectator and enjoyer of it. I knew no churlish properties nor bounds nor divisions; but all properties and divisions were mine, all treasures and the possessors of them.

So that, with much ado, I was corrupted and made to learn the dirty devices of this world. Which now I unlearn, and become, as it were, a little child again that I may enter into the kingdom of God.

With New and Open Eyes (A Poem)

Upon those pure and virgin apprehensions which I had in my infancy, I made this poem:

> That childish thoughts such jogs inspire,
> Does make my wonder, and his glory higher,
>   His bounty, and my wealth more great
> It shews his kingdom, and his work complete.
>   In which there is not anything,
> Not meet to be the joy of cherubim.

>   He in our childhood with us walks,
> And with our thoughts mysteriously he talks;
>   He often visits our minds,
> But cold acceptance in us ever finds:
>   We send him often grieved away,
> Who else would show us all his kingdom's joy.

>   O Lord, I wonder at your love,
> Which did my infancy so early move:
>   But more at that which did forbear
> And move so long, though slighted many a year:
>   But most of all, at last that you
> Yourself should me convert, I scarce know how.

Your gracious motions oft in vain
Assaulted me: my heart did hard remain
    Long time! I sent my God away
Grieved much, that he could not give me his joy.
    I careless was, nor did regard
The end for which he all those thoughts prepared.

    But now, with new and open eyes,
I see beneath, as if above the skies,
    And as I backward look again
See all his thoughts and mine most clear and plain.
    He did approach, he me did woo;
I wonder that my God this thing would do,

    From nothing taken first, I was;
What wondrous things his glory brought to pass!
    Now in the world I him behold,
And me, enveloped in precious gold;
    In deep abysses of delights,
In present hidden glorious benefits.

    These thoughts his goodness long before
Prepared as precious and celestial store
    With curious art in me inlaid,
That childhood might itself alone be said
    My Tutor, Teacher, Guide to be,
Instructed then even by the Deity.

Enjoying What We Naturally Saw at Our Birth

Our Saviour's meaning, when he said, "He must be born again[90] and become a little child that will enter into the kingdom of heaven,"[91] is deeper far than is generally believed. It is not only in a careless reliance upon divine providence that we are to become little children, or in the feebleness and shortness of our anger and simplicity of our passions, but in the peace and purity of all our soul. Which purity also is a deeper thing than is commonly apprehended. For we must disrobe ourselves of all false colors, and unclothe our souls of evil habits. All our thoughts must be infant-like and clear—the powers of our soul free from the leaven of this world, and disentangled from men's conceits and customs.

Grit in the eye or yellow jaundice will not let a man see those objects truly that are before it. And therefore it is requisite that we should be as very strangers to the thoughts, customs, and opinions of men in this world, as if we were but little children. So those things would appear to us only which do to children when they are first born.

Ambitions, trades, luxuries, inordinate affections,[92] casual and accidental riches invented since the fall, would be gone; and only those things appear which did to Adam in Paradise, in the same light and in the same colors: God in his works, glory in the light, love in our parents, men, ourselves, and the face of heaven—every man naturally seeing those things, to the enjoyment of which he is naturally born.

I Will Show You My Steps to Enjoying the Universe

Everyone provides objects, but few prepare senses whereby, and light wherein, to see them. Since therefore we are born to be a burning and shining light, and whatever men learn of others, they see in the light of others' souls: I will in the light of my soul show you the universe. Perhaps it is celestial and will teach you how beneficial we may be to each other.

I am sure it is a sweet and curious light to me, which had I wanted, I would have given all the gold and silver in all worlds to have purchased. But it was the gift of God and could not be bought with money. And by what steps and degrees I proceeded to that enjoyment of all eternity which now I possess, I will likewise show you. A clear and familiar light it may prove unto you.

Wholly Forgetting My Treasures

The first light which shined in my infancy in its primitive and innocent clarity was totally eclipsed insomuch that I was fain to learn all again. If you ask me how it was eclipsed? Truly by the customs and manners of men, which like contrary winds blew it out. By an innumerable company of other objects: rude, vulgar, and worthless things, that like so many loads of earth and dung did overwhelm and bury it. By the impetuous torrent of wrong desires in all others whom I saw or knew that carried me away and alienated me from it. By a whole sea of other matters and concernments that covered and drowned it. Finally, by the evil influence of a bad education that did not foster and cherish it.

All men's thoughts and words were about other matters. They all prized new things which I did not dream of. I was a stranger and unacquainted with them; I was little and reverenced their authority; I was weak and easily guided by their example; ambitious also, and desirous to prove myself to them. And finding not one syllable in any man's mouth of those things, by degrees they vanished—my thoughts (as indeed what is more fleeting than a thought?) were blotted out, and at last all the celestial, great, and stable treasures to which I was born, as wholly forgotten, as if they had never been.

More Prone to Good & Excellent Things

Had any man spoken of it, it had been the most easy thing in the world to have taught me, and to have made me believe that heaven and earth was God's house, and that he gave it to me. That the sun was mine, and that men were mine, and that cities and kingdoms were mine also. That earth was better than gold, and that water, every drop of it was a precious jewel. And that these were great and living treasures, and that all riches whatsoever else was dross in comparison.

From whence I clearly find how docible our nature is in natural things, were it rightly entreated. And that our misery proceeds ten thousand times more from the outward bondage of opinion and custom than from any inward corruption or depravation of nature. And that it is not our parents' loins, so much as our parents' lives, that enthrals and blinds us. Yet is all our corruption derived from Adam inasmuch as all the evil examples and inclinations of the world arise from his sin.

But I speak it in the presence of God and of our Lord Jesus Christ: in my pure primitive virgin light, while my apprehensions were natural and unmixed, I cannot remember but that I was ten thousand times more prone to good and excellent things than evil. But I was quickly tainted and fell by others.

The Riches of Nature

It was a difficult matter to persuade me that the tinseled ware upon a hobby horse was a fine thing. They did impose upon me, and obtrude their gifts that made me believe a ribbon or a feather curious. I could not see where was the curiousness or fineness. And to teach me that a purse of gold was at any value seemed impossible—the art by which it becomes so, and the reasons for which it is accounted so, were so deep and hidden to my inexperience.

So that nature is still nearest to natural things and farthest off from pre-ternatural; and to esteem that the reproach of nature, is an error in them only who are unacquainted with it. Natural things are glorious, and to know them glorious, but to call things preternatural natural, monstrous. Yet all those do it, who esteem gold, silver, houses, lands, clothes, etc., the riches of nature, which are indeed the riches of invention.

Nature knows no such riches, but art and error make them. Not the God of nature, but sin only was the parent of them. The riches of nature are our souls and bodies with all their faculties, senses, and endowments. And it had been the easiest thing in the whole world to teach me that all felicity consisted in the enjoyment of all the world, that it was prepared for me before I was born, and that nothing was more divine and beautiful.

Drowning the Knowledge of Heaven and Earth

Thoughts are the most present things to thoughts, and of the most powerful influence. My soul was only apt and disposed to great things; but souls to souls are like apples to apples—one being rotten rots another. When I began to speak and go, nothing began to be present to me, but what was present to me in their thoughts. Nor was anything present to me any other way than it was so to them.

The glass of imagination was the only mirror wherein anything was represented or appeared to me. All things were absent which they talked not of. So I began among my play-fellows to prize a drum, a fine coat, a penny, a gilded book, etc., who before never dreamed of any such wealth. Goodly objects to drown all the knowledge of heaven and earth!

As for the heavens and the sun and stars: they disappeared and were no more unto me than the bare walls. So that the strange riches of man's invention quite overcame the riches of nature, being learned more labori-ously and in the second place.

Making Children Possessors of Heaven & Earth

By this let nurses, and those parents that desire holy children, learn to make them possessors of heaven and earth betimes, to remove silly objects from before them, to magnify nothing but what is great indeed, and to talk of God to them, and of his works and ways, before they can either speak or go. For nothing is so easy as to teach the truth, because the nature of the thing confirms the doctrine: as when we say the sun is glorious, a man is a beautiful creature—sovereign over beasts and fowls and fishes, the stars minister unto us, the world was made for you, etc.

But to say, "This house is yours, and these lands are another man's, and this bauble is a jewel, and this gew-gaw a fine thing, this rattle makes music, etc.," is deadly, barbarous, and uncouth to a little child; and makes him suspect all you say, because the nature of the thing contradicts your words. Yet does that blot out all noble and divine ideas, unsettle his foundation, render him uncertain in all things, and divide him from God. To teach him those objects are little vanities, and that though God made them by the ministry of man, yet better and more glorious things are more to be esteemed, is natural and easy.

Indians Nearer to God in Simplicity

By this you may see who are the rude and barbarous Indians. For verily there is no savage nation under the cope of heaven that is more absurdly barbarous than the Christian world. They that go naked and drink water and live upon roots are like Adam or angels in comparison of us.

But they indeed that call beads and glass buttons jewels, and dress themselves with feather, and buy pieces of brass and broken hafts of knives of our merchants, are somewhat like us. But we pass them in barbarous opinions and monstrous apprehensions, which we nickname civility and the mode amongst us. I am sure those barbarous people that go naked, come nearer to Adam, God, and angels in the simplicity of their wealth, though not in knowledge.

Making Men to Live Without God in the World

You would not think how these barbarous inventions spoil your knowledge. They put grubs and worms in men's heads that are enemies to all pure and true apprehensions, and eat out all their happiness. They make it impossible for them, in whom they reign, to believe there is any excellency in the works of God, or to taste any sweetness in the nobility of nature, or to prize any common, though never so great a blessing.

They alienate men from the life of God, and at last make them to live without God in the world.[93] To live the life of God is to live to all the works of God, and to enjoy them in his image, from which they are wholly diverted that follow fashions. Their fancies are corrupted with other gingles.

Idle Talk & Worthless Vanities

Being swallowed up therefore in the miserable gulf of idle talk and worthless vanities, thenceforth I lived among dreams and shadows, like a prodigal son feeding upon husks with swine. A comfortless wilderness full of thorns and troubles the world was, or worse: a waste place covered with idleness and play, and shops, and markets, and taverns.

As for churches, they were things I did not understand, and schools were a burden—so that there was nothing in the world worth the having or enjoying, but my game and sport, which also was a dream, and being passed wholly forgotten. So that I had utterly forgotten all goodness, bounty, comfort, and glory: which things are the very brightness of the glory of God, for lack of which therefore he was unknown.

Inquisitive About an Unknown Happiness

Yet sometimes in the midst of these dreams, I should come a little to myself, so far as to feel I wanted something, secretly to expostulate with God for not giving me riches, to long after an unknown happiness, to grieve that the world was so empty, and to be dissatisfied with my present state because it was vain and forlorn. I had heard of angels and much admired that here upon earth nothing should be but dirt and streets and gutters; for as for the pleasures that were in great men's houses, I had not seen them, and it was my real happiness they were unknown. For because nothing deluded me, I was the more inquisitive.

What I Imagined When I was 4 Years Old

Once I remember (I think I was about 4 years old when) I thus reasoned with myself, sitting in a little obscure room in my father's poor house: if there be a God, certainly he must be infinite in goodness: and that I was prompted to by a real whispering instinct of nature. And if he be infinite in goodness, and a perfect being in wisdom and love, certainly he must do most glorious things and give us infinite riches—how comes it to pass therefore that I am so poor? Of so scanty and narrow a fortune, enjoying few and obscure comforts?

I thought I could not believe him a God to me unless all his power were employed to glorify me. I knew not then my soul or body; nor did I think of the heavens and the earth, the rivers and the stars, the sun or the seas. All those were lost and absent from me. But when I found them made out of nothing for me, then I had a God indeed whom I could praise and rejoice in.

Questions About Heaven & Earth

Sometimes I should be alone and without employment, when suddenly my soul would return to itself, and forgetting all things in the whole world which mine eyes had seen, would be carried away to the ends of the earth. And my thoughts would be deeply engaged with enquiries: How the earth did end? Whether walls did bound it, or sudden precipices? Or whether the heavens by degrees did come to touch it, so that the face of the earth and heaven were so near that a man with difficulty could creep under? Whatever I could imagine was inconvenient, and my reason being posed was quickly wearied. What also upheld the earth (because it was heavy) and kept it from falling: whether pillars or dark waters? And if any of these, what then upheld those, and what again those, of which I saw there would be no end? Little did I think that the earth was round and the world so full of beauty, light, and wisdom. When I saw that, I knew by the perfection of the work there was a God, and was satisfied and rejoiced. People underneath, and fields and flowers, with another sun and another day, pleased me mightily; but more when I knew it was the same sun that served them by night, that served us by day.

Thinking About Creation

Sometimes I should soar above the stars, and enquire how the heavens ended, and what was beyond them? Concerning which by no means could I receive satisfaction. Sometimes my thoughts would carry me to the creation, for I had heard now that the world which at first I thought was eternal, had a beginning. How therefore that beginning was, and why it was, why it was no sooner, and what was before, I mightily desired to know. By all which I easily perceive that my soul was made to live in communion with God in all places of his dominion,[94] and to be satisfied with the highest reason in all things. After which it so eagerly aspired, that I thought all the gold and silver in the world but dirt in comparison of satisfaction in any of these.

Sometimes I wondered why men were made no bigger? I would have had a man as big as a giant, a giant as big as a castle, and a castle as big as the heavens. Which yet would not serve, for there was infinite space beyond the heavens, and all was defective and but little in comparison. And for him to be made infinite, I thought it would be to no purpose, and it would be inconvenient. Why also there was not a better sun and better stars, a better sea and better creatures, I much admired. Which thoughts produced that poem upon moderation, which afterwards was written. Some part of the verses are these:

Our Greatness is Not in Our Size, But in Our Souls

In making bodies love could not express
Itself, or art, unless it made them less.
O what a monster had in man been seen,
Had every thumb or toe a mountain been!
What worlds must he devour when he did eat?
What oceans drink! yet could not all his meat,
Or stature, make him like an angel shine;
Or make his soul in glory more divine.
A soul it is that makes us truly great,
Whose little bodies make us more complete.
An understanding that is infinite,
An endless, wide, and everlasting sight,
That can enjoy all things and nothing exclude,
Is the most sacred greatness may be viewed.
'Twas inconvenient that his bulk should be
An endless hill; he nothing then could see:

No figure have, no motion, beauty, place,
No color, feature, member, light, or grace.
A body like a mountain is but cumber.
An endless body is but idle lumber:
It spoils converse, and time itself devours,
While meat in vain, in feeding idle powers;
Excessive bulk being most injurious found,
To those conveniences which men have crowned:
His wisdom did his power here repress,
God made man greater while he made him less.

Infinite Worth in Limited Beings

The excellencies of the sun I found to be of another kind than that splendor after which I sought, even in unknown and invisible services. And that God, by moderation wisely bounding his almighty power, had to my eternal amazement and wonder, made all bodies far greater than if they were infinite: there not being a sand nor mote in the air that is not more excellent than if it were infinite.

How rich and admirable then is the kingdom of God, where the smallest is greater than an infinite treasure! Is not this incredible? Certainly to the placits and doctrines of the schools: till we all consider that infinite worth shut up in the limits of a material being is the only way to a real infinity. God made nothing infinite in bulk, but everything there where it ought to be. Which, because moderation is a virtue observing the golden mean, in some other parts of the former poem is thus expressed:

Bounding Things to Make Them Beautiful (A Poem)

His power bounded, greater is in might,
Than if let loose, 'twere wholly infinite.

He could have made an endless sea by this,
But then it had not been a sea of bliss.
Did waters from the center to the skies
Ascend, 'twould drown whatever else we prize.
The ocean bounded in a finite shore,
Is better far because it is no more.
No use nor glory would in that be seen,
His power made it endless in esteem.
Had not the Sun been bounded in its sphere,
Did all the world in one fair flame appear,
And were that flame a real Infinite
'Twould yield no profit, splendor, nor delight.
Its corps confined, and beams extended be
Effects of wisdom in the Deity.
One star made infinite would all exclude,
An earth made infinite could ne'er be viewed:
But one being fashioned for the other's sake,
He, bounding all, did all most useful make
And which is best, in profit and delight
Though not in bulk, they all are infinite.

First Visit to a Noble Dining Room

These liquid, clear satisfactions were the emanations of the highest reason, but not achieved till a long time afterwards. In the meantime, I was sometimes, though seldom, visited and inspired with new and more vigorous desires after that bliss which nature whispered and suggested to me. Every new thing quickened my curiosity and raised my expectation.

I remember once, the first time I came into a magnificent or noble dining room and was left there alone, I rejoiced to see the gold and state and carved imagery—but when all was dead, and there was no motion, I was weary of it and departed dissatisfied. But afterwards, when I saw it full of lords and ladies, and music and dancing, the place which once seemed not to differ from a solitary den, had now entertainment, and nothing of tediousness but pleasure in it.

By which I perceived (upon a reflection made long after) that men and women are, when well understood, a principal part of our true felicity. By this I found also that nothing that stood still could by doing so be a part of happiness; and that affection, though it were invisible, was the best of motions. But the august and glorious exercise of virtue was more solemn and divine, which yet I saw not. And that all men and angels should appear in heaven.

My Change from Fearing the Universe to Enjoying It

Another time, in a lowering and sad evening, being alone in the field when all things were dead and quiet, a certain want and horror fell upon me beyond imagination. The unprofitableness and silence of the place dissatisfied me; its wideness terrified me; from the utmost ends of the earth, fears surrounded me. How did I know but dangers might suddenly arise from the East, and invade me from the unknown regions beyond the seas? I was a weak and little child, and had forgotten there was a man alive in the earth.

Yet something also of hope and expectation comforted me from every border. This taught me that I was concerned in all the world; and that in the remotest borders, the causes of peace delight me; and the beauties of the earth when seen were made to entertain me; that I was made to hold a communion with the secrets of divine providence in all the world; that a remembrance of all the joys I had from my birth ought always to be with me; that the presence of cities, temples, and kingdoms ought to sustain me; and that to be alone in the world was to be desolate and miserable. The comfort of houses and friends, the clear assurance of treasures everywhere, God's care and love, his goodness, wisdom, and power, his presence and watchfulness in all the ends of the earth, were my strength and assurance forever. And that these things being absent to my eye, were my joys and consolations—as present to my understanding as the wideness and emptiness of the universe which I saw before me.

All Kingdoms Became Accessible

When I heard of any new kingdom beyond the seas, the light and glory of it pleased me immediately. It rose up within me, and I was enlarged wonderfully. I entered into it: I saw its commodities, rarities, springs, meadows, riches, inhabitants, and became possessor of that new room as if it had been prepared for me, so much was I magnified and delighted in it.

When the Bible was read, my spirit was present in other ages. I saw the light and splendor of them: the land of Canaan, the Israelites entering into it, the ancient glory of the Amorites, their peace and riches, their cities, houses, vines and fig-trees, the long prosperity of their kings, their milk and honey, their slaughter and destruction, with the joys and triumphs of God's people; all which entered into me, and God among them.

I saw all and felt all in such a lively manner, as if there had been no other way to those places but in spirit only. This showed me the liveliness of interior presence, and that all ages were for most glorious ends, accessible to my understanding, yea with it, yea within it. For without changing place, in myself I could behold and enjoy all those—anything when it was proposed, though it was a thousand ages ago, being always before me.

Learning That Every Kingdom Contains Wonders

When I heard any news, I received it with greediness and delight, because my expectation was awakened with some hope that my happiness and the thing I wanted was concealed in it. Glad tidings, you know, from a far country, brings us our salvation—and I was not deceived. In jury was Jesus killed, and from Jerusalem the Gospel came. Which when I once knew, I was very confident that every kingdom contained like wonders and causes of joy, though that was the fountain of them. As it was the first fruits, so was it the pledge of what I shall receive in other countries.

Thus also, when any curious cabinet, or secret in chemistry, geometry, or physic was offered to me, I diligently looked into it. But when I saw it to the bottom and not my happiness, I despised it. These imaginations and this thirst of news occasioned these reflections.

A Poem: 'On News'

I

News from a foreign country came,
As if my treasure and my wealth lay there:
So much it did my heart enflame
'Twas wont to call my soul into mine ear!
Which thither went, to meet
The approaching sweet:
And on the threshold stood,
To entertain the unknown good.
It hovered there,
As if 'twould leave mine ear,
And was so eager to embrace
The joyful tidings as they came,

'Twould almost leave its dwelling place,
    To entertain the same.

2

    As if the tidings were the things,
My very joys themselves, my foreign treasure,
    Or else did bear them on their wings;
With so much joy they came, with so much pleasure.
      My soul stood at the gate
          To recreate
        Itself with bliss: and to
      Be pleased with speed. A fuller view
         It fain would take
       Yet journeys back would make
Unto my heart: as if 'twould fain
Go out to meet, yet stay within
To fit a place, to entertain,
      And bring the tidings in.

3

    What sacred instinct did inspire
My soul in childhood with a hope so strong?
    What secret force moved my desire,
To expect my joys beyond the seas, so young?
        Felicity I knew
           Was out of view
         And being here alone,
      I saw that happiness was gone
         From me! For this

I thirsted absent bliss,
And thought that sure beyond the seas,
Or else in something near at hand
I knew not yet, (since nought did please
I knew) my bliss did stand.

4

But little did the infant dream
That all the treasures of the world were by:
And that himself was so the cream
And crown of all, which round about did lie:
Yet thus it was. The gem,
The diadem,
The ring enclosing all
That stood upon this earthly ball;
The heavenly eye,
Much wider than the sky,
Wherein they all included were
The glorious soul that was the king
Made to possess them, did appear
A small and little thing!

My Desire for a Book from Heaven

Among other things, there befell me a most infinite desire of a book from heaven. For observing all things to be rude and superfluous here upon earth, I thought the ways of felicity to be known only among the holy angels; and that unless I could receive information from them, I could never be happy. This thirst hung upon me a long time, till at last I perceived that the God of angels had taken care of me and prevented my desires. For he had sent the book I wanted before I was born, and prepared it for me, and also commended and sent it unto me in a far better manner than I was able to imagine.

Had some angel brought it to me, which was the best way wherein I could then desire it, it would have been a peculiar favor, and I should have thought myself therein honored above all mankind. It would have been the soul of this world, the light of my soul, the spring of life, and a fountain of happiness. You cannot think what riches and delights I promised myself therein. It would have been a mint of rarities, curiosities, and wonders: to have entertained the powers of my soul, to have directed me in the way of life, and to have fed me with pleasures unknown to the whole world.

Thousands in the World Enjoying Communion with God

Had some angel brought it miraculously from heaven and left it at my foot, it had been a present meet for seraphims. Yet had it been a dream, in comparison of the glorious way wherein God prepared it. I must have spent time in studying it, and with great diligence have read it daily to drink in the precepts and instructions it contained. It had in a narrow, obscure manner come unto me, and all the world had been ignorant of felicity but I.

Whereas now there are thousands in the world—of whom I, being a poor child, was ignorant—that in temples, universities, and secret closets, enjoy felicity: whom I saw not in shops, or schools, or trades; whom I found not in streets or at feasts or taverns, and therefore thought not to be in the world; who enjoy communion with God and have fellowship with the angels every day. And these I discerned to be a great help unto me.

What I Found in the Bible

This put me upon two things: upon inquiring into the matter contained in the Bible, and into the manner wherein it came unto me. In the matter, I found all the glad tidings my soul longed after in its desire of news; in the manner, that the wisdom of God was infinitely greater than mine, and that he had appeared in his wisdom exceeding my desires.

Above all things I desired some great lord or mighty king, that having power in his hand to give me all kingdoms, riches, and honors, was willing to do it. And by that book, I found that there was an eternal God who loved me infinitely, that I was his son, that I was to overcome death and to live forever, that he created the world for me, that I was to reign in his throne and to inherit all things. Who would have believed this, had not that book told me? It told me also that I was to live in communion with him in the image of his life and glory, that I was to enjoy all his treasures and pleasures in a more perfect manner than I could devise, and that all the truly amiable and glorious persons in the world were to be my friends and companions.

Giving Myself to What I Found in the Bible

Upon this I had enough. I desired no more the honors and pleasures of this world, but gave myself to the unlimited and clear fruition of that, and to this day see nothing wanting to my felicity but mine own perfection. All other things are well; I only, and the sons of men about me, are disordered.

Nevertheless, could I be what I ought, their very disorders would be my enjoyments. For all things should work together for good to them that love God.[95] And if the disorders, then certainly the troubles; and if the troubles, much more the vanities of men would be mine. Not only their enjoyments, but their very errors and distractions increasing my felicity. So that being heir of the whole world alone, I was to walk in it as in a strange, marvelous, and amiable possession, and alone to render praises unto God for its enjoyment.

Fashions & Tinselled Vanities Became Mine

This taught me that those fashions and tinseled vanities, which you and I despise heretofore, fetching a little course about, became ours. And that the wisdom of God in them also was very conspicuous. For it becomes his goodness to make all things treasures, and his power is able to bring light out of darkness and good out of evil. Nor would his love endure, but that I also should have a wisdom whereby I could draw order out of confusion.

So that it is my admiration and joy, that while so many thousand wander in darkness, I am in the light; and that while so many dote upon false treasures and pierce themselves through with many sorrows, I live in peace and enjoy the delights of God and heaven.

My Unbelief

In respect of the matter, I was very sure that angels and cherubims could not bring unto me better tidings than were in the Scriptures contained, could I but believe them to be true. But I was dissatisfied about the manner, and that was the ground of my unbelief. For I could not think that God, being love, would neglect his son—and therefore surely I was not his son, nor he love, because he had not ascertained me more carefully, that the Bible was his book from heaven.

Yet I was encouraged to hope well, because the matter was so excellent, above my expectation. And when I searched into it, I found the way infinitely better than if all the angels in heaven had brought it to me.

Reasons Why God's Manner of Revelation Was Best

Had the angels brought it to me alone, these several inconveniences had attended the vision:

(1) It had been but one sudden act wherein it was sent to me, whereas now God has been all ages in preparing it;

(2) It had been done by inferior ministers, whereas now it is done by God himself;

(3) Being Satan is able to transform himself into an angel of light,[96] I had been still dubious till having recourse to the excellency of the matter; by it I was informed and satisfied;

(4) Being corrupted, that one miracle would have been but like a single spark upon green wood—it would have gone out immediately; whereas I needed a thousand miracles to seal it, yea and to awaken me to the meditation of the matter that was revealed to me;

(5) Had it been revealed no other way, all the world had been dark and empty round about me; whereas now it is my joy and my delight and treasure, being full of knowledge and light and glory;

(6) Had it been revealed at no other time, God had now only been good unto me; whereas he has manifested his love in all ages, and been carefully and most wisely revealing it from the beginning of the world;

(7) Had he revealed it to no other person, I had been weak in faith, being solitary and sitting alone like a sparrow upon the house-top,[97] who now have the concurrent and joint affections of kingdoms and ages, yea, notwithstanding the disadvantage of this weakness, I must have gone abroad and published this faith to others, both in love to God and love to men. For I must have done my duty, or the book would have done me no good, and love to God and men must have been my duty, for without that I could never be happy.

(8) Yea, finally, had not the book been revealed before, neither had God been glorious nor I blessed, for he had been negligent of other persons, his goodness had been defective to all ages—whom now I know to be God by the universality of his love unto mankind

and the perfection of his wisdom to every person.

Imagining the Difficulties of Being the Only Man With This Book From Heaven

To talk now of the necessity of bearing all calamities and persecutions in preaching is little. To consider the reproaches, mockings, and derisions I must have endured of all the world, while they scoffed at me for pretending to be the only man that had a book from heaven, is nothing. Nor is it much to mention the impossibility of convincing others—all the world having been full of darkness, and God always silent before.

All ages had been void of treasure had not the Bible been revealed till the other day, wherein now I can expatiate with perfect liberty, and everywhere see the love of God to all mankind as love to me alone. All the world being adorned with miracles, prophets, patriarchs, apostles, martyrs, revelations from heaven, lively examples, holy souls, divine affairs for my enjoyment. The glory of God and the light of heaven appearing everywhere as much as it would have done in that seeming instant, had the book I desired come unto me any other way.

Light of Heaven in This World

You will not believe what a world of joy this one satisfaction and pleasure brought me. Thenceforth I thought the light of heaven was in this world. I saw it possible, and very probable, that I was infinitely beloved of Almighty God, the delights of Paradise were round about me, heaven and earth were open to me, all riches were little things; this one pleasure being so great that it exceeded all the joys of Eden. So great a thing it was to me to be satisfied in the manner of God's revealing himself unto mankind. Many other inquiries I had concerning the manner of his revealing himself, in all which I am infinitely satisfied.

CHAPTER 19

MY YEARS AT THE UNIVERSITY

Meeting Glorious Secrets & Persons at the University

Having been at the University and received there the taste and tincture of another education, I saw that there were things in this world of which I never dreamed: glorious secrets and glorious persons past imagination. There I saw that Logic, Ethics, Physics, Metaphysics, Geometry, Astronomy, Poesy, Medicine, Grammar, Music, Rhetoric, all kinds of arts, trades, and mechanisms that adorned the world, pertained to felicity; at least there I saw those things which afterwards I knew to pertain unto it, and was delighted in it. There I saw into the nature of the sea, the heavens, the sun, the moon and stars, the elements, minerals, and vegetables. All which appeared like the king's daughter, all glorious within;[98] and those things which my nurses and parents should have talked of there were taught unto me.

We Didn't Study Things So As to Enjoy Them

Nevertheless some things were defective too. There was never a tutor that did professly teach Felicity, though that be the mistress of all other sciences. Nor did any of us study these things but as aliena, which we ought to have studied as our enjoyments. We studied to inform our knowledge, but knew not for what end we so studied. And for lack of aiming at a certain end, we erred in the manner. Howbeit there we received all those seeds of knowledge that were afterwards improved, and our souls were awakened to a discerning of their faculties and exercise of their powers.

Studying with the Most Excellent Manners

The manner is in everything of greatest concernment. Whatever good thing we do, neither can we please God unless we do it well; nor can he please us, whatever good he does, unless he do it well. Should he give us the most perfect things in heaven and earth to make us happy, and not give them to us in the best of all possible manners, he would but displease us; and it were impossible for him to make us happy.

It is not sufficient therefore for us to study the most excellent things unless we do it in the most excellent of manners. And what that is, it is impossible to find till we are guided thereunto by the most excellent end, with a desire of which I flagrantly burned.

My Inquiry Into the Excellence of Things

The best of all possible ends is the glory of God, but happiness was what I thirsted after. And yet I did not err, for the glory of God is to make us happy. Which can never be done but by giving us most excellent natures and satisfying those natures: by creating all treasures of infinite value, and giving them to us in an infinite manner, to wit, both in the best that to omnipotence was possible. This led me to inquire whether all things were excellent and of perfect value, and whether they were mine in propriety?

Studying Things Out of Both Interest & Treasure

It is the glory of God to give all things to us in the best of all possible manners. To study things therefore under the double notion of interest and treasure is to study all things in the best of all possible manners. Because in studying so, we inquire after God's glory and our own happiness. And indeed enter into the way that leads to all contentments, joys, and satisfactions; to all praises, triumphs, and thanksgivings; to all virtues, beauties, adorations, and graces; to all dominion, exaltation, wisdom, and glory; to all holiness, union, and communication with God; to all patience and courage and blessedness, which it is impossible to meet any other way.

So that to study objects for ostentation, vain knowledge, or curiosity is fruitless impertinence, though God himself and angels be the object. But to study that which will oblige us to love him, and feed us with nobility and goodness toward men—that is blessed. And so is it to study that which will lead us to the temple of wisdom and seat us in the throne of glory.

Studying Things in Order to See God

Many men study the same things which have not the taste of, nor delight in them. And their palates vary according to the ends at which they aim. He that studies polity, men, and manners, merely that he may know how to behave himself and get honor in this world, has not that delight in his studies as he that contemplates these things that he might see the ways of God among them, and walk in communion with him. The attainments of the one are narrow; the other grows a celestial king of all kingdoms. Kings minister unto him, temples are his own, thrones are his peculiar treasure. Governments, officers, magistrates, and courts of judicature are his delights in a way ineffable and a manner inconceivable to the other's imagination.

He that knows the secrets of nature with Albertus Magnus, or the motions of the heavens with Galileo, or the cosmography of the moon with Hevelius, or the body of man with Galen, or the nature of diseases with Hippocrates, or the harmonies in melody with Orpheus, or of poesy with Homer, or of grammar with Lilly, or of whatever else with the greatest artist—he is nothing if he knows them merely for talk or idle speculation, or transient and external use. But he that knows them for value, and knows them his own, shall profit infinitely. And therefore, of all kinds of learnings, humanity and divinity are the most excellent.

What I Learn By Studying Humanity

By humanity we search into the powers and faculties of the soul, inquire into the excellencies of human nature, consider its wants, survey its inclinations, propensities, and desires, ponder its principles, proposals, and ends, examine the causes and fitness of all, the worth of all, the excellency of all. Whereby we come to know what man is in this world, what his sovereign end and happiness, and what is the best means by which he may attain it. And by this we come to see what wisdom is: which namely is a knowledge exercised in finding out the way to perfect happiness, by discerning man's real wants and sovereign desires.

We come moreover to know God's goodness, in seeing into the causes wherefore he implanted such faculties and inclinations in us, and the objects and ends prepared for them. This leads us to Divinity.

For God gave man an endless intellect to see all things, and a proneness to covet them, because they are his treasures;

and an infinite variety of apprehensions and affections, that he might have an all-sufficiency in himself to enjoy them;

a curiosity profound and insatiable to stir him up to look into them;

an ambition great and everlasting to carry him to the highest honors, thrones, and dignities;

an emulation whereby he might be animated and quickened by all examples;

a tenderness and compassion whereby he may be united to all persons;

a sympathy and love to virtue;

a tenderness of his credit in every soul, that he might delight to be honored in all persons;

an eye to behold eternity and the omnipresence of God, that he might see eternity and dwell within it;

a power of admiring, loving, and prizing, that seeing the beauty and goodness of God, he might be united to it forevermore.

What I Learn by Studying Divinity

In Divinity we are entertained with all objects from everlasting to everlasting because we are with him whose outgoings are from everlasting, which is to contemplate God and to walk with him in all his ways, and therefore to be entertained with all objects as he is the fountain, governor, and end of them. We are to contemplate God in the unity of his essence, in the trinity of persons, in his manifold attributes, in all his works, internal and external, in his counsels and decrees, in the work of creation, and in his works of providence.

And man, as he is a creature of God, capable of celestial blessedness, and a subject in his kingdom in his fourfold estate of innocence, misery, grace, and glory.

In the estate of innocence, we are to contemplate the nature and manner of his happiness, the laws under which he was governed, the joys of paradise, and the immaculate powers of his immortal soul.

In the estate of misery, we have his fall, the nature of sin, original and actual; his manifold punishments, calamity, sickness, death, etc.

In the estate of grace, the tenor of the new covenant, the manner of its exhibition under the various dispensations of the Old and New Testament, the mediator of the covenant, the conditions of it, faith and repentance, the sacraments or seals of it, the Scriptures, ministers, and sabbaths, the nature and government of the Church, its histories and successions from the beginning to the end of the world, etc.

In the estate of glory, the nature of separate souls, their advantages, excellencies, and privileges, the resurrection of the body, the day of judgment, and life everlasting. Wherein further we are to see and understand the communion of saints, heavenly joys, and our society with angels—to all which I was naturally born, to the fruition of all which I was by grace redeemed, and in the enjoyment of all which I am to live eternally.

What I Learn by Studying Natural Philosophy

Natural philosophy teaches us the causes and effects of all bodies simply and in themselves. But if you extend it a little further, to that indeed which its name imports—signifying the love of nature—it leads us into a diligent inquisition into all natures, their qualities, affections, relations, causes and ends, so far forth as by nature and reason they may be known. And this noble science, as such, is most sublime and perfect. It includes all Humanity and Divinity together. God, angels, men, affections, habits, actions, virtues, everything as it is a solid entire object singly proposed, being a subject of it, as well as material and visible things.

But taking it as it is usually bounded in its terms, it treats only of corporeal things, as heaven, earth, air, water, fire, the sun and stars, trees, herbs, flowers, influences, winds, fowls, beasts, fishes, minerals and precious stones, with all other beings of that kind. And as thus it is taken, it is nobly subservient to the highest ends, for it opens the riches of God's kingdom and the natures of his territories, works, and creatures in a wonderful manner, clearing and preparing the eyes of the enjoyer.

What I Learn by Studying Ethics

Ethics teach us the mysteries of morality and the nature of affections, virtues, and manners, as by them we may be guided to our highest happiness. The former for speculation; this for practice. The former furnishes us with riches; this with honors and delights. The former feasts us; and this instructs us. For by this we are taught to live honorably among men, and to make ourselves noble and useful among them. It teaches us how to manage our passions, to exercise virtues, and to form our manners, so as to live happily in this world.

And all these put together discover the materials of religion to be so great that it plainly manifests the revelation of God to be deep and infinite.

For it is impossible for language, miracles, or apparitions to teach us the infallibility of God's word, or to show us the certainty of true religion, without a clear sight into truth itself—that is unto the truth of things. Which will themselves, when truly seen by the very beauty and glory of them, best discover and prove religion.

CHAPTER 20

MY YEARS IN THE COUNTRY

Going Into the Country to Study Happiness

When I came into the country, and being seated among silent trees and meads and hills, had all my time in mine own hands, I resolved to spend it all, whatever it cost me, in the search of happiness, and to satiate that burning thirst which nature had enkindled in me from my youth. In which I was so resolute, that I chose rather to live upon ten pounds a year, and to go in leather clothes, and feed upon bread and water, so that I might have all my time clearly to myself, than to keep many thousands per annum in an estate of life where my time would be devoured in care and labor.

And God was so pleased to accept of that desire, that from that time to this, I have had all things plentifully provided for me, without any care at all, my very study of felicity making me more to prosper than all the care in the whole world. So that through his blessing I live a free and a kingly life as if the world were turned again into Eden, or much more, as it is at this day.

A Poem About Overcoming Lust & Sin

I

A life of Sabbaths here beneath!
Continual jubilees and joys!
The days of heaven, while we breathe
On earth! where sin all bliss destroys:
This is a triumph of delights
That does exceed all appetites:
No joy can be compared to this,
It is a life of perfect bliss.

2

Of perfect bliss! How can it be?
To conquer Satan, and to reign
In such a vale of misery,
Where vipers, stings, and tears remain,
Is to be crowned with victory.
To be content, divine, and free,
Even here beneath is great delight
And next the beatific sight.

3

But inward lusts do oft assail,
Temptations work us much annoy
We'll therefore weep, and to prevail
Shall be a more celestial joy.
To have no other enemy
But one; and to that one to die:[99]
To fight with that and conquer it,
Is better than in peace to sit.

4

'Tis better for a little time;
For he that all his lusts doth quell,
Shall find this life to be his prime
And vanquish sin, and conquer Hell.
The next shall be his double joy;
And that which here seemed to destroy
Shall in the other life appear
A root of bliss; a pearl each tear.

Descending Into Humility

Thus you see I can make merry with calamities, and while I grieve at sins and war against them, abhorring the world, and myself more, descend into the abyss of humility, and there admire a new offspring and torrent of joys—God's mercies. Which accept our fidelity in bloody battles, though every wound defile and poison; and when we slip or fall, turns our true penitent tears into solid pearl that shall abide with him forevermore. But oh let us take heed that we never willingly commit a sin against so gracious a Redeemer, and so great a Father.

A Poem About How Sin Destroys My Soul

I

Sin!

O only fatal woe,

That makes me sad and mourning go!

That all my joys do spoil,

His kingdom and my soul defile!

I never can agree

With thee!

2

You!

Only you! O you alone,

And my obdurate heart of stone,

The poison and the foes

Of my enjoyments and repose,

The only bitter ill,

Does kill !

3
Oh!
I cannot meet with you,
Nor once approach your memory,
But all my joys are dead,
And all my sacred treasures fled
As if I now did dwell
In Hell.

4
Lord!
O hear how short I breathe!
See how I tremble here beneath
A sin! Its ugly face
More terror, than its dwelling place
Contains (O dreadful sin!)
Within!

A Poem About My Battle With Sin: "The Recovery"

Sin! will you vanquish me?
And shall I yield the victory?
Shall all my joys be spoil'd,
And pleasures soil'd
By thee?
Shall I remain
As one that's slain
And never more lift up the head?
Is not my Saviour dead?

His blood, thy bane, my balsam, bliss, joy, wine,
Shall thee destroy; heal, feed, make me divine.

By Jesus, I Can Kill Sin

I cannot meet with sin but it kills me, and 'tis only by Jesus Christ that I can kill it and escape. Would you blame me to be confounded, when I have offended my eternal Father, who gave me all the things in heaven and earth? One sin is a dreadful stumbling-block in the way to heaven. It breeds a long parenthesis in the fruition of our joys. Do you not see, my friend, how it disorders and disturbs my proceeding? There is no calamity but sin alone.

I Saw Myself Like Some Traveler

When I came into the country and saw that I had all time in my own hands, having devoted it wholly to the study of felicity, I knew not where to begin or end; nor what objects to choose, upon which most profitably I might fix my contemplation. I saw myself like some traveler that had destined his life to journeys, and was resolved to spend his days in visiting strange places: who might wander in vain unless his undertakings were guided by some certain rule, and that innumerable millions of objects were presented before me, unto any of which I might take my journey. Fain would I have visited them all, but that was impossible.

What then should I do? Even imitate a traveler, who because he cannot visit all coasts, wildernesses, sandy deserts, seas, hills, springs and mountains, chooses the most populous and flourishing cities, where he might see the fairest prospects, wonders, and rarities, and be entertained with greatest courtesy, and where indeed he might most benefit himself with knowledge, profit, and delight, leaving the rest, even the naked and empty places unseen. For which cause I made it my prayer to God Almighty that he, whose eyes are open upon all things, would guide me to the fairest and divinest.

My Faith In God's Goodness (As Revealed in Obvious & Common Things)

And what rule do you think I walked by? Truly a strange one, but the best in the whole world. I was guided by an implicit faith in God's goodness, and therefore led to the study of the most obvious and common things. For thus I thought within myself: God being, as we generally believe, infinite in goodness, it is most consonant and agreeable with his nature that the best things should be most common. For nothing is more natural to infinite goodness than to make the best things most frequent, and only things worthless scarce.

Then I began to inquire what things were most common. Air, light, heaven and earth, water, the sun, trees, men and women, cities, temples, etc.: these I found common and obvious to all. Rubies, pearls, diamonds, gold and silver: these I found scarce, and to the most denied. Then began I to consider and compare the value of them which I measured by their serviceableness, and by the excellencies which would be found in them should they be taken away. And in conclusion, I saw clearly that there was a real value in all the common things; in the scarce, a feigned.

Invisible Common Things

Besides these common things I have named, there were others as common, but invisible. The laws of God, the soul of Man, Jesus Christ and his Passion on the Cross, with the ways of God in all ages. And these, by the general credit they had obtained in the world, confirmed me more. For the ways of God were transient things—they were past and gone; our Saviour's sufferings were in one particular, obscure place; the laws of God were no object of the eye, but only found in the minds of men. These therefore which were so secret in their own nature, and made common only by the esteem men had of them, must of necessity include unspeakable worth for which they were celebrated of all, and so generally remembered.

As yet I did not see the wisdom and depths of knowledge, the clear principles and certain evidences whereby the wise and holy, the ancients and the learned that were abroad in the world, knew these things—but was led to them only by the fame which they had vulgarly received. Howbeit I believed that there were unspeakable mysteries contained in them, and though they were generally talked of, their value was unknown. These therefore I resolved to study, and no other, but to my unspeakable wonder, they brought me to all the things in heaven and in earth, in time and eternity, possible and impossible, great and little, common and scarce; and discovered them all to be infinite treasures.

The Importance of Relationships Among Things

That anything may be found to be an infinite treasure, its place must be found in eternity and in God's esteem. For as there is a time, so there is a place for all things. Everything in its place is admirable, deep, and glorious; out of its place, like a wandering bird,[100] is desolate and good for nothing. How therefore it relates to God and all creatures must be seen before it can be enjoyed. And this I found by many instances.

The sun is good only as it relates to the stars, to the seas, to your eye, to the fields, etc. As it relates to the stars, it raises their influences; as to the seas, it melts them and makes the waters flow; as to your eye, it brings in the beauty of the world; as to the fields, it clothes them with fruits and flowers. Did it not relate to others, it would not be good. Divest it of these operations and divide it from these objects, it is useless and good for nothing, and therefore worthless, because worthless and useless go together. A piece of gold cannot be valued unless we know how it relates to clothes, to wine, to victuals, to the esteem of men and to the owner. Some little piece, in a kingly monument, severed from the rest, has no beauty at all. It enjoys its value in its place, by the ornament it gives to, and receives from, all the parts.

By this I discerned that even a little knowledge could not be had in the mystery of felicity, without a great deal. And that, that was the reason why so many were ignorant of its nature, and why so few did attain it. For by the labor required to much knowledge, they were discouraged; and for lack of much, did not see any glorious motives to allure them.

Our Instinctive Desire for an Unknown Felicity

Therefore of necessity they must at first believe that felicity is a glorious though an unknown thing. And certainly it was the infinite wisdom of God that did implant by instinct so strong a desire of felicity in the soul, that we might be excited to labor after it, though we know it not—the very force wherewith we covet it, supplying the place of understanding. That there is a felicity, we all know by the desires after; that there is a most glorious felicity, we know by the strength and vehemence of those desires. And that nothing but felicity is worthy of our labor, because all other things are the means only which conduce unto it.

I was very much animated by the desires of philosophers, which I saw in heathen books aspiring after it. But the misery is: it was unknown. An altar was erected to it like that in Athens with this inscription: TO THE UNKNOWN GOD.[101]

The Perfection of Felicity's Objects and Manner

Two things in perfect felicity I saw to be requisite, and that felicity must be perfect, or not felicity. The first was the perfection of its objects in nature, serviceableness, number, and excellency. The second was the perfection of the manner wherein they are enjoyed for sweetness, measure, and duration. And unless in these I could be satisfied, I should never be contented: especially about the latter.

For the manner is always more excellent than the thing. And it far more concerns us that the manner wherein we enjoy be complete and perfect, than that the matter which we enjoy be complete and perfect. For the manner, as we contemplate its excellency, is itself a great part of the matter of our enjoyment.

I Asked About God's Treasures

In discovering the matter or objects to be enjoyed, I was greatly aided by remembering that we were made in God's image. For thereupon it must of necessity follow that God's treasures be our treasures, and his joys our joys. So that by inquiring what were God's, I found the objects of our felicity, God's treasures being ours. For we were made in his image that we might live in his similitude.

And herein I was mightily confirmed by the Apostle's blaming the Gentiles, and charging it upon them as a very great fault that they were alienated from the life of God.[102] For hereby I perceived that we were to live the life of God when we lived the true life of nature according to knowledge, and that, by blindness and corruption, we had strayed from it. Now God's treasures are his own perfections and all his creatures.

I Asked About How God Enjoyed His Treasures

The image of God implanted in us guided me to the manner wherein we were to enjoy. For since we were made in the similitude of God, we were made to enjoy after his similitude. Now to enjoy the treasures of God in the similitude of God is the most perfect blessedness God could devise. For the treasures of God are the most perfect treasures, and the manner of God is the most perfect manner.

To enjoy therefore the treasures of God after the similitude of God is to enjoy the most perfect treasures in the most perfect manner. Upon which I was most infinitely satisfied in God, and knew there was a Deity because I was satisfied. For in exerting himself wholly in achieving thus an infinite felicity, he was infinitely delightful, great, and glorious, and my desires so august and insatiable that nothing less than a Deity could satisfy them.

I Saw All Things in Their Proper Places

This spectacle once seen, will never be forgotten. It is a great part of the beatific vision. A sight of happiness is happiness. It transforms the soul and makes it heavenly; it powerfully calls us to communion with God, and weans us from the customs of this world. It puts a luster upon God and all his creatures, and makes us to see them in a divine and eternal light.

I no sooner discerned this but I was (as Plato said, *In summâ Rationis arce quies habitat*) seated in a throne of repose and perfect rest. All things were well in their proper places—I alone was out of frame and had need to be mended. For all things were God's treasures in their proper places, and I was to be restored to God's image. Whereupon you will not believe how I was withdrawn from all endeavors of altering and mending outward things. They lay so well, I thought, they could not be mended; but I must be mended to enjoy them.

I Saw the Greatest Thing God Could Make

The image of God is the most perfect creature. Since there cannot be two Gods, the utmost endeavor of almighty power is the image of God. It is no blasphemy to say that God cannot make a God. The greatest thing that he can make is his image: a most perfect creature, to enjoy the most perfect treasures in the most perfect manner. A creature endued with the most divine and perfect powers, for measure, kind, number, duration, and excellency, is the most perfect creature—able to see all eternity with all its objects, and as a mirror to contain all that it sees; able to love all it contains, and as a sun to shine upon its caves; able by shining to communicate itself in beams of affection, and to illustrate all it illuminates with beauty and glory; able to be wise, holy, glorious, blessed in itself, as God is; being adorned inwardly with the same kind of beauty, and outwardly superior to all creatures.

I Began to See the Richness & Greatness of Everything

Upon this I began to believe that all other creatures were such that God was himself in their creation—that is almighty power wholly exerted—and that every creature is indeed as it seemed in my infancy, not as it is commonly apprehended. Everything being sublimely rich and great and glorious. Every spire of grass is the work of his hand. And I in a world where everything is mine, and is far better than the greater sort of children esteem diamonds and pearls to be. Gold and silver being the very refuse of nature and the worst things in God's kingdom, howbeit truly good in their proper places.

Being Satisfied in God

To be satisfied in God is the highest difficulty in the whole world, and yet most easy to be done. To make it possible that we should be satisfied in God was an achievement of infinite weight before it was attempted, and the most difficult thing in all worlds before it was achieved. For we naturally expect infinite things of God, and can be satisfied only with the highest reason. So that the best of all possible things must be wrought in God, or else we shall remain dissatisfied. But it is most easy at present, because God is.

For God is not a being compounded of body and soul, or substance and accident, or power and act, but is all act; pure act, a simple being whose essence is to be, whose being is to be perfect so that he is most perfect towards all and in all. He is most perfect for all and by all. He is in nothing imperfect, because his being is to be perfect. It is impossible for him to be God and imperfect, and therefore do we so ardently and infinitely desire his absolute perfection.

How God Exerts His Power

Neither is it possible to be otherwise. All his power being turned into act, it is all exerted: infinitely and wholly. Neither is there any power in him which he is not able and willing to use, or which he cannot wisely guide to most excellent ends. So that we may expect most angelical and heavenly rarities in all the creatures. Were there any power in God unemployed, he would be compounded of power and act. Being therefore God is all act, he is a God in this: that himself is power exerted. An infinite act because infinite power infinitely exerted. An eternal act because infinite power eternally exerted.

Wherein consists the generation of his Son: the perfection of his love, and the immutability of God. For God by exerting himself begot his Son, and doing it wholly for the sake of his creatures, is perfect love; and doing it wholly from all eternity, is an eternal act, and therefore unchangeable.

God Has Always Propagated Himself

With this we are delighted because it is absolutely impossible that any power dwelling with love should continue idle. Since God therefore was infinitely and eternally communicative, all things were contained in him from all eternity.

As Nazianzen in his 38th Oration admirably expressed it in these words, "Because it was by no means sufficient for goodness to move only in the contemplation of itself, but it became what was good to be diffused and propagated, that more might be affected with the benefit (for this was the part of the highest goodness). First, he thought upon angelical and celestial virtues, and that thought was the work which he wrought by the Word and fulfilled by the Spirit. (*Atque ita Secundi Splendores procreati primi splendoris Administri.*)" And so were there second splendors created and made to minister to the first splendor, so that all motions, successions, creatures, and operations, with their beginnings and ends, were in him from everlasting. To whom nothing can be added because from all eternity he was whatsoever to all eternity he can be. All things being now to be seen and contemplated in his bosom; and advanced therefore into a diviner light, being infinitely older and more precious than we were aware. Time itself being in God eternally.

I Discovered These Great Thoughts Throughout the Entire Bible

Little did I imagine that, while I was thinking these things, I was conversing with God. I was so ignorant that I did not think any man in the world had had such thoughts before. Seeing them therefore so amiable, I wondered not a little that nothing was spoken of them in former ages. But as I read the Bible, I was here and there surprised with such thoughts, and found by degrees that these things had been written of before, not only in the Scriptures but in many of the Fathers, and that this was the way of communion with God in all saints, as I saw clearly in the person of David.

I thought a new light darted into all his Psalms, and finally spread abroad over the whole Bible. So that things, which for their obscurity I thought not in being, were there contained; things, which for their greatness were incredible, were made evident; and things obscure plain. God by this means bringing me into the very heart of his kingdom.

Moses, Jacob, Adam, & Abraham Enjoyed Heaven & Earth

There I saw Moses blessing the Lord for the precious things of heaven, for the dew and for the deep that couches beneath, and for the precious fruits brought forth by the sun, and for the precious things put forth by the moon, and for the chief things of the ancient mountains, and for the precious things of the lasting hills, and for the precious things of the earth, and fullness thereof.[103]

There I saw Jacob with awful apprehensions admiring the glory of the world, when awaking out of his dream he said, "How dreadful is this place. This is none other than the house of God, and the gate of heaven."[104]

There I saw God leading forth Abraham, and showing him the stars of heaven, and all the countries round about him, and saying, "All these will I give you, and your seed after you."[105]

There I saw Adam in Paradise, surrounded with the beauty of heaven and earth, void of all earthly comforts, to wit, such as were devised: gorgeous apparel, palaces, gold and silver, coaches, musical instruments, etc.; and entertained only with celestial joys: the sun and moon and stars, beasts and fowls and fishes, trees and fruits and flowers, with the other naked and simple delights of nature. By which I evidently saw that the way to become rich and blessed was not by heaping accidental and devised riches to make ourselves great in the vulgar manner, but to approach more near, or to see more clearly with the eye of our understanding, the beauties and glories of the whole world. And to have communion with the Deity in the riches of God and nature.

I Saw the Importance of Seeing & Loving Things Perfectly

I saw moreover that it did not so much concern us what objects were before us, as with what eyes we beheld them, with what affections we esteemed them, and what apprehensions we had about them. All men see the same objects, but do not equally understand them. Intelligence is the tongue that discerns and tastes them, knowledge is the light of heaven, love is the wisdom and glory of God, life extended to all objects is the sense that enjoys them. So that knowledge, life, and love are the very means of all enjoyment, which above all things we must seek for and labor after.

All objects are in God eternal, which we by perfecting our faculties are made to enjoy. Which then are turned into act, when they are exercised about their objects; but without them are desolate and idle, or discontented and forlorn. Whereby I perceived the meaning of the definition wherein Aristotle describes felicity, when he says, "Felicity is the perfect exercise of perfect virtue in a perfect life." For that life is perfect when it is perfectly extended to all objects, and perfectly sees them, and perfectly loves them— which is done by a perfect exercise of virtue about them.

CHAPTER 21

MY MENTOR, DAVID
(A JOURNEY THROUGH THE PSALMS)

My Poetic Tribute to David

I

In Salem dwelt a glorious king,
Raised from a shepherd's lowly state;
That did his praises like an angel sing
    Who did the world create.
By many great and bloody wars
He was advanced unto thrones:
But more delighted in the stars
Than in the splendor of his precious stones;
Nor gold nor silver did his eye regard:
The works of God were his sublime reward.

2

A warlike champion he had been,
And many feats of chivalry
Had done: in kingly courts his eye had seen
    A vast variety
Of earthly joys: Yet he despis'd
Those fading honors, and false pleasures
Which are by mortals so much prized;
And placed his happiness in other treasures:
No state of life which in this world we find
Could yield contentment to his greater mind.

3

His fingers touched his trembling lyre,
And every quavering string did yield
A sound that filled all the Jewish choir,

And echoed in the field.
No pleasure was so great to him
As in a silent night to see
The moon and stars: A cherubim
Above them, even here, he seemed to be:
Enflam'd with love it was his great desire,
To sing, contemplate, ponder, and admire.

4
He was a prophet, and foresaw
Things extant in the world to come:
He was a judge, and ruled by a law
    That than the honeycomb
    Was sweeter far:[106] he was a sage,
And all his people could advise;
    An oracle, whose every page
Contained in verse the greatest mysteries;
But most he then enjoyed himself when he
Did as a poet praise the Deity.

5
A shepherd, soldier, and divine,
A judge, a courtier, and a king,
Priest, angel, prophet, oracle, did shine
    At once when he did sing.
    Philosopher and poet too
    Did in his melody appear;
    All these in him did please the view
Of those that did his heavenly music hear:

And every drop that from his flowing quill
Came down, did all the world with nectar fill.

6

He had a deep and perfect sense
Of all the glories and the pleasures
That in God's works are hid: the excellence
 Of such transcendent treasures
 Made him on earth a heavenly king,
 And filled his solitudes with joy;
 He never did more sweetly sing
Than when alone, though that doth mirth destroy:
Sense did his soul with heavenly life inspire,
And made him seem in God's celestial choir.

7

Rich, sacred deep and precious things
Did here on earth the man surround:
With all the glory of the King of Kings
 He was most strangely crowned.
 His clear soul and open sight
 Among the Sons of God did see
 Things filling angels with delight:
His ear did hear their heavenly melody,
And when he was alone he all became
That bliss implied, or did increase his fame.

8

All arts he then did exercise;
And as his God he did adore
By secret ravishments above the skies
    He carried was before
    He died. His soul did see and feel
    What others know not; and became,
    While he before his God did kneel,
A constant, heavenly, pure, seraphic flame.
Oh that I might unto his throne aspire,
And all his joys above the stars admire!

I Found a Soulmate in David

When I saw those objects celebrated in his psalms which God and nature had proposed to me, and which I thought chance only presented to my view, you cannot imagine how unspeakably I was delighted to see so glorious a person, so great a prince, so divine a sage, that was a man after God's own heart,[107] by the testimony of God himself, rejoicing in the same things, meditating on the same, and praising God for the same. For by this I perceived we were led by one spirit, and that following the clue of nature into this labyrinth, I was brought into the midst of celestial joys. And that to be retired from earthly cares and fears and distractions, that we might in sweet and heavenly peace contemplate all the works of God, was to live in heaven, and the only way to become what David was—a man after God's own heart. There we might be enflamed with those causes for which we ought to love him. There we might see those choice foods which feed the soul with angels' food. There we might bathe in those streams of pleasure that flow at his right hand forevermore.

Psalm 8: Every Man's Inheritance

That hymn of David in the eighth Psalm was supposed to be made by night, wherein he celebrates the works of God, because he mentions the moon and stars, but not the sun in his meditation.

When I consider the heavens which you have made, the moon and stars which are the work of your fingers, what is man that you are mindful of him, or the Son of man that you visit him? You have made him a little lower than the angels, and have crowned him with glory and honor. You have given him dominion over the works of your hands; you have put all things in subjection under his feet: all sheep and oxen, yea and the beasts of the fields, the fowls of the air, and the fishes of the sea, and whatsoever passes through the paths of the sea.[108]

This glory and honor wherewith man is crowned ought to affect every person that is grateful with celestial joy; and so much the rather because it is every man's proper and sole inheritance.

Psalm 19: The Glory of Heaven & Earth

His joyful meditation in the nineteenth Psalm directs every man to consider the glory of heaven and earth.

The heavens declare the glory of God, and the firmament shows his handiwork. Day unto day utters speech, and night unto night shows knowledge. There is no speech nor language where their voice is not heard. Their line is gone throughout all the earth, and their voice to the end of the world. In them has he set a tabernacle for the sun, which is as a bridegroom coming out of his chamber, and rejoices as a strong man to run his race. His going forth is from the end of the heaven and his circuit to the ends of it; and nothing is hid from the heat thereof.[109]

From thence he proceeds to the laws of God, as things more excellent in their nature than his works.

The Law of the Lord is perfect, converting the soul; the testimony of the Lord is sure, making wise the simple. The statutes of the Lord are right, rejoicing the heart; the commandment of the Lord is pure, enlightening the eyes. The fear of the Lord is clean, enduring forever; the judgments of the Lord are true and righteous altogether. More to be desired are they than gold, yea, than much fine gold; sweeter also than honey and the honeycomb.[110]

Whereby he plainly shows that divine and kingly delights are, in the laws and works of God, to be taken by all those that would be angelical and celestial creatures. For that in the kingdom of heaven, everyone being disentangled from particular relations and private riches, as if he were newly taken out of nothing to the fruition of all eternity, was in these alone to solace himself as his peculiar treasures.

Psalm 22: All Nations Praising God

You that fear the Lord, praise him; all you seed of Jacob, glorify him; and fear him all you seed of Israel. For he has not despised nor abhorred the affliction of the afflicted, neither has he hid his face from him; but when he cried unto him he heard. My praise shall be of you in the great congregation; I will pay my vows before them that fear him. The meek shall eat and be satisfied. They shall praise the Lord that seek him; your heart shall live forever. All the ends of the world shall remember and turn unto the Lord; all the kindreds of the nations shall worship before you. For the kingdom is the Lord's, and he is the governor among the nations. All they that be fat upon earth shall eat and worship. All they that go down to the dust shall bow before him, and none can keep alive his own soul. A seed shall serve him; it shall be counted to the Lord for a generation. They shall come and declare his righteousness to a people that shall be born, that he has done this.[111]

Here he shows that it was his desire and delight to have all nations praising God, and that the condescension of the Almighty, in stooping down to the poor and needy, was the joy of his soul. He prophesies also of the conversion of the Gentiles to the knowledge of Jesus Christ, which to see was to him an exceeding pleasure.

Psalms 24 & 28: He Saw God's Pleasure With the World

The earth is the Lord's and the fullness thereof, the round world and they that dwell therein.[112]

He observes here that God, by a comprehensive possession and by way of eminence, enjoys the whole world; all mankind and all the earth, with all that is therein, being his peculiar treasures. Since therefore we are made in the image of God to live in his similitude, as they are his, they must be our treasures—we being wise and righteous over all as he is.

Because they regard not the works of the Lord nor the operations of his hands, therefore shall he destroy them, and not build them up.[113]

Psalm 33: The Psalmist Affirms God's Works

By the word of the Lord were the heavens made, and all the host of them by the breath of his mouth. He gathers the waters of the sea together; he lays up the depth in storehouses. Let all the earth fear the Lord; let all the inhabitants of the world stand in awe of him. For he spoke, and it was done; he commanded, and it stood fast.[114]

He frequently meditates upon the works of God, and affirms the contemplation of them to beget his fear in our hearts. For that he being great in strength, not one fails.

Psalms 35 & 36: God's Mercy, Faithfulness & Lovingkindness

All my bones shall say, Lord, who is like unto you, who delivered the poor from him that is too strong for him; yea, the poor and the needy from him that spoils him![115]

Your mercy, O Lord, is above the heavens, and your faithfulness reaches to the clouds. Your righteousness is like the great mountains; your judgments are a great deep. O Lord, you preserve man and beast. How excellent is your lovingkindness, O God! Therefore the children of men put their trust in the shadow of your wings. They shall be abundantly satisfied with the fatness of your house, and you will make them drink of the river of your pleasures. For with you is the fountain of life. In your light we shall see light.[116]

The judgments of God, and his lovingkindness, his mercy and faithfulness, are the fatness of his house, and his righteousness being seen in the light of glory is the torrent of pleasure at his right hand forevermore.

Psalm 45: Entering God's Palace

Hearken, O Daughter, and consider and incline your ear. Forget
also my own people and your father's house. So shall the king
greatly desire your beauty, for he is your Lord, and worship
you him.[117]

The king's daughter is all glorious within; her clothing is of
wrought gold. She will be brought unto the king in raiment of
needlework; the virgins, her companions that follow her, shall be
brought unto you. With gladness and rejoicing shall they be
brought; they will enter into the king's palace. Instead of your
fathers shall be your children, whom you may make princes in all
the earth.[118]

The Psalmist here sings an Epithalamium upon the marriage between
Christ and his Church, whom he persuades to forsake her country and her
father's house, together with all the customs and vanities of this world, and
to dedicate herself wholly to our Saviour's service. Since she is in exchange
to enter into his palace and become a bride to so glorious a person. The
bridegroom and the bride, the palace (which is all the world) with all that
is therein, being David's joy and his true possession. Nay every child of this
bride is, if a male, a prince over all the earth; if a female, bride to the king
of heaven. And every soul that is a spouse of Jesus Christ, esteems all the
saints her own children and her own bowels.

Psalm 46: Praising God's Grace & His Works

There is a river, the streams whereof shall make glad the City of
God, the holy place of the tabernacle of the Most High.[119]

He praises the means of grace which, in the midst of this world, are great consolations, and, in all distresses, refresh our souls.

> Come behold the works of the Lord, what desolations he has made in the earth.[120]

He exhorts us to contemplate God's works, which are so perfect, that when his secret and just judgments are seen, the very destruction of nations and laying waste of cities shall be sweet and delightful.

Psalms 47 & 48

> O clap your hands, all you people, shout unto God with the voice of triumph. For the Lord most high is terrible, he is a great king over all the earth.[121]

> He shall choose our inheritance for us, the excellency of Jacob whom he loved.[122]

> Beautiful for situation, the joy of the whole earth, is Mount Zion on the sides of the north, the city of the great king. God is known in her palaces for a refuge.[123]

> Walk about Zion and go round about her; tell the towers thereof; mark you well her bulwarks; consider her palaces, that you may tell it to the generation following. For this God is our God forever and ever. He will be our guide even unto death.[124]

Psalm 49: The Vanity of False Imaginations

As in the former psalms, he proposes true and celestial joys, so in the following, he discovers the vanity of false imaginations.

They that trust in their wealth, and boast themselves in the multitude of their riches, none of them can by any means redeem his brother, or give unto God a ransom for him. For the redemption of their soul is precious and it ceases forever.[125]

For he sees that wise men die; likewise the fool and brutish person perish and leave their wealth to others. Their inward thought is that their houses shall continue forever, and their dwelling places to all generations. They call their lands after their own names.[126]

This their way is their folly, yet their posterity reprove their sayings. Like sheep, they are laid in the grave; death shall feed sweetly on them, and the upright shall have dominion over them in the morning, and their beauty shall consume in the grave from their dwelling.[127]

Man that is in honor and understands not, is like the beast that perishes.[128]

Psalm 50: Hindrances to Praising God

Hear, O my people, and I will speak; O Israel, and I will testify against you. I am God, even your God. I will not reprove you for your sacrifices or your burnt offerings, to have been continually before me. I will take no bullock out of your house, nor he-goats out of your folds. For every beast of the forest is mine, and the cattle upon a thousand hills. I know all the fowls of the mountains, and the wild beasts of the field are mine. If I were hungry, I would not tell you; for the world is mine, and the fullness thereof. Will I eat the flesh of bulls or drink the blood of goats? Offer unto God thanksgiving, and pay your vows to the Most High. And call upon me in the day of trouble; I will deliver you, and you shall glorify me.[129]

When I was a little child, I thought that everyone that lifted up his eyes to behold the sun, did me, in looking on it, wonderful service. And certainly, being moved thereby to praise my Creator, it was in itself a service wonderfully delightful. For since God so much esteems praises that he prefers them above thousands of rams and tens of thousands of rivers of oil, if I love him with that inflamed ardor and zeal I ought, his praises must needs be delightful to me above all services and riches whatsoever.

That which hinders us from seeing the glory and discerning the sweetness of praises hinders us also from knowing the manner how we are concerned in them. But God knows infinite reasons for which he prefers them. If I should tell you what they are, you would be apt to despise them. Divine and heavenly mysteries being thirsted after till they are known, but by corrupted nature undervalued. Howbeit since grace corrects the perverseness of nature, and tastes in a better manner, it shall not be long till somewhere we disclose them.

The World Created to Praise God

Are not praises the very end for which the world was created? Do they not consist as it were of knowledge, complacency, and thanksgiving? Are they not better than all the fowls and beasts and fishes in the world? What are the cattle upon a thousand hills but carcases, without creatures that can rejoice in God and enjoy them? It is evident that praises are infinitely more excellent than all the creatures because they proceed from men and angels. For as streams do, they derive an excellency from their fountains, and are the last tribute that can possibly be paid to the Creator. Praises are the breathings of interior love, the marks and symptoms of a happy life: overflowing gratitude, returning benefits, an oblation of the soul, and the heart ascending upon the wings of divine affection to the throne of God.

God is a spirit and cannot feed on carcases; but he can be delighted with thanksgivings, and is infinitely pleased with the emanations of our joy, because he himself is admired and his works are esteemed. What can be more acceptable to love than that it should be prized and magnified? Because therefore God is love, and his measure infinite, he infinitely desires to be admired and beloved, and so our praises enter into the very secret of his eternal bosom, and mingle with him who dwells in that light which is inaccessible. What strengths are there even in flattery to please a great affection? Are not your bowels moved, and your affections melted with delight and pleasure, when your soul is precious in the eye of those you love? When your affection is pleased, your love prized, and they satisfied? To prize love is the highest service in the whole world that can be done unto it. But there are a thousand causes moving God to esteem our praises, more than we can well apprehend. However, let these inflame you and move you to praise him night and day forever.

Psalm 51: Deep & Serious Groans

Of our Saviour it is said, "Sacrifice and offering you would not, but a body have you prepared me,"[130] all sacrifices being but types and figures of himself, and himself infinitely more excellent than they all. Of a broken heart also it is said,

You desire not sacrifice else I would give it. You delight not in burnt offering. The sacrifices of God are a broken spirit; a broken and contrite heart, O God, you will not despise.[131]

One deep and serious groan is more acceptable to God than the creation of a world. In spiritual things, we find the greatest excellency. As praises, because they are the pledges of our mutual affection, so groans, because they are pledges of a due contrition, are the greatest sacrifices. Both proceed from love, and in both we manifest and exercise our friendship. In contrition we show our penitence for having offended, and by that are fitted to rehearse his praises. All the desire wherewith he longs after a returning sinner, makes him to esteem a broken heart. What can more melt and dissolve a lover than the tears of an offending and returning friend? Here also is the saying verified, "The falling out of lovers is the beginning of love—the renewing, the repairing, and the strengthening of it."

Praises & Pentinence

An enlarged soul that sees all the world praising God, or penitent by bewailing their offences and converting to him, has his eye fixed upon the joy of angels. It needs nothing but the sense of God to inherit all things. We must borrow and derive it from him by seeing his, and aspiring after it. Do but clothe yourself with divine resentments and the world shall be to you the valley of vision,[132] and all the nations and kingdoms of the world shall appear in splendor and celestial glory.

Psalms 58 & 59: Vengeance of the Wicked

The righteous shall rejoice when he sees the vengeance; he shall wash his feet in the blood of the wicked.[133]

But I will sing of your power, yea I will sing aloud of your mercy in the morning. For you have been my defense in the day of my trouble.[134]

The deliverances of your former life are objects of your felicity, and so is the vengeance of the wicked. With both which, in all times and places, you are ever to be present in your memory and understanding. For lack of considering its objects, the soul is desolate.

Psalms 63 & 65: Dwelling in God's Courts

My soul thirsts for you; my flesh longs for you in a dry and thirsty land where no water is. To see your power and your glory so as I have seen you in the sanctuary. Because your lovingkindness is better than life, my lips shall praise you. Thus will I bless you while I live; I will lift up my hands in your name. My soul shall be satisfied as with marrow and fatness, and my mouth shall praise you with joyful lips.[135]

O you that hears prayer, unto you shall all flesh come.[136]

Blessed is the man whom you choose and cause to approach unto you, that he may dwell in your courts. We shall be satisfied with the goodness of this house, even of this holy temple.[137]

See how in the 65th Psalm, he introduces the meditation of God's visible works sweetly into the tabernacle and makes them to be the fatness of his house, even of his holy temple. God is seen when his love is manifested. God is enjoyed when his love is prized. When we see the glory of his wisdom and goodness and his power exerted, then we see his glory. And these we cannot see till we see their works. When therefore we see his works, in them as in a mirror we see his glory.

Psalm 66: All Nations Praising God

Make a joyful noise unto God, all ye lands; sing forth the honor of his name, make his praise glorious. Say unto God, "How terrible are you in your works? Through the greatness of your power shall your enemies submit themselves unto you. All the earth shall worship you, and sing unto you; they shall sing to your name." Come and see the works of God, he is terrible in his doing towards the children of man.[138]

The prospect of all nations praising him is far sweeter than the prospect of the fields or silent heavens serving them, though you see the skies adorned with stars, and the fields covered with corn and flocks of sheep and cattle. When the eye of your understanding shines upon them, they are yours in him, and all your joys.

Psalm 74: More of God's Treasures

God is my king, of old working salvation in the midst of the earth. He divided the sea by his strength. He broke the heads of Leviathan in pieces.[139]

His heart is always abroad in the midst of the earth, seeing and rejoicing in his wonders there. His soul is busied in the ancient works of God for his people Israel.

The day is yours, the night also is yours; you have prepared the light and the sun. You have set all the borders of the earth. You have made summer and winter.[140]

He proposes more objects of our felicity in which we ought to meet the goodness of God, that we might rejoice before him. The day and night, the light and the sun, are God's treasures, and ours also.

Psalm 78: Celestial Light in Our Memories & Minds

In the 78th Psalm, he commands all ages to record the ancient ways of God and recommends them to our meditation, showing the ordinance of God: that fathers should teach their children and they another generation, which certainly since they are not to be seen in the visible world but only in the memory and minds of men. The memory and mind are a strange region of celestial light, and a wonderful place, as well as a large and sublime one, in which they may be seen. What is contained in the souls of men being as visible to us as the very heavens.

Psalm 84: Preferring a Day in God's Courts

In the 84th Psalm, he longs earnestly after the tabernacle of God,[141] and prefers a day in his courts above a thousand.[142] Because there, as Deborah speaks in her song, was the place of drawing waters, that is of repentance, and of rehearsing the righteous acts of the Lord,[143] which it is more blessed to do than to inherit the palaces of wicked men.

Psalm 86: The Excellency of God's Works

> Among the Gods, there is none like unto you. Neither are there any works like unto your works. All nations whom you have made shall come and worship you, O Lord, and shall glorify your name. For you are great, and do wondrous things. You are God alone.[144]

This is a glorious meditation, wherein the Psalmist gives himself liberty to examine the excellency of God's works—and finding them infinitely great and above all that can be besides, rejoices and admires the goodness of God, and rests satisfied with complacency in them. That they were all his, he knew well, being the gifts of God made unto him, and that he was to have communion with God in the enjoyment of them. But their excellency was a thing unsearchable and their incomparableness above all imagination, which he found by much study to his infinite delectation.

Psalms 103-107, 119: Living in Heaven by Enjoying God's Works

In his other Psalms, he proceeds to speak of the works of God over and over again: sometimes stirring up all creatures to praise God for the very delight he took in their admirable perfections, sometimes showing God's goodness and mercy by them, and sometimes rejoicing himself and triumphing in them. By all this, teaching us what we ought to do, that we might become divine and heavenly.

In the 103rd Psalm, he opens the nature of God's present mercies, both towards himself in particular and towards all in general, turning emergencies in this world into celestial joys.

In the 104th Psalm, he insists wholly upon the beauty of God's works in the creation, making all things in heaven and earth, and in the heaven of heavens, in the wilderness and the sea, his private and personal delights.

In the 105th and 106th Psalms, he celebrates the ways of God in former ages with as much vehemence, zeal, and pleasure as if they were new things, and as if he were present with them, seeing their beauty and tasting their delight that very moment.

In the 107th Psalm, he contemplates the ways of God in the dispensations of his providence over travelers, sick men, seamen, etc., showing that the way to be much in heaven is to be much employed here upon earth in the meditation of divine and celestial things. For such are these, though they seem terrestrial. All which he concludes thus: "Whoever considers these things, even he shall understand the lovingkindness of the Lord."[145]

In the 119th Psalm, like an enamoured person, and a man ravished in spirit with joy and pleasure, he treats upon divine laws, and over and over again makes mention of their beauty and perfection. By all which we may see what inward life we ought to lead with God in the temple. And that to be much in the meditation of God's works and laws, to see their excellency, to taste their sweetness, to behold their glory, to admire and rejoice and overflow with praises, is to live in heaven. But unless we have a communion with David in a rational knowledge of their nature and excellency, we can never understand the grounds of his complacency, or depth of his resentments.

Pleasing God in Our Daily Circumstances

In our outward life towards men, the Psalmist also is an admirable precedent: in weeping for those that forget God's law, in publishing his praises in the congregation of the righteous, in speaking of his testimonies without cowardice or shame even before princes, in delighting in the saints, in keeping promises though made to his hurt, in tendering the life of his enemies and clothing himself with sackcloth when they were sick,[146] in showing mercy to the poor, in enduring the songs and mockings of the drunkards,[147] in taking care to glorify the author of all bounty with a splendid temple and musical instruments in this world, in putting his trust and confidence in God among all his enemies, evermore promoting his honor and glory, instructing others in the excellency of his ways, and endeavoring to establish his worship in Israel.

Thus ought we, to the best of our power, to express our gratitude and friendships to so great a benefactor in all the effects of love and fidelity—

doing his pleasure with all our might and promoting his honor with all our power.

Psalms 145-150: The Nature of God's Kingdom

There are Psalms more clear wherein he expresses the joy he takes in God's works and the glory of them. Wherein he teaches us at diverse times and in diverse manner to ponder on them. Among which the 145th Psalm (and so onward to the last) are very eminent. In which he opens the nature of God's kingdom, and so vigorously and vehemently excites all creatures to praise him, and all men to do it with all kind of musical instruments by all expressions,[148] in all nations for all things, as ten thousand vents were not sufficient to ease his fullness, as if all the world were but one celestial temple in which he was delighted, as if all nations were present before him and he saw God face to face in this earthly tabernacle, as if his soul like an infinite ocean were full of joys, and all these but springs and channels over-flowing. So purely, so joyfully, so powerfully, he walked with God—all creatures, as they brought a confluence of joys unto him, being pipes to ease him.

The Kingdom of God Was Always Around Him

His soul recovered its pristine liberty and saw through the mud walls of flesh and blood. Being alive, he was in the spirit all his days. While his body therefore was enclosed in this world, his soul was in the temple of eternity, and clearly beheld the infinite life and omnipresence of God: having con-versation with invisible, spiritual, and immaterial things, which were its companions, itself being invisible, spiritual, and immaterial.

Kingdoms and ages did surround him as clearly as the hills and moun-tains, and therefore the kingdom of God was ever round about him.

Everything was one way or other his sovereign delight and transcendent pleasure, as in heaven everything will be everyone's peculiar treasure.

David's Faith in Prophecies

He saw these things only in the light of faith, and yet rejoiced as if he had seen them by the light of heaven, which argued the strength and glory of his faith. And whereas he so rejoiced in all the nations of the earth for praising God, he saw them doing it in the light of prophesy, not of history. Much more therefore should we rejoice, who see these prophecies fulfilled, since the fulfilling of them is so blessed, divine, and glorious, that the very prevision of their accomplishment transported and ravished this glorious person. But we wither and, for lack of sense, shrivel up into nothing, who should be filled with the delights of ages.

Reigning in God's Kingdom

By this we understand what it is to be the Sons of God and what it is to live in communion with him, what it is to be advanced to his throne, and to reign in his kingdom, with all those other glorious and marvelous expressions that are applied to men in the holy Scriptures.

To be the Sons of God is not only to enjoy the privileges and the freedom of his house, and to bear the relation of children to so great a Father, but it is to be like him, and to share with him in all his glory and in all his treasures. To be like him in spirit and understanding; to be exalted above all creatures as the end of them; to be present as he is by sight and love, without limit and without bounds, with all his works; to be holy towards all and wise towards all, as he is. Prizing all his goodness in all with infinite ardor, that as glorious and eternal kings being pleased in all, we might reign over all forevermore.

Being Present with God's Omnipresence

This greatness both of God towards us, and of ourselves towards him, we ought always as much as possible to retain in our understanding. And when we cannot effectually keep it alive in our senses, to cherish the memory of it in the center of our hearts, and do all things in the power of it. For the angels, when they come to us, so fulfill their outward ministry, that within they nevertheless maintain the beatific vision—ministering before the throne of God and among the sons of men at the same time. The reason whereof St. Gregory says is this:

> Though the spirit of an angel be limited and circumscribed in itself, yet the Supreme Spirit, which is God, is uncircumscribed. He is everywhere and wholly everywhere, which makes their knowledge to be dilated everywhere. For being wholly everywhere, they are immediately present with his omnipresence in every place and wholly. It fills them forever.

Our Joy, Courage, Zeal, & Fidelity

This sense that God is so great in goodness, and we so great in glory as to be his sons, and so rich as to live in communion with him, and so individually united to him, that he is in us and we in him, will make us do all our duties not only with incomparable joy but courage also. It will fill us with zeal and fidelity, and make us to overflow with praises. For which one cause alone, the knowledge of it ought infinitely to be esteemed.

For to be ignorant of this is to sit in darkness and to be a child of darkness. It makes us to be without God in the world,[149] exceeding weak, timorous and feeble, comfortless and barren, dead and unfruitful, lukewarm, indifferent, dumb, unfaithful. To which I may add that it makes us uncertain. For so glorious is the face of God and true religion, that it is impossible to see it but in transcendent splendor. Nor can we know that God is till we see him infinite in goodness. Nothing therefore will make us certain of his being but his glory.

Abiding in all of God's Attributes, Thoughts, Creatures, & Works

To enjoy communion with God is to abide with him in the fruition of his divine and eternal glory, in all his attributes, in all his thoughts, in all his creatures, in his eternity, infinity, almighty power, sovereignty, etc. In all those works which from all eternity he wrought in himself; as the generation of his Son, the proceeding of the Holy Ghost, the eternal union and communion of the blessed Trinity, the counsels of his bosom, the attainment of the end of all his endeavors, wherein we shall see ourselves exalted and beloved from all eternity.

We are to enjoy communion with him in the creation of the world, in the government of angels, in the redemption of mankind, in the dispensations of his providence, in the incarnation of his Son, in his passion, resurrection, and ascension, in his shedding abroad the Holy Ghost, in his government of the Church, in his judgment of the world, in the punishment of his enemies, in the rewarding of his friends, in eternal glory. All these therefore particularly ought to be near us, and to be esteemed by us as our riches; being those delectable things that adorn the house of God which is eternity; and those living fountains, from whence we seek forth the streams of joy, that everlastingly overflow to refresh our souls.

V.
PRINCIPLES FOR YOUR OWN JOURNEY

CHAPTER 22

THE PRINCIPLE OF TWO KINDS OF CHRISTIANS

Principles for Action & Contemplation

Having spoken so much concerning his entrance and progress in felicity, I will in this century speak of the principles with which your friend endued himself to enjoy it. For besides contemplative, there is an active happiness, which consists in blessed operations. And as some things fit a man for contemplation, so there are others fitting him for action—which, as they are infinitely necessary to practical happiness, so are they likewise infinitely conducive to contemplative itself.

Acting on Our Principles to Do Great Things

He thought it a vain thing to see glorious principles lie buried in books unless he did remove them into his understanding; and a vain thing to remove them unless he did revive them, and raise them up by continual exercise. Let this therefore be the first principle of your soul — that to have no principles or to live beside them is equally miserable. And that philosophers are not those that speak but do great things.

A Philosopher, A Christian, & A Divine

He thought that to be a philosopher, a Christian, and a divine, was to be one of the most illustrious creatures in the world—and that no man was a man in act, but only in capacity, that was not one of these, or rather all. For either of these three include the other two. A divine includes a philosopher and a Christian; a Christian includes a divine and a philosopher; a philosopher includes a Christian and a divine. Since no man therefore can be a man unless he be a philosopher, nor a true philosopher unless he be a Christian, nor a perfect Christian unless he be a divine, every man ought to spend his time in studying diligently Divine Philosophy.

Divine Philosophy

This last principle needs a little explication. Not only because Philosophy is condemned for vain, but because it is superfluous among inferior Christians, and impossible, as some think, unto them. We must distinguish therefore of philosophy and of Christians also. "Some philosophy," as Saint Paul says, "is vain",[150] but then it is vain philosophy. But there is also a Divine Philosophy, of which no books in the world are more full than his own. That we are naturally the Sons of God (I speak of primitive and upright nature); that the Son of God is the first beginning of every creature; that we are to be changed from glory to glory into the same image;[151] that we are spiritual kings; that Christ is the express image of his Father's person;[152] that by him all things are made whether they are visible or invisible—is the highest philosophy in the world; and so is it also to treat, as he does, of the nature of virtues and Divine Laws.

Yet no man, I suppose, will account these superfluous or vain, for in the right knowledge of these, eternal life consists. And till we see into the beauty and blessedness of God's laws, the glory of his works, the excellency of our soul, etc., we are but children of darkness, at least but ignorant and imperfect—neither able to rejoice in God as we ought, nor to live in communion with him.

Rather we should remember that Jesus Christ is the wisdom of the Father[153] and that, since our life is hid with Christ in God,[154] we should spend our days in studying wisdom, that we might be like unto him; that the treasures of heaven are the treasures of wisdom; and that they are hid in Christ. As it is written, "In him are hid all the treasures of wisdom and knowledge."[155]

Two Sorts of Christians

In distinguishing of Christians, we ought to consider that Christians are of two sorts: perfect or imperfect—intelligent and mature, or weak and inexperienced (I will not say ignorant, for an ignorant Christian is a contradiction in nature). I say not that an imperfect Christian is the most glorious creature in the whole world; nor that it is necessary for him, if he loves to be imperfect, to be a Divine Philosopher. But he that is perfect is a Divine Philosopher—and the most glorious creature in the whole world.

Is not a philosopher a lover of wisdom? That is the signification of the very word, and sure it is the essence of a Christian, or very near it, to be a lover of wisdom. Can a Christian be so degenerate as to be a lover of imperfection? Does not your very nature abhor imperfection? Tis true that a Christian, so far as he is defective and imperfect, may be ignorant; yet still he is a lover of wisdom and a studier of it. He may be defective, but so far as he is defective he is no Christian—for a Christian is not a Christian in his blemishes, but his excellencies. Nor is a man indeed a man in his ignorances, but his wisdom. Blemishes may mar a man and spoil a Christian, but they cannot make him. Defects may be in him and cleave unto him, but they are to be shaken off and repented. Every man therefore according to his degree, so far forth as he is a Christian, is a philosopher.

Understanding & Full Assurance

Furthermore, does not St. Paul command us, in understanding to be men?[156] That implies that with little understanding we are but children, and without understanding are not men—but dreams and shadows, insignificant shells and mere apparitions. Does he not earnestly pray that their hearts may be comforted, being knit together in love, unto all the riches of the full assurance of understanding, to the acknowledgment of the mystery of God and of the Father and of Christ?[157] This plainly shows that, though a weak Christian may believe great things by an implicit faith, yet it is very desirable his faith should be turned into assurance; and that cannot be but by the riches of knowledge and understanding.

For he may believe that God is, and that Jesus Christ is his Saviour, and that his soul is immortal, and that there are joys in heaven, and that the scriptures are God's Word, and that God loves him, etc., so far as to yield obedience in some measure. But he can never come to a full assurance of all this, but by seeing the riches of the full assurance (i.e., those things which are called the riches of the full assurance). For being known, they give us assurance of the truth of all things: the glory of God's laws, the true dignity of his own soul, the excellency of God's ways, the magnificent goodness of his works, and the real blessedness of the state of grace. All which a man is so clearly to see, that he is not more sensible of the reality of the sunbeams. How else should he live in communion with God—to wit, in the enjoyment of them? For a full assurance of the reality of his joys is infinitely necessary to the possession of them.

Taking Time to Study God & Happiness

This digression steals me a little further. Is it not the shame and reproach of nature, that men should spend so much time in studying trades and be so ready skilled in the nature of clothes, of grounds, of gold and silver, etc., and to think it much to spend a little time in the study of God, themselves, and happiness? What have men to do in this world, but to make themselves happy? Shall it ever be praised and despised? Verily, happiness being the sovereign and supreme of our concerns, should have the most peculiar portion of our time, and other things what she can spare.

It more concerns me to be divine than to have a purse of gold. And therefore as Solomon said, "We must dig for her as for gold and silver,"[158] and that is the way to understand the fear of the Lord and to find the knowledge of God. It is a strange thing that men will be such enemies to them-selves. Wisdom is the principal thing, yet all neglect her. "Wherefore get wisdom, and with all your getting get understanding. Exalt her and she shall promote you; she shall bring you to honor when you embrace her. She will give to your head an ornament of grace; a crown of glory shall she deliv-er to you."[159] Had you certain tidings of a mine of gold, would the care of your ordinary affairs detain you, could you have it for the digging?

Nothing more ruins the world than a conceit that a little knowledge is sufficient. Which is a mere lazy dream to cover our sloth or enmity against God. Can you go to a mine of gold and not to wisdom; to dig for it without being guilty—either of a base despondency and distrust of wisdom that she will not bring you to such glorious treasures as is promised, or else of a vile and lazy humor that makes you despise them because of the little but long labor you apprehend between?

Nothing keeps men out of the temple of honor but that the temple of virtue stands between. But this was his principle that loved happiness, and is your friend: **I came into this world only that I might be happy. And what-soever it cost me, I will be happy.** A happiness there is, and it is my desire to enjoy it.

Practicing Virtue

Philosophers are not only those that contemplate happiness, but prac-tice virtue. He is a philosopher that subdues his vices, lives by reason, orders his desires, rules his passions, and submits not to his senses, nor is guided by the customs of this world. He despises those riches which men esteem; he despises those honors which men esteem; he forsakes those pleasures which men esteem.

And having proposed to himself a superior end than is commonly dis-cerned, bears all discouragements, breaks through all difficulties, and lives unto it—that having seen the secrets and the secret beauties of the highest reason, orders his conversation and lives by rule, though in this age it be held never so strange that he should do so. Only he is divine because he does this upon noble principles: because God is, because heaven is, because Jesus Christ has redeemed him, and because he loves him. Not only because virtue is amiable and felicity delightful, but for that also.

Two Sorts of Christians: Deferring Happiness or Enjoying Happiness Now

Once more, we will distinguish of Christians. There are Christians that place and desire all their happiness in another life, and there is another sort of Christians that desire happiness in this. The one can defer their enjoyment of wisdom till the world to come, and dispense with the increase and perfection of knowledge for a little time. The other are instant and impatient of delay, and would fain see that happiness here which they shall enjoy hereafter. Not the vain happiness of this world—falsely called happiness and truly vain—but the real joy and glory of the blessed, which consists in the enjoyment of the whole world in communion with God. Not this only, but the invisible and eternal which they earnestly covet to enjoy immediately; for which reason they daily pray your kingdom come, and travail towards it by learning wisdom as fast as they can.

Whether the first sort be Christians indeed, look you to that. They have much to say for themselves. Yet certainly they that put off felicity with long delays are to be much suspected. For it is against the nature of love and desire to defer. Nor can any reason be given why they should desire it at last, and not now. If they say, "because God has commanded them," that is false, for he offers it now—now they are commanded to have their conversation in heaven;[160] now they may be full of joy and full of glory. You are not straitened in me, but in your own bowels.[161] Those Christians that can defer their felicity may be contented with their ignorance.

Riches Should be Servants of Happiness

He that will not exchange his riches now, will not forsake them hereafter. He must forsake them, but will hardly be persuaded to do it willingly. He will leave them but not forsake them—for which cause two dishonors cleave unto him; and if at death, eternally. First, he comes off the stage unwillingly, which is very unhandsome; and secondly, he prefers his riches above his happiness.

Riches are but servants unto happiness; when they are impediments to it, they cease to be riches. As long as they are conducive to felicity they are desirable, but when they are incompatible are abominable. For what end are riches endeavored? Why do we desire them, but that we may be more happy? When we see the pursuit of riches destructive to felicity, to desire them is of all things in nature the most absurd and the most foolish. I ever thought that nothing was desirable for itself but happiness, and that whatever else we desire, it is of value only in relation and order to it.

CHAPTER 23

PRINCIPLES OF RETIREMENT AND SOLITUDE

Enjoying Happiness After Seeking It

That maxim also which your friend used is of very great and divine concernment: **I will first spend a great deal of time in seeking happiness, and then a great deal more in enjoying it.** For if happiness be worthy to be sought, it is worthy to be enjoyed.

As no folly in the world is more vile than that pretended by alchemists—of having the philosopher's stone and being contented without using it—so is no deceit more odious than that of spending many days in studying, and none in enjoying, happiness. That base pretence is an argument of falsehood and mere forgery in them—that after so much toil in getting it, they refuse to use it. Their pretence is that they are so abundantly satisfied in having it, that they care not for the use of it. So the neglect of any man that finds it shows that indeed he has lost happiness. That which he has found is counterfeitware if he neglect to use it. Tis only because he cannot—true happiness being too precious to be despised.

Shall I forsake all riches and pleasures for happiness, and pursue it many days and months and years, and then neglect and bury it when I have it? I will now spend days and nights in possessing it, as I did before in seeking it. It is better being happy than asleep.

Don't Boast About Your Happiness

Happiness was not made to be boasted, but enjoyed. Therefore though others count me miserable, I will not believe them if I know and feel myself to be happy—nor fear them. I was not born to approve myself to them, but God. A man may enjoy great delights, without telling them.

> *Tacitus si pasci potuisset Corvus, haberet*
> *Plus dapis & rixae minus invidiaeque.*
> Could but the crow in lonely silence eat,
> She then would have less envy and more meat.

Heaven is a place where our happiness shall be seen of all. We shall there enjoy the happiness of being seen in happiness without the danger of ostentation. But here, men are blind and corrupted and cannot see; if they could, we are corrupted, and in danger of abusing it. I knew a man that was mightily derided in his pursuit of happiness till he was understood, and then admired; but he lost all by his miscarriage.

Why Men Despise Open Happiness

One great discouragement to felicity—or rather to great souls in the pursuit of felicity—is the solitariness of the way that leads to her temple. A man that studies happiness must sit alone like a sparrow upon the house-top, and like a pelican in the wilderness.[162] And the reason is because all men praise happiness and despise it. Very few shall a man find in the way of wisdom; and few indeed that, having given up their names to wisdom and felicity, will persevere in seeking it. Either he must go on alone or go back for company. People are tickled with the name of it, and some are persuaded to enterprise a little, but quickly draw back when they see the trouble; yea, cool of themselves without any trouble.

Those mysteries which, while men are ignorant of, they would give all the gold in the world for, I have seen when known to be despised. Not as if the nature of happiness were such that it did need a veil, but the nature of man is such that it is odious and ungrateful. For those things which are most glorious when most naked, are by men when most nakedly revealed, most despised. So that God is fain for his very name's sake, lest his beauties should be scorned, to conceal her beauties; and for the sake of men, which naturally are more prone to pry into secret and forbidden things than into open and common.

Felicity is amiable under a veil, but most amiable when most naked. It has its times and seasons for both. There is some pleasure in breaking the shell, and many delights in our addresses previous to the sweets in the possession of her. It is some part of felicity that we must seek her.

Being Happy Alone & In Company

In order to this, he furnished himself with this maxim: **It is a good thing to be happy alone. It is better to be happy in company, but good to be happy alone.**

Men owe me the advantage of their society, but if they deny me that just debt, I will not be unjust to myself and side with them in bereaving me. I will not be discouraged, lest I be miserable for company. More company increases happiness but does not lighten or diminish misery.

Inward Apprehensions

In order to interior or contemplative happiness, it is a good principle that: **apprehensions within are better than their objects.**

Mornay's simile of the saw is admirable. If a man would cut with a saw, he must not apprehend it to be a knife, but a thing with teeth; otherwise he cannot use it. He that mistakes his knife to be an auger, or his hand to be his meat, confounds himself by misapplications. These mistakes are ocular. But far more absurd ones are unseen.

To mistake the world, or the nature of one's soul, is a more dangerous error. He that thinks the heavens and the earth not his can hardly use them; and he that thinks the sons of men impertinent to his joy and happiness can scarcely love them. But he that knows them to be instruments and what they are, will delight in them; and is able to use them.

Whatever we misapprehend, we cannot use; nor well enjoy what we cannot use. Nor can anything be our happiness th\at we cannot enjoy. Nothing therefore can be our happiness but that alone which we rightly apprehend. To apprehend God our enemy destroys our happiness. Inward apprehensions are the very light of blessedness, and the cement of souls and their objects.

Things Prized Are Enjoyed

Of what vast importance right principles are we may see by this: **Things prized are enjoyed.**

All things are ours; all things serve us and minister to us, could we find the way. Nay they are ours and serve us so perfectly, that they are best enjoyed in their proper places: even from the sun to a sand, from a cherubim to a worm. I will not except gold and silver and crowns and precious stones, nor any delights or secret treasures in closets and palaces. For if otherwise, God would not be perfect in bounty. But suppose the world were all yours—if this principle be rooted in you, to prize nothing that is yours, it blots out all at one dash and bereaves you of a whole world in a moment.

Prizing Daily & Common Joys

If God be yours, and all the joys and inhabitants in heaven—if you be resolved to prize nothing great and excellent, nothing sublime and eternal, you lay waste your possessions and make vain your enjoyment of all permanent and glorious things. So that you must be sure to inure yourself frequently to these principles and to impress them deeply:

I will prize all I have, and nothing shall with me be less esteemed because it is excellent.

A daily joy shall be more my joy because it is continual.

A common joy is more my delight because it is common. For all mankind are my friends, and everything is enriched in serving them.

A little grit in the eye destroys the sight of the very heavens, and a little malice or envy a world of joys.

One wry principle in the mind is of infinite consequence.

I will ever prize what I have, and so much the more because I have it. To prize a thing when it is gone breeds torment and repining; to prize it while we have it joy and thanksgiving.

CHAPTER 24

PRINCIPLES OF CHARITY

Principles for Communication & Conversation

All these relate to enjoyment, but those principles that relate to com-munication are more excellent. These are principles of retirement and soli-tude; but the principles that aid us in conversation are far better and help us, though not so immediately to enjoyment, in a far more blessed and divine manner. For it is more blessed to give than to receive;[163] and we are more happy in communication than enjoyment, but only that communica-tion is enjoyment—as indeed, what we give we best receive. For the joy of communicating and the joy of receiving makes perfect happiness. And therefore are the sons of men our greatest treasures, because they can give and receive treasures, perhaps infinite, as well as affections. But this I am sure: they are our treasures, and therefore is conversation so delightful because they are the greatest.

Loving Others as Ourselves

The world is best enjoyed and most immediately while we converse blessedly and wisely with men. I am sure it were desirable that they could give and receive infinite treasures; and perhaps they can. For whomsoever I love as myself, to him I give myself and all my happiness—which I think is infinite—and I receive him and all his happiness. Yea, in him I receive God, for God delights me for being his blessedness: so that a man obliges me infinitely that makes himself happy, and by making himself happy, gives me himself and all his happiness. Besides this, he loves me infinitely as God does; and he dare do no less for God's sake. Nay he loves God for lov-ing me, and delights in him for being good to me. So that I am magnified in his affections, represented in his understanding, tenderly beloved, caressed, and honored—and this makes society delightful.

But here upon earth it is subject to changes. And therefore this principle is always to be firm, as the foundation of bliss: **God only is my sovereign happiness and friend in the world.**

Conversation is full of dangers, and friendships are mortal among the sons of men. But communion with God is infinitely secure, and he my happiness.

Thinking Oneself a Happy Physician Amidst a Generation of Vipers

He from whom I received these things, always thought, that to be happy in the midst of a generation of vipers was become his duty—for men and he are fallen into sin. Were all men wise and innocent, it were easy to be happy—for no man would injure and molest another. But he that would be happy now, must be happy among ungrateful and furious persons. That knowledge which would make a man happy among just and holy persons is not useful now. And those principles are only profitable that will make a man happy not only in peace, but blood.

On every side we are environed with enemies, surrounded with reproaches, encompassed with wrongs, besieged with offences, receiving evil for good, being disturbed by fools, and invaded with malice. This is the true estate of this world, which lying in wickedness, as our Saviour witnesses, yields no better fruits than the bitter clusters of folly and perverseness—the grapes of Sodom, and the seeds of Gomorrah.[164]

Blind wretches that wound themselves offend me. I need therefore the oil of pity and the balm of love to remedy and heal them. Did they see the beauty of holiness[165] or the face of happiness, they would not do so. To think the world therefore a general Bedlam or place of madmen, and oneself a physician, is the most necessary point of present wisdom—an important imagination and the way to happiness.

Extracting Good Out of Evil

He thought within himself that this world was far better than Paradise, had men eyes to see its glory and their advantages. For the very miseries and sins and offences that are in it are the materials of his joy and triumph and glory. So that he is to learn a diviner art that will now be happy, and that is like a royal chemist—to reign among poisons, to turn scorpions into fishes, weeds into flowers, bruises into ornaments, poisons into cordials. And he that cannot learn this art—of extracting good out of evil—is to be accounted nothing. Heretofore, to enjoy beauties and be grateful for benefits was all the art that was required to felicity; but now a man must, like a God, bring light out of darkness and order out of confusion. Which we are taught to do by his wisdom, that rules in the midst of storms and tempests.

The Charity of Paradise

He generally held that whosoever would enjoy the happiness of Paradise must put on the charity of Paradise, and that nothing was his felicity but his duty. He called his house the house of Paradise—not only because it was the place wherein he enjoyed the whole world, but because it was everyone's house in the whole world. For observing the methods and studying the nature of charity in Paradise, he found that all men would be brothers and sisters throughout the whole world, and evermore love one another as their own selves, though they had never seen each other before. From whence it would proceed that every man approaching him would be as welcome as an angel, and the coming of a stranger as delightful as the sun—all things in his house being as much the foreigner's as they were his own, especially if he could infuse any knowledge or grace unto him.

Living Upon God's Provision

To establish himself thoroughly in this principle, he made much of another. For he saw that in Paradise a great help to this kind of life was the cheapness of commodities, and the natural fertility of the then innocent and blessed ground. By which means it came to pass that every man had enough for himself, and all. But that now, the earth being cursed and barren, there was danger of want, a necessity of toil and labor and care and maintenance of servants. Therefore he concluded that the charity of men ought to supply the earth's sterility—who could never want, were they all of a mind and liberal to each other.

But since this also fails, and men's hearts are cursed and barren as the ground, what is wanting in them God will supply. And that to live upon God's provisions is the most glorious dependence in the whole world. And so he made the love of God his true foundation, and built not his hopes on the charity of men, but fled unto God as his best refuge[166]—which he thought it very safe and blessed to do, because the trial of his faith was more glorious, and the love of God supplied the defect of charity in men, and he that had commanded had faithfully promised and was able to perform.

Universal Charity Blowing Away Sins & Vices

He thought the stars as fair now as they were in Eden, the sun as bright, the sea as pure; and nothing pestered the world with miseries and destroyed its order, peace, and beauty but sins and vices. Rapine, covetousness, envy, oppression, luxury, ambition, pride etc., filled the world with briars and thorns, desolations, wars, complaints, and contentions, and that this made enormities to be vices. But universal charity, did it breathe among men, would blow all these away, as the wind does chaff and stubble; and that then the heavens would be as serene and fair, and the lands as rich as ever they were. And that, as all things were improved by the work of redemption, trades and occupations that were left behind would be pleasant ornaments and innocent recreations; for whence have we all our cities, palaces, and temples, whence all our thrones and magnificent splendors, but from trades and occupations?

The Bright Star of Order & Charity

But order and charity in the midst of these, is like a bright star in an obscure night, like a summer's day in the depth of winter, like a sun shining among the clouds, like a giant among his enemies that receives strength from their numbers, like a king sitting in the midst of an army. By how much the more scarce it is, by so much the more glorious. By how much the more assaulted, by so much the more invincible. By how much the more lonely, by so much the more pitied of God and heaven. And surely he, who being perfect love, designed the felicity of the world with so much care in the beginning, will now be more tender of the soul that is like him in its deordination.

The Worse a Person, The More to be Loved

He thought that men were more to be beloved now than before. And, which is a strange paradox, the worse they are the more they were to be beloved. The worse they are, the more they were to be pitied and tendered and desired, because they had more need and were more miserable, though the better they are, they are more to be delighted in.

But his true meaning in that saying was this: **Comparing them with what they were before they were fallen, they are more to be beloved.** They are now worse, yet more to be beloved. For Jesus Christ has been crucified for them. God loved them more, and he gave his Son to die for them and for me also—which are strong obligations leading us to greater charity. So that men's unworthiness and our virtue are alike increased.

Every Man a Representative of Mankind

He conceived it his duty, and much delighted in the obligation, that he was to treat every man in the whole world as representative of mankind and that he was to meet in him, and to pay unto him, all the love of God, angels, and men.

Treating Every Person Like Christ

He thought that he was to treat every man in the person of Christ. That is both as if himself were Christ in the greatness of his love, and also as if the man were Christ, he was to use him having respect to all others. For the love of Christ is to dwell within him, and every man is the object of it. God and he are to become one spirit, that is one in will, and one in desire. Christ must live within him. He must be filled with the Holy Ghost, which is the God of love, he must be of the same mind with Christ Jesus, and led by his Spirit. For on the other side he was well acquainted with this mystery—that every man being the object of our Saviour's love, was to be treated as our Saviour, who has said, "Inasmuch as you have done it to the least of these my brothers, you have done it unto me."[167] And thus he is to live upon earth among sinners.

Doing the Most Good to Others (Especially the Poor)

He had another saying: **He lives most like an angel that lives least upon himself and does most good to others.**

For the angels neither eat nor drink, and yet do good to the whole world. Now a man is an incarnate angel. And he that lives in the midst of riches as a poor man himself—enjoying God and Paradise, or Christendom which is better, conversing with the poor and seeing the value of their souls through their bodies, and prizing all things clearly with a due esteem—is arrived here to the estate of immortality. He cares little for the delicacies either of food or raiment himself, and delights in others. God, angels, and men are his treasures. He sees through all the mists and veils of invention, and possesses here beneath the true riches. And he that does this always is a rare phoenix. But he confessed that he had often cause to bewail his infirmities.

Falling Short of Our Principles

I speak not his practices but his principles. I should too much praise your friend did I speak his practices, but it is no shame for any man to declare his principles, though they are the most glorious in the world. Rather they are to be shamed that have no glorious principles, or that are ashamed of them. This he desired me to tell you because of modesty.

But with all that, indeed his practices are so short of these glorious principles, that to relate them would be to his shame; and that therefore you would never look upon him but as clothed in the righteousness[168] of Jesus Christ. Nevertheless I have heard him often say that he never allowed himself in swerving from any of these, and that he repented deeply every miscarriage, and moreover firmly resolved as much as was possible never to err or wander from them again.

Doing the Excellent Things We Know

I heard him often say that holiness and happiness were the same, and he quoted a mighty place of scripture, "All her ways are pleasantness and her paths are peace."[169] But he delighted in giving the reason of scripture and therefore said that holiness and wisdom in effect were one, for no man could be wise that knew excellent things without doing them. Now to do them is holiness and to do them wisdom. No man therefore can be further miserable than he severs from the ways of holiness and wisdom.

Being a Blessing to Mankind

If he might have had but one request of God Almighty, it should have been above all other that he might be a blessing to mankind. That was his daily prayer above all his petitions. He wisely knew that it included all petitions—for he that is a blessing to mankind must be blessed, that he may be so, and must inherit all their affections and in that their treasures. He could not help it.

But he so desired to love them and to be a joy unto them, that he protested often that he could never enjoy himself but as he was enjoyed of others, and that above all delight in all worlds, he desired to be a joy and blessing to others. Though for this he was not to be commended, for he did but right to God and nature, who had implanted in all that inclination.

Giving Away Riches

The desire of riches was removed from himself pretty early. He often protested, if he had a palace of gold and a paradise of delights, besides that he enjoyed, he could not understand a farthing worth of benefit that he should receive thereby unless in giving it away. But for others he sometimes could desire riches till at last perceiving the root of covetousness in him, and that it would grow as long as it was shrouded under that mould. He rooted it quite up with this principle: **Sometimes it may so happen that to contemn the world in the whole lump was as acceptable to God as first to get it with solicitude and care, and then to retail it out in particular charities.**

His Friend's Feelings About Riches

After this, he could say with Luther that covetousness could never fasten the least hold upon him. And concerning his friends, even to the very desire of seeing them rich, he could say, as Phocion the poor Athenian did of his children: "Either they will be like me or not. If they are like me, they will not need riches; if they are not, they will be but needless and hurtful superfluities."

The Foolishness of a Miser

He desired no other riches for his friends but those which cannot be abused—to wit, the true treasures: God and heaven and earth and angels and men, etc. with the riches of wisdom and grace to enjoy them.

And it was his principle: **That all the treasures in the whole world would not make a miser happy.** A miser is not only a covetous man but a fool. Any needy man, that wants the world, is miserable. He wants God and all things.

The Riches of Nakedness

He thought also that no poverty could befall him that enjoyed Paradise. For when all the things are gone which man can give, a man is still as rich as Adam was in Eden, who was naked there. A naked man is the richest creature in all worlds, and can never be happy till he sees the riches of his very nakedness. He is very poor in knowledge that thinks Adam poor in Eden. See here how one principle helps another. All our disadvantages contracted by the fall are made up and recompensed by the love of God.

PRINCIPLES OF OUR FREE CHOICE & EFFORT

Heaven Established by Principles, Not Place

'Tis not change of place, but glorious principles well practiced, that establish heaven in the life and soul. An angel will be happy anywhere and a devil miserable—because the principles of the one are always good, of the other, bad. From the center to the utmost bounds of the everlasting hills, all is heaven before God and full of treasure; and he that walks like God in the midst of them, blessed.

Actions to Make All Things Beautiful in Their Places

Love God, angels, and men; triumph in God's works; delight in God's laws; take pleasure in God's ways in all ages; correct sins; bring good out of evil; subdue your lusts; order your senses; conquer the customs and opinions of men and render good for evil—you are in heaven everywhere. Above the stars earthly things will be celestial joys, and here beneath will things delight you that are above the heavens—all things being infinitely beautiful in their places and wholly yours in all their places. Your riches will be as infinite in value and excellency as they are in beauty and glory, and, that is, as they are in extent.

The Objects of Our Joy and the Objects of Our Care

Thus he was possessor of the whole world and held it his treasure, not only as the gift of God, but as the theatre of virtues. Esteeming it principally his because it upheld and ministered to many objects of his love and goodness. Towards whom, before whom, among whom he might do the work of fidelity and wisdom, exercise his courage and prudence, show his temperance, and bring forth the fruits of faith and repentance. For all those are the objects of our joy that are the objects of our care. They are our true treasures about whom we are wisely employed.

God Left Man's Heart to Himself

He had one maxim of notable concernment, and that was that: **God, having reserved all other things in his own disposal, had left his heart to him.**

Those things that were in God's care, he would commit to God; those things that were committed to his, he would take care about. He said therefore that he had but one thing to do, and that was to order and keep his heart, which alone being well-guided would order all other things blessedly and successfully. The things about him were innumerable and out of his power, but they were in God's power. And if he pleased God in that which was committed to him, God would be sure to please him in things without committed to God. For he was faithful that had promised.[170] In all that belonged to him, God was perfect—all the danger being lest we should be imperfect in ours and unfaithful in those things that pertain to us.

Keeping Your Heart

Having these principles, nothing was more easy than to enjoy the world. Which being enjoyed, he had nothing more to do than to spend his life in praises and thanksgivings. All his care being to be sensible of God's mercies and to behave himself as the friend of God in the universe.[171]

If anything were amiss, he still would have recourse to his own heart—and he found nothing but that out of frame. By restoring which, all things were rectified and made delightful. As much as that had swerved from the rule of justice, equity, and right, so far was he miserable, and no more—so that by experience he found the words of the wise man true and worthy of all acceptance: "In all your keeping, keep your heart, for out of it are the issues of life and death."[172]

God Made Man a Free Agent

One thing he saw, which is not commonly discerned, and that is that **God made man a free agent for his own advantage, and left him in the hand of his own counsel that he might be the more glorious.**

It is hard to conceive how much this tended to his satisfaction. For all the things in heaven and earth being so beautiful, and made, as it were, on purpose for his own enjoyment, he infinitely admired God's wisdom, in that it salved his and all men's exigencies, in which it fully answered his desires. For his desire was that all men should be happy as well as he. And he admired his goodness, which had enjoined no other duty than what pertained to the more convenient fruition of the world which he had given, and at the marvelous excellency of his love in committing that duty to the sons of men to be performed freely.

For thereby he adventured such a power into the hands of his creatures, which angels and cherubim wonder at, and which, when it is understood, all eternity will admire the bounty of giving. For he thereby committed to their hands a power to do that which he infinitely hated—which nothing certainly could move him to entrust them with, but some infinite benefit which might be attained thereby. What that was, if you desire to know: it was the excellency, dignity, and exaltation of his creature.

Our Power to Infinitely Please God or Infinitely Displease Him

O adorable and eternal God! Have you made me a free agent! And enabled me if I please to offend you infinitely! What other end could you intend by this, but that I might please you infinitely! That having the power of pleasing or displeasing, I might be the friend of God! Of all exaltations in all worlds this is the greatest. To make a world for me was much; to prepare eternal joys for me was more. But to give me a power to displease you or to set a sin before your face which you infinitely hate, to profane eternity or to defile your works, is more stupendous than all these.

What other could you intend by it but that I might infinitely please you? And having the power of pleasing or displeasing, might please you and myself infinitely in being pleasing! Hereby you have prepared a new fountain and torrent of joy greater than all that went before, seated us in the throne of God, made us your companions, endued us with a power most dreadful to ourselves, that we might live in sublime and incomprehensible blessedness forevermore. For the satisfaction of our goodness is the most sovereign delight of which we are capable. And that, by our own actions we should be well pleasing to you, is the greatest felicity nature can contain.

O you who are infinitely delightful to the sons of men, make me and the sons of men infinitely delightful to you. Replenish our actions with amiableness and beauty, that they may be answerable to yours, and like yours in sweetness and value. That as you in all your works are pleasing to us, we in all our works may be so to you—our own actions as they are pleasing to you being an offspring of pleasures sweeter than all.

Whatever Satisfies Goodness

This he thought a principle at the bottom of nature, that: **Whatsoever satisfied the goodness of nature, was the greatest treasure.**

Certainly men therefore err because they know not this principle. For all inclinations and desires in the soul flow from and tend to the satisfaction of goodness. 'Tis strange that an excess of goodness should be the fountain of all evil. An ambition to please, a desire to gratify, a great desire to delight others being the greatest snare in the world. Hence is it that all hypocrisies and honors arise—I mean esteem of honors. Hence all imitations of human customs; hence all compliances and submissions to the vanities and errors of this world.

For men being mistaken in the nature of felicity, and we by a strong inclination prone to please them, follow a multitude to do evil. We naturally desire to approve ourselves to them, and above all things covet to be excellent, to be greatly beloved, to be esteemed and magnified—and therefore endeavor what they endeavor, prize what they prize, magnify what they desire, desire what they magnify—ever doing that which will render us accepted to them, and coveting that which they admire and praise, that so we might be delightful. And the more there are that delight in us, the more great and happy we account ourselves.

The Happiness of Giving

This principle of nature, when you remove the rust it has contracted by corruption, is pure gold, and the most orient jewel that shines in man. Few consider it either in itself or in the design of the implanter. No man doubts but it is blessed to receive: to be made a glorious creature and to have worlds given to one is excellent. But to be a glorious creature and to give, is a blessedness unknown. It is a kind of paradox in our Saviour, and not (as we read of) revealed upon earth, but to St. Paul from heaven, "It is more blessed to give than to receive."[173] It is a blessedness too high to be understood. To give is the happiness of God; to receive, of man.

But O the mystery of his lovingkindness, even that also has he imparted to us. Will you that I ascend higher? In giving us himself, in giving us the world, in giving us our souls and bodies, he has done much; but all this had been nothing unless he had given us a power to have given him ourselves, in which is contained the greatest pleasure and honor. We love ourselves earnestly, and therefore rejoice to have palaces and kingdoms. But when we have these, yea heaven and earth—unless we can be delightful and joyous to others, they will be of no value.

One soul to whom we may be pleasing is of greater worth than all dead things. Some unsearchable good lies in this, without which the other is but a vile and desolate estate; so that to have all worlds, with a certain sense that they are infinitely beautiful and rich and glorious, is miserable vanity—and leaves us forlorn—if all things are dead, or if ourselves are not Divine and illustrious creatures.

Man's Liberty

O the superlative bounty of God! Where all power seems to cease, he proceeds in goodness, and is wholly infinite, unsearchable, and endless. He seems to have made as many things depend upon man's liberty, as his own. When all that could be wrought by the use of his own liberty were attained, by man's liberty he attained more.

This is incredible, but experience will make it plain. By his own liberty he could but create worlds and give himself to creatures, make images and endow them with faculties, or seat them in glory. But to see them obedient or to enjoy the pleasure of their amity and praises, to make them fountains of actions like his own (without which indeed they could not be glorious) or to enjoy the beauty of their free imitation—this could by no means be without the liberty of his creatures intervening. Nor indeed could the world be glorious, or they blessed, without this attainment. For can the world be glorious unless it be useful? And to what use could the world serve him, if it served not those that in this were supremely glorious—that they could obey and admire and love and praise and imitate their Creator? Would it not be wholly useless without such creatures? In creating liberty therefore and giving it to his creatures, he glorified all things: himself, his work, and the subjects of his kingdom.

We Are Blessed When We Are a Blessing

You may feel in yourself how conducive this is to your highest happiness. For that you should be exalted to the fruition of worlds, and, in the midst of innumerable most glorious creatures, be vile and ungrateful, injurious and dishonorable, hateful and evil, is the greatest misery and dissatisfaction imaginable. But to be the joy and delight of innumerable thousands, to be admired as the similitude of God, to be amiable and honorable, to be an illustrious and beautiful creature, to be a blessing—O the good we perceive in this! O the suavity! O the contentment! O the infinite and unspeakable pleasure! Then indeed we reign and triumph when we are delighted in. Then are we blessed when we are a blessing.

When all the world is at peace with us and takes pleasure in us, when our actions are delightful and our persons lovely, when our spirits amiable and our affections inestimable—then are we exalted to the throne of glory. For things when they are useful are most glorious, and it is impossible for you or me to be useful but as we are delightful to God and his attendants. And that the head of the world, or the end for which all worlds were made, should be useless, as it is improportioned to the glory of the means and methods of his exaltation, so is it the reproach of his nature and the utter undoing of all his glory. It is improportionable to the beauty of his ways, who made the world, and to the expectation of his creatures.

Receiving & Appreciating What God Gives

By this you may see that the works or actions flowing from your own liberty are of greater concernment to you than all that could possibly happen besides. And that it is more to your happiness what you are, than what you enjoy. Should God give himself and all worlds to you, and you refuse them, it would be to no purpose. Should he love you and magnify you, should he give his Son to die for you and command all angels and men to love you, should he exalt you in his throne and give you dominion over all his works—and you neglect them, it would be to no purpose. Should he make you in his image, and employ all his wisdom and power to fill eternity with treasures, and you despise them, it would be in vain.

In all these things you have to do; and therefore your actions are great and magnificent, being of infinite importance in all eyes. While all creatures stand in expectation, what will be the result of your liberty? Your exterior works are little in comparison of these. And God infinitely desires you should demean yourself wisely in these affairs, that is, rightly. Esteeming and receiving what he gives, with veneration and joy and infinite thanksgiving. Many other works there are, but this is the great work of all works to be performed.

Consider whether more depends upon God's love to you, or your love to him. From his love, all the things in heaven and earth flow unto you; but if you love neither him nor them, you bereave yourself of all, and make them infinitely evil and hurtful to you. So that upon your love naturally depends your own excellency and the enjoyment of his. It is by your love that you enjoy all his delights, and are delightful to him.

CHAPTER 26

PRINCIPLES OF SELF-LOVE

Self-Love & Love of God

It is very observable by what small principles infusing them in the beginning, God attains infinite ends. By infusing the principle of self-love, he has made a creature capable of enjoying all worlds: to whom, did he not love himself, nothing could be given. By infusing grateful principles and inclinations to thanksgiving, he has made the creature capable of more than all worlds, yea, of more than enjoying the Deity in a simple way—though we should suppose it to be infinite.

For to enjoy God as the fountain of infinite treasures, and as the giver of all, is infinite pleasure. But he, by his wisdom infusing grateful principles, has made us upon the very account of self-love to love him more than ourselves. And us, who without self-love could not be pleased at all—even as we love ourselves, he has so infinitely pleased that we are able to rejoice in him and to love him more than ourselves. And by loving him more than ourselves, in very gratitude and honor, to take more pleasure in his felicity than in our own, by which way we best enjoy him.

To see his wisdom, goodness, and power employed in creating all worlds for our enjoyment, and infinitely magnified in beautifying them for us, and governing them for us, satisfies our self-love; but with all, it so obliges us that in love to him, which it creates in us, it makes us more to delight in those attributes as they are his, than as they are our own. And the truth is, without this we could not fully delight in them, for the most excellent and glorious effect of all had been unachieved. But now there is an infinite union between him and us, he being infinitely delightful to us, and we to him. For he infinitely delights to see creatures act upon such illustrious and eternal principles, in a manner so divine, heroic, and most truly blessed; and we delight in seeing him giving us the power.

Receiving All Things in Heaven & Earth

That I am to receive all the things in heaven and earth is a principle not to be slighted. That in receiving, I am to behave myself in a divine and illustrious manner, is equally glorious. That God and all eternity are mine is surely considerable; that I am his, is more.

How ought I to adorn myself, who am made for his enjoyment? If man's heart be a rock of stone, these things ought to be engraven in it with a pen of a diamond, and every letter to be filled up with gold, that it may eternally shine in him and before him! Wherever we are living, whatever we are doing, these things ought always to be felt within him. Above all trades, above all occupations, this is most sublime. This is the greatest of all affairs. Whatever else we do, it is only in order to this end that we may live conveniently to enjoy the world and God within it—which is the sovereign employment including and crowning all: the celestial life of a glorious creature, without which all other estates are servile and impertinent.

Man Was Made Good

Man being to live in the image of God, and thus of necessity to become productive of glorious actions, was made good, that he might rejoice in the fruits which himself did yield. That goodness which by error and corruption becomes a snare, being in the clear and pure estate of innocence, the fountain and the channel of all his joys.

Being Faithful With Our Freedom

Thus you see how God has perfectly pleased me. It ought also to be my care perfectly to please him. He has given me freedom, and adventured the power of sinning into my hands. It ought to be a principle engraven in me: **to use it nobly, to be illustrious and faithful, to please him in the use of it, to consult his honor, and having all the creatures in all worlds by his gift** ministering unto me, to behave myself as a faithful friend to so great a Majesty, so bountiful a Lord, so divine a benefactor.

Nothing is so easy as to yield one's assent to glorious principles, nothing so clear in upright nature, nothing so obscure to find in perverted, nothing so difficult to practice at all. In the rubbish of depraved nature they are lost, though when they are found by anyone, and shown, like jewels they shine by their native splendor.

Restored to Adam's Original Principles

If you ask, "What is become of us since the fall?", because all these things now lately named seem to pertain to the estate of innocence; truly now we have super-added treasures, Jesus Christ, and are restored to the exercise of the same principles upon higher obligations. I will not say with more advantage, though perhaps obligations themselves are to us advantage. For what enabled Adam to love God? Was it not that God loved him? What constrained him to be averse from God? Was it not that God was averse from him? When he was fallen, he thought God would hate him and be his enemy eternally. And this was the miserable bondage that enslaved him. But when he was restored, O the infinite and eternal change! His very love to himself made him to praise his eternal love: I mean his redeemer's. Do we not all love ourselves? Self-love makes us to love those that love us, and to hate all those that hate us. So that obligations themselves are to us advantage. How we come to lose those advantages, I will not stand here to relate. In a clear light it is certain no man can perish. For God is more delightful than he was in Eden. Then he was as delightful as was possible, but he had not that occasion, as by sin was afforded, to superadd many more delights than before. Being more delightful and more amiable, he is more desirable, and may now be more easily, yea strongly, beloved. For the amiableness of the object enables us to love it.

Principles of Our Blessings

It was your friend's delight to meditate on the principles of upright nature, and to see how things stood in Paradise before they were muddied and blended and confounded. For now they are lost and buried in ruins, nothing appearing but fragments, that are worthless shreds and parcels of them. To see the entire piece ravishes the angels. It was his desire to recover them and to exhibit them again to the eyes of men.

Above all things, he desired to see those principles which a stranger in this world would covet to behold upon his first appearance. And that is, what principles those were by which the inhabitants of this world are to live blessedly and to enjoy the same. He found them very easy and infinitely noble—very noble and productive of unspeakable good, were they well pursued. We have named them, and they are such as these:

A man should know the blessings he enjoys.
A man should prize the blessings which he knows.
A man should be thankful for the benefits which he prizes.
A man should rejoice in that for which he is thankful.

These are easy things, and so are those also which are drowned in a deluge of errors and customs: **That blessings, the more they are, are the sweeter; the more they serve, if lovers and friends, the more delightful.**

Yet these are the hard lessons, in a perverse and retrograde world, to be practiced, and almost the only lessons necessary to its enjoyment.

Self-Love is the Basis of All Love

He was a strict and severe applier of all things to himself, and would first have his self-love satisfied, and then his love of all others. It is true that self-love is dishonorable, but then it is when it is alone. And self-endedness is mercenary, but then it is when it ends in oneself. It is more glorious to love others, and more desirable, but by natural means to be attained.

That pool must first be filled that shall be made to overflow. He was ten years studying before he could satisfy his self-love. And now finds nothing more easy than to love others better than oneself, and that to love mankind so is the comprehensive method to all felicity. For it makes a man delightful to God and men, to himself and spectators—and God and men delightful to him, and all creatures infinitely in them.

But as not to love oneself at all is brutish, or rather absurd and stonish (for the beasts do love themselves), so has God by rational methods enabled us to love others better than ourselves, and thereby made us the most glorious creatures. Had we not loved ourselves at all, we could never have been obliged to love anything. So that self-love is the basis of all love. But when we do love ourselves, and self-love is satisfied infinitely in all its desires and possible demands, then it is easily led to regard the benefactor more than itself, and for his sake overflows abundantly to all others. So that God, by satisfying my self-love, has enabled and engaged me to love others.

CHAPTER 27
PRINCIPLES FOR LOVING OTHERS

Loving Another More Than Myself

No man loves, but he loves another more than himself. In mean instances this is apparent. If you come into an orchard with a person you love, and there be but one ripe cherry, you prefer it to the other. If two lovers delight in the same piece of meat, either takes pleasure in the other, and more esteems the beloved's satisfaction.

What ails men that they do not see it? In greater cases this is evident. A mother runs upon a sword to save her beloved. A father leaps into the fire to fetch out his beloved. Love brought Christ from heaven to die for his beloved. It is in the nature of love to despise itself, and to think only of its beloved's welfare. Look to it—it is not right love that is otherwise. Moses[174] and St. Paul[175] were no fools. God make me one of their number. I am sure nothing is more acceptable to him than to love others so as to be willing to imperil even one's own soul for their benefit and welfare.

Inheriting Others' Joys Through Love

Nevertheless it is infinitely rewarded, though it seems difficult. For by this love do we become heirs of all men's joys, and co-heirs with Christ. For what is the reason of your own joys, when you are blessed with benefits? Is it not self-love? Did you love others as you love yourself, you would be as much affected with their joys. Did you love them more, more. For according to the measure of your love to others will you be happy in them. For, according thereto, you will be delightful to them, and delighted in your felicity. The more you love men, the more delightful you will be to God, and the more delight you will take in God, and the more you will enjoy him. So that the more like you are to him in goodness, the more abundantly you will enjoy his goodness. By loving others you live in others to receive it.

Love Receives What it Gives Away

Shall I not love him infinitely for whom God made the world and gave his Son? Shall I not love him infinitely who loves me infinitely? Examine yourself well, and you will find it a difficult matter to love God so as to die for him, and not to love your brother so as to die for him in like manner. Shall I not love him infinitely whom God loves infinitely, and commends to my love, as the representative of himself, with such a saying, "What you do to him is done unto me?"[176] And if I love him so, can I forbear to help him?

Verily had I but one crown in the world, being in an open field where both he and I were ready to perish, and it were necessary that one of us must have it all or be destroyed—though I knew not where to have relief, he should have it, and I would die with comfort. I will not say, "How small a comfort so small a succor is, did I keep it;" but, "How great a joy, to be the occasion of another's life!" Love knows not how to be timid, because it receives what it gives away, and is unavoidably the end of its own afflictions and another's happiness. Let him that pleases, keep his money—I am more rich in this noble charity to all the world, and more enjoy myself in it, than he can be in both the Indies.

Learning From Jesus How to Love

Is it unnatural to do what Jesus Christ has done? He that would not in the same cases do the same things can never be saved. For unless we are led by the Spirit of Christ, we are none of his.[177] Love in him that in the same cases would do the same things, will be an oracle always inspiring and teaching him what to do, how far to adventure upon all occasions. And certainly he whose love is like his Saviour's, will be far greater than any that is now alive, in goodness and love to God and men.

This is a sure rule: **Love studies not to be scanty in its measures, but how to abound and overflow with benefits.** He that pinches and studies to spare is a pitiful lover, unless it be for other's sakes. Love studies to be pleasing, magnificent, and noble, and would in all things be glorious and divine unto its object. Its whole being is to its object, and its whole felicity in its object, and it has no other thing to take care for. It does good to its own soul while it does good to another.

Love in the Midst of Disadvantages

Here upon earth, it is under many disadvantages and impediments that maim it in its exercise, but in heaven it is most glorious. And it is my happiness that I can see it on both sides the veil or screen. There it appears in all its advantages, for every soul being full and fully satisfied—at ease, in rest, and wanting nothing—easily overflows and shines upon all. It is its perfect interest so to do, and nothing hinders it, self-love therefore being swallowed up and made perfect in the love of others.

But here it is pinched and straitened by wants. Here it is awakened and put in mind of itself. Here it is divided and distracted between two. It has a body to provide for, necessities to relieve, and a person to supply. Therefore is it in this world the more glorious, if in the midst of these disadvantages it exert itself in its operations. In the other world it swims down the stream, and acts with its interest. Here therefore is the place of its trial where its operations and its interests are divided. And if our Lord Jesus Christ, as some think, knew the glory to which he should ascend by dying for others, and that all was safe which he undertook, because in humbling himself to the death of the cross he did not forsake but attain his glory: the like fate shall follow us, only let us expect it after death as he did. And remember that this and the other life are made of a piece, but this is the time of trial, that, of rewards.

The greatest disadvantages of love are its highest advantages. In the great hazards, it achieves to itself the greatest glory. It is seldom considered, but a love to others stronger than what we bear to ourselves, is the mother of all the heroic actions that have made histories pleasant, and beautified the world.

Allowing Room for Love

Since love will thrust in itself as the greatest of all principles, let us at last willingly allow it room. I was once a stranger to it; now I am familiar with it as a daily acquaintance. 'Tis the only heir and benefactor of the world. It seems it will break in everywhere, as that without which the world could not be enjoyed. Nay as that without which it would not be worthy to be enjoyed. For it was beautified by love, and commands the love of a donor to us. Love is a phoenix that will revive in its own ashes, inherit death, and smell sweetly in the grave.

Love Needs Expression

These two properties are in it—that it can attempt all and suffer all. And the more it suffers, the more it is delighted; and the more it attempts, the more it is enriched. For it seems that all love is so mysterious that there is something in it which needs expression and can never be understood by any manifestation (of itself, in itself), but only by mighty doings and sufferings. This moved God the Father to create the world, and God the Son to die for it. Nor is this all.

There are many other ways whereby it manifests itself as well as these, there being still something infinite in it behind: in its laws, in its tenderness, in its provisions, in its caresses, in its joys as well as in its hazards, in its honors as well as in its cares. Nor does it ever cease till it has poured out itself in all its communications. In all which it ever rights and satisfies itself; for above all things in all worlds it desires to be magnified, and takes pleasure in being glorified before its object. For which cause also it does all those things, which magnify its object and increase its happiness.

A Riddle About Love

Whether love principally intends its own glory or its object's happiness is a great question, and of the more importance, because the right ordering of our own affections depends much upon the solution of it. For on the one side, to be self-ended is mercenary and base and slavish; and to do all things for one's own glory is servile and vainglory. On the other, God does all things for himself, and seeks his glory as his last end, and is himself the end whom he seeks and attains in all his ways.

How shall we reconcile this riddle? Or untie this knot? For some men have taken occasion hereby, seeing this in love: to affirm that there is no true love in the world, but it is all self-love whatsoever a man does. Implying also that it was self-love in our Saviour that made him to undertake for us. Whereupon we might justly question whether it were more for his own ends or more for ours? As also, whether it were for his own end that God created the world or more for ours? For an extraordinary amount of our duty and felicity hangs upon this point, and whatsoever sword unties this Gordian knot will open a world of benefit and instruction to us.

True Glory

God does desire glory as his sovereign end—but true glory. From whence it follows that he does sovereignly and supremely desire both his own glory and man's happiness. Though that be miraculous, yet it is very plain. For true glory is to love another for his own sake, and to prefer his welfare and to seek his happiness. Which God does because it is true glory. So that he seeks the happiness of angels and men as his last end, and in that his glory—to wit, his true glory. False and vain glory is inconsistent with his nature, but true glory is the very essence of his being. Which is love unto his beloved, love unto himself, love unto his creatures.

How God Loves Himself And Others

How can God be love unto himself without the imputation of self-love? Did he love himself under any other notion than as he is the lover of his beloved, there might be some danger. But the reason why he loves himself being because he is love, nothing is more glorious than his self-love. For he loves himself because he is infinite and eternal love to others. Because he loves himself he cannot endure that his love should be displeased. And loving others vehemently and infinitely, all the love he bears to himself is tenderness towards them. All that wherein he pleases himself is delightful to them. He magnifies himself in magnifying them.

And in fine, his love unto himself is his love unto them, and his love unto them is love unto himself. They are individually one, which it is very amiable and beautiful to behold, because therein the simplicity of God does evidently appear. The more he loves them, the greater he is and the more glorious. The more he loves them, the more precious and dear they are to him. The more he loves them, the more joys and treasures he possesses. The more he loves them, the more he delights in their felicity. The more he loves them, the more he rejoices in all his works for serving them—and in all his kingdoms for delighting them. And being love to them the more he loves himself, and the more jealous he is lest himself should be displeased, the more he loves and tenders them and secures their welfare. And the more he desires his own cry, the more good he does for them, in the more divine and genuine manner. You must love after his similitude.

CHAPTER 28

PRINCIPLES RELATED TO LOVE & THE SOUL

Love's Principles

He from whom I derived these things delighted always that I should be acquainted with principles that would make me fit for all ages. And truly in love there are enough of them. For since nature never created anything in vain, and love of all other is the most glorious, there is not any relic or parcel of that that shall be unused. It is not like gold made to be buried and concealed in darkness, but like the sun to communicate itself wholly in its beams unto all. It is more excellent and more communicative. It is hid in a center and nowhere at all, if we respect its body.

But if you regard its soul, it is an interminable sphere, which as some say of the sun, is *infinities infinita*, in the extension of its beams—being equally vigorous in all places, equally near to all objects, equally acceptable to all persons, and equally abundant in all its overflowing: infinitely everywhere. This of naked and divested love in its true perfection. Its own age is too little to contain it; its greatness is spiritual, like the Deity's. It fills the world, and exceeds what it fills. It is present with all objects, and tastes all excellencies, and meets the infiniteness of God in everything. So that in length it is infinite as well as in breadth, being equally vigorous at the utmost bound to which it can extend as here, and as wholly there as here, and wholly everywhere. Thence also it can see into further spaces; things present and things to come; height and depth being open before it, and all things in heaven, eternity, and time, equally near.

The Visible Image of Love

Were not love the darling of God, this would be a rash and a bold sally. But since it is his image, and the love of God—I may almost say the God of God, because his beloved—all this happens unto love. And this love is your true self when you are in act what you are in power: the great Daemon of the world, the end of all things, the desire of angels and of all nations. A creature so glorious, that having seen it, it puts an end to all curiosity and swallows up all admiration. Holy, wise, and just towards all things, blessed in all things, the Bride of God, glorious before all, his offspring and first born, and so like him, that being described, one would think it he.

I should be afraid to say all this of it, but that I know him—how he delights to have it magnified, and how he has magnified it infinitely before because it is his bride and firstborn. I will speak only a little of its violence and vigor afar off. It can love an act of virtue in the utmost Indies and hate a vice in the highest heavens. It can see into hell and adore the justice of God among the damned. It can behold and admire his love from everlasting. It can be present with his infinite and eternal love. It can rejoice in the joys which it foresees: can love Adam in Eden, Moses in the wilderness, Aaron in the tabernacle, David before the Ark, St. Paul among the nations, and Jesus either in the manger or on the cross. All these it can love with violence. And when it is restored from all that is earthly and sensual to its true spiritual being, it can love these, or any of these, as violently as any person in the living age.

Our Love Can Be Omnipresent

Shall it not love violently what God loves, what Jesus Christ loves, what all saints and angels love? Moses glorified God in a wonderful manner: he prophesied of Christ, he plagued the Egyptians, he brought the Israelites out of the land of Egypt, he guided them in the wilderness, he gave us the law, he loved the people more than his own life, yea, than his own self and all the possible glory that might have accrued to him.

And what shall we think of Christ himself? Shall not all our love be where he is? Shall it not wholly follow and attend him? Yet shall it not forsake other objects, but love them all in him, and him in them, and them the more because of him, and him the more because of them; for by him it is redeemed to them. So that as God is omnipresent, our love shall be at once with all: that is we, having these strengths to animate and quicken our affection.

To Love All is Glorious

To love one person with a private love is poor and miserable; to love all is glorious. To love all persons in all ages, all angels, all worlds, is divine and heavenly. To love all cities and all kingdoms, all kings and all peasants, and every person in all worlds with a natural intimate familiar love, as if him alone, is blessed. This makes a man effectually blessed in all worlds, a delightful lord of all things, a glorious friend to all persons, a concerned person in all transactions, and ever present with all affairs. So that he must ever be filled with company, ever in the midst of all nations, ever joyful and ever blessed.

The greatness of this man's love no man can measure; it is stable like the sun, it endures forever as the moon, it is a faithful witness in heaven. It is stronger and greater than all private affections. It represents every person in the light of eternity, and loves him with the love of all worlds, with a love conformable to God's—guided to the same ends, and founded upon the same causes. Which however lofty and divine it is, is ready to humble itself into the dust to serve the person beloved. And by how much the more sublime and glorious it is, is so much the sweeter and truly delightful: majesty and pleasure concurring together.

Love Makes Us Sons of God

Now you may see what it is to be a Son of God more clearly. Love in its glory is the friend of the Most High. It was begotten of him, and is to sit in his throne, and to reign in communion with him. It is to please him and to be pleased by him, in all his works, ways, and operations. It is ordained to hold an eternal correspondence with him in the highest heavens. It is here in its infancy, there in its manhood and perfect stature. He wills and commands that it should be reverenced of all, and takes pleasure to see it admired in its excellencies.

If love thus displayed be so glorious a being, how much more glorious and great is he that is sovereign Lord of all Lords, and the heavenly king of all these? So many monarchs under one Supreme, mightily set forth the glory of his kingdom. If you ask by what certainty, or by what rules we discover this? As by the seed we conjecture what plant will arise, and know by the acorn what tree will grow forth, or by the eagle's egg what kind of bird—so do we by the powers of the soul upon earth, know what kind of being, person, and glory it will be in the heavens. Its blind and latent power shall be turned into act, its inclinations shall be completed, and its capacities filled, for by this means is it made perfect. A spiritual king is an eternal spirit.

Love in the abstract is a soul exerted. Neither do you esteem yourself to be any other than love alone. God is love, and you are never like him till you are so: love unto all objects in like manner.

Sitting in the Throne of God

To sit in the throne of God is the most supreme estate that can befall a creature. It is promised in the Revelations. But few understand what is promised there, and but few believe it.

Our Throne is the Omnipresence & Eternity of God

To sit in the throne of God is to inhabit eternity. To reign there is to be pleased with all things in heaven and earth from everlasting to everlasting, as if we had the sovereign disposal of them. For he is to dwell in us, and we in him, because he lives in our knowledge and we in his. His will is to be in our will; and our will is to be in his will, so that both being joined and becoming one, we are pleased in all his works as he is—and herein the image of God perfectly consists.

No artist makes a throne too wide for the person. God is the greatest and divinest artist. Thrones proper and fit for the persons, are always prepared by the wisest kings. For little bodies, bodily thrones; for spirits, invisible. God's throne is his omnipresence, and that is infinite, who dwells in himself, or in that light which is inaccessible. The omnipresence, therefore, and the eternity of God are our throne, wherein we are to reign forevermore. His infinite and eternal love are the borders of it, which everywhere we are to meet, and everywhere to see forevermore.

In this throne our Saviour sits—who is the Alpha and Omega, the first and the last,[178] the Amen, and the faithful witness[179] who said, "The Glory which you have given me, I have given them, that they may be one, as we are one."[180] In him the fullness of the Godhead dwells bodily.[181] If that be too great to be applied to men, remember what follows, "His Church is the fullness of him that fills all in all."[182] The fullness of the Godhead dwells in him for our sakes. And if yet it seems too great to be enjoyed, by the surpassing excellency of his eternal power, it is made more than ours. For in him we shall more enjoy it than if it were infinitely and wholly all in ourselves.

Objects Magnify Our Souls

If anything yet remains that is dreadful or terrible or doubtful, that seems to startle us, there is more behind that will more amaze us. For God is infinite in the expression of his love; as we shall all find to our eternal comfort. Objects are so far from diminishing, that they magnify the faculties of the soul beholding them. A sand in your conception conforms your soul, and reduces it to the size and similitude of a sand; a tree apprehended is a tree in your mind; the whole hemisphere and the heavens magnify your soul to the wideness of the heavens; all the spaces above the heavens enlarge it wider to their own dimensions.

And what is without limit makes your conception unlimited and end-less. The infinity of God is infinitely profitable as well as great, as glorious as incomprehensible, so far from straitening that it magnifies all things. And must be seen in you, or God will be absent. Nothing less than infinite is God, and as finite he cannot be enjoyed.

God Made Us Worthy of His Love

But what is there more that will more amaze us? Can anything be behind such glorious mysteries? Is God more sovereign in other excellen-cies? Has he shown himself glorious in anything besides? Verily there is no end of all his greatness—his understanding is infinite, and his ways innu-merable. "How precious," says the psalmist, "are your thoughts to me, O God; when I would count them, they are more than can be numbered."[183]

There is no man that reckons them up in order unto you. O my Lord, I will endeavor it, and I will glorify you forevermore. The most perfect laws are agreeable only to the most perfect creatures. Since therefore your laws are the most perfect of all that are possible, so are your creatures. And if infinite power be wholly expressed, O Lord, what creatures! what creatures shall we become! What divine, what illustrious beings—souls worthy of so great a love, blessed forever. Made worthy, though not found; for love either finds or makes an object worthy of itself.

For which cause Picus Mirandula admirably says, in his tract *De Dignitate Hominis*,

> "I have read in the monuments of Arabia, that Abdala,
> the Saracen, being asked,

Quid in hâc quasi mundanâ Scenâ admirandum maxime spectaretur?
'What in this world was most admirable?,' answered,
'Man'—That whom he saw nothing more to be admired."

Which sentence of his is seconded by that of Mercurius Trismegistus,
Magnum, O Asclepiades, Miraculum, Homo;
Man is a great and wonderful miracle.

Ruminating upon the reason of these sayings, those things did not satisfy me, which many have spoken concerning the excellency of human nature. As that man was:
Creaturarum Internuncius; Superis familiaris, Inferiorum Rex; sensuum perspicaciâ, Rationis Indagine, Intelligentiae Lumine, Naturae Interpres, Stabilis Aevi et fluxi Temporis Interstitium, et (qd. Persae dicunt) | Mundi Copula immo Hymenaeus.

A messenger between the creatures, Lord of inferior things, and familiar to those above; by the keenness of his sense, the piercing of his reasons, and the light of knowledge, the interpreter of nature, a seeming interval between time and eternity, and the inhabitant of both, the golden link or tie of the world, yea, the Hymenaeus marrying the Creator and his creatures together; made as David witnessed a little lower than the angels.[184]

All these things are great, but they are not the principal. That is, they are not those which rightly challenge the name and title of most admirable. And so he goes on, admiring and exceeding all that had been spoken before concerning the excellency of man. Why do we not rather admire the angels and the choirs above the heaven? At length I seemed to understand why man was the most happy and therefore the most worthy to be admired of all the creatures—and to know that estate, which in the order of things he enjoys, not only above the beasts but above the stars, and that might be envied even of the supra-celestial spirits, which he styles, *ultra-mundanis mentibus invidiosam.*

God's Preparation For Creating Man

The supreme architect and our Everlasting Father—having made the world, this most glorious house and magnificent temple of his divinity, by the secret laws of his hidden wisdom—he adorned the regions above the heavens with most glorious spirits, the spheres he enlivened with eternal souls, the dreggy parts of the inferior world he filled with all kinds of herds of living creatures. *Sed Opere Consummato.* But his work being completed, he desired someone that might weigh and reason, and love the beauty, and admire the vastness of so great a work.

All things therefore being (as Moses and Timaeus witness) already finished, at last he thought of creating man. But there was not in all the platforms before conceived, any being after whom he might form this new offspring. Nor in all his treasures, what he might give this new son by way of inheritance, nor yet a place in all the regions of the world, wherein this contemplator of the universe might be seated. All things were already full; all things were already distributed into their various orders of supreme, middle, and inferior.

But it was not the part of infinite power to fail as defective in the last production. It was not the part of infinite wisdom, for want of council, to fluctuate in so necessary an affair. It was not the part of infinite goodness or sovereign love, that he, who should be raised up to praise the divine bounty in other things, should condemn it in himself.

Statuit tandem opt. Opifex, ut cui dari nihil proprium poterat communis esset, quod privatum singulis fuit:

The wisest and best of workmen appointed therefore that he, to whom nothing proper to himself could be added, should have something of all that was peculiar to everything—and therefore he took man, the image of all his work, and placing him in the middle of the world, spoke thus unto him:

God's Commission to Adam

"O Adam, we have given you neither a certain seat, nor a private face, nor a peculiar office, that whatsoever seat or face or office you desire you may enjoy. All other things have a nature bounded within certain laws; you only are loose from all, and according to your own council in the hand of which I have put you, may choose and prescribe what nature you will to yourself. I have placed you in the middle of the world, that from thence you may behold on every side more commodiously everything in the whole world. We have made you neither heavenly nor earthly, neither mortal nor immortal, that being the honored former and framer of thyself, you may shape yourself into what nature yourself pleases!"

Man's Unlimited Options

"O infinite liberality of God the Father! O admirable and supreme felicity of man! To whom it is given to have what he desires and to be what he wishes. The brutes, when they are brought forth, bring into the world with them what they are to possess continually. The spirits that are above were, either from the beginning or a little after, that which they are about to be to all eternities.

Nascenti Homini omnigena vitae germina indidit Pater: God infused the seeds of every kind of life into man. Whatever seeds everyone chooses, those spring up with him, and the fruits of those shall he bear and enjoy. If sensual things are chosen by him, he shall become a beast; if reasonable, a celestial creature; if intellectual, an angel and a Son of God; and if being content with the lot of no creatures, he withdraws himself into the center of his own unity, he shall be one spirit with God, and dwell above all in the solitary darkness of his eternal Father."

Deformity or Excellency is Within Creatures

This Picus Mirandula spoke in an oration made before a most learned assembly in a famous university. Any man may perceive that he permits his fancy to wander a little undisciplined after the manner of a poet, but most deep and serious things are secretly hidden under his free and luxuriant language. The changeable power he ascribes to man is not to be referred to his body, for as he wisely says, Neither does the bark make a plant, but its stupid and nothing-perceiving nature. Neither does the skin make a beast, but his brutish and sensual nature. Neither does separation from a body make an angel, but his spiritual intelligence.

So neither does his rind or coat or skin or body make a man to be this or that, but the interior stupidness or sensuality or angelical intelligence of his soul make him accordingly a plant, a beast, or an angel. The deformity or excellency is within.

Man Was First in Intention, Last in Execution

Neither is it to be believed that God filled all the world with creatures before he thought of man. But by that little fable, he teaches us the excel-

lency of man. Man is the end, and therefore the perfection of all the creatures; but as Eusebius Pamphilus says (in the Nicene Council): He was first
in the intention, though last in the execution.

All angels were spectators as well as he. All angels were free agents as
well as he (as we see by their trial and the fall of some). All angels were seated in as convenient a place as he. But this is true—that he was the end of all
and the last of all, and the comprehensive head and the bond of all, and in
that, more excellent than all the angels. As for whom the visible and invisible worlds were made, and to whom all creatures ministered—as one also
that contained more species in his nature than the angels, which is not, as
some have thought, derogatory, but perfective to his being.

It is true also that God has prevented him, and satisfied all wishes, in
giving him such a being as he now enjoys. And that for infinite reasons it
was best that he should be in a changeable estate, and have power to choose
what himself listed. For he may so choose as to become one spirit with
God Almighty.

Love's Healing Influences

By choosing, a man may be turned and converted into love. Which, as
it is a universal sun filling and shining in the eternity of God, so is it infinitely more glorious than the sun is—not only shedding abroad more amiable, arid, delightful beams, illuminating and comforting all objects (yea
glorifying them in the supreme and sovereign manner) —but is of all sen-
sibles the most quick and tender, being able to feel like the long-legged spi-
der at the utmost end of its divaricated feet, and to be wholly present in
every place where any beam of itself extends. The sweetness of its healing
influences is inexpressible. And of all beings, such a being would I choose
to be forever: one that might inherit all in the most exquisite manner and
be the joy of all in the most perfect measure.

Man is the Greatest Miracle

Nazianzen professed himself to be a lover of right reason, and by it did undertake even to speak oracles. Even so may we, by the reason, discover all the mysteries of heaven. And what our author here observes is very considerable: "That man by retiring from all externals and withdrawing into himself in the center of his own unity becomes most like unto God."

What Mercurius said in the dialogue is most true: "Man is of all other the greatest miracle. Yea verily, should all the miracles that ever were done be drawn together, man is a miracle greater than they."

And as much may be written of him alone as of the whole world. The dividing of the sea, the commanding of the sun, the making of the world is nothing to the single creation of one soul. There is so much wisdom and power expressed in its faculties and inclinations. Yet is this greatest of all miracles unknown because men are addicted only to sensible and visible things.

So great a world in explication of its parts is easy, but here the dimensions of innumerable worlds are shut up in a center. Where it should lodge such innumerable objects, as it does by knowing; whence it should derive such infinite streams as flow from it by loving; how it should be a mirror of all eternity, being made of nothing; how it should be a fountain or a sun of eternity out of which such abundant rivers of affection flow, it is impossible to declare. But above all—how, having no material or bodily existence, its substance, though invisible, should be so rich and precious. The consideration of one soul is sufficient to convince all the Atheists in the whole world.

The Richness of the Soul's Communications

The abundance of its beams, the reality of its beams, the freedom of its beams, the excellence and value of its beams are all transcendent. They shine upon all the things in heaven and earth and cover them all with celestial waters—waters of refreshment, beams of comfort. They flow freely from a mind desiring to be obedient, pleasing, and good.

The soul communicates itself wholly by them and is richer in its communications than all odors and spices whatsoever. It contains in its nature the influences of the stars by way of eminence, the splendor of the sun, the verdure of trees, the value of gold, the luster of precious stones, the sense of beasts and the life of angels, the fatness of feasts, the magnificence of palaces, the melody of music, the sweetness of wine, the beauty of the excellent, the excellency of virtue, and the glory of cherubim. The harmony and the joys of heaven appear in love, for all these were made for her, and all these are to be enjoyed in her.

The Sweetest Thing in the World

Whether it be the soul itself, or God in the soul, that shines by love, or both, it is difficult to tell. But certainly the love of the soul is the sweetest thing in the world. I have often admired what should make it so excellent. If it be God that loves, it is the shining of his essence. If it be the soul, it is his image. If it be both, it is a double benefit.

Our Souls Are Mirrors, Reflecting God's Love

That God should love in the soul is most easy to believe, because it is most easy to conceive. But it is a greater mystery that the soul should love in itself. If God loves in the soul, it is the more precious; if the soul loves, it is the more marvelous. If you ask how a soul that was made of nothing can return so many flames of love? Where it should have them, or out of what ocean it should communicate them?

It is impossible to declare—for it can return those flames upon all eternity, and upon all the creatures and objects in it—unless we say, "As a mirror returns the very self-same beams it receives from the sun, so the soul returns those beams of love that shine upon it from God." For as a looking-glass is nothing in comparison of the world, yet contains all the world in it and seems a real fountain of those beams which flow from it, so the soul is nothing in respect of God, yet all eternity is contained in it and it is the real fountain of that love that proceeds from it. They are the sunbeams which the glass returns, yet they flow from the glass and from the sun within it. The mirror is the wellspring of them because they shine from the sun within the mirror, which is as deep within the glass as it is high within the heavens.

And this shows the exceeding richness and preciousness of love—it is the love of God shining upon, and dwelling in, the soul. For the beams that shine upon it reflect upon others and shine from it.

God Made Us With Our Own Love

That the soul shines of itself is equally manifest, for it can love with a love distinct from God's. It can love irregularly; and no irregular love is the love of God. It can forbear to love while God loves. It can love while God forbears. It can love a wicked man, wickedly and in his wickedness. This shows plainly that it can love regularly, with a love that is not merely the reflection of God's. For which cause it is not called a mirror, but esteemed more a real fountain.

Cant.: My love is a spring shut up, a fountain sealed.[185] That is, shut up like a letter, and concealed yet. But in the kingdom of heaven, her contents and secrets shall be known, and her beauty read of all men. Her own waters whence she should receive them: it is most admirable, considering the reality and beauty of them.

But in this God has magnified his infinite power, that he has made them. Made them freely, made them her own, out of herself to flow from her—creatures as it were to which she herself gives their existence. For indeed she could not love, were not her beams of love her own. Before she loves, they are not; when she loves, they are. And so she gives them their being. Being good herself because she can love. Who else would be a dry and withered stick, having neither life nor value.

But now she can exalt a creature above all the things in heaven and earth in herself: esteem it most dear, admire it, honor it, tender it, desire it, delight in it, be united to it, prefer it, forsake all things for it, give all things to it, die for it. It can languish after it when absent, take pleasure in it when present, rejoice in its happiness, live only to it, study to please it, delight in suffering for it, feed it with pleasures, honors, and caresses, do all things for its sake, esteem gold and pearl but dross in comparison, lay crowns and sceptres at its feet, make it a lord of palaces, delight in its own beauties, riches, and pleasures, as they feed only and satisfy its beloved, be ravished with it. It can desire infinitely that good things should be added to it.

And all this shall we enjoy in every soul in the kingdom of heaven. All there being like so many suns shining upon one. All this goodness is so like God's, that nothing can be more. And yet that it is distinct from his is manifest because it is the return or recompense of it—the only thing which for and above all worlds he infinitely desires.

The Goal of Heaven and Earth

Here upon earth souls love what God hates, and hate what God loves. Did they keep their eye open always upon what he loves, and see his love to them and to all, they could not choose but love as he does. And were they mirrors only that return his love, one would think it impossible, while he shines upon them, to forbear to shine; but they are like the eye, mirrors with lids—and the lid of ignorance or inconsideration interposing, they are oftentimes eclipsed or shine only through some crannies. So that here upon earth having free power to hold open or shut their lids, to send or turn away their beams, they may love me or forbear.

The loss of their love is an evil past imagination, for it is the removal of the end of heaven and earth, the extinction of a sun infinitely more glorious than that in the heavens. The sun was made to serve this more divine and glorious creature. The love of this creature is the end of heaven and earth, because the end for which heaven and earth were made was for it. And in recompense for all that God has done for it is to love me. So that God has glorified me by giving me a communion with himself in the end for which the world was made. And has made that creature to love me, and given me so great a certainty of its love and title to it, that first it must cease to love itself or to love God before it bereave me. It must cease to be wise, and forfeit all its interest in heaven and earth, before it can cease to love me. In doing it, it ruins itself and apostatizes from all its happiness.

Extending God's Grace to Sinners

In the estate of innocence, the love of man seemed nothing but the beams of love reverted upon another. For they loved no person but of whom he was beloved. All that he loved was good, and nothing evil. His love seemed the goodness of a being expressed in the soul, or apprehended in the lover, and returned upon itself.

But in the estate of misery (or rather grace), a soul loves freely and purely of its own self, with God's love, things that seem incapable of love—naught and evil. For as God showed his eternity and omnipotence in that he could shine upon nothing and love an object when it was nothing or evil—as he did Adam when he raised him out of nothing and mankind when he redeemed them from evil—so now we can love sinners and them that deserve nothing at our hands. Which as it is a diviner love and more glorious than the other, so were we redeemed to this power, and it was purchased for us with a greater price.

Obliging God For His Good & Generous Intent

It is a generous and heavenly principle, that where a benefit is fairly intended we are equally obliged for the intention or success. He is an ungrateful debtor that measures a benefactor by the success of his kindness. A clear soul and a generous mind is as much obliged for the intent of his friend, as the prosperity of it—and far more, if we separate the prosperity from the intent. For the goodness lies principally in the intention.

Since therefore God intended me all the joys in heaven and earth, I am as much obliged for them as if I received them. Whatever intervening accident bereaved me of them, he really intended them. And in that I contemplate the riches of his goodness. Whether men's wickedness in the present age, or my own perverseness, or the fall of Adam, he intended me all the joys of Paradise, and all the honors in the world, whatever hinders me. In the glass of his intention therefore I enjoy them all, and I do confess my obligation. It is as great as if nothing had intervened, and I had wholly received them.

Seeing and knowing him to be infinitely wise and great and glorious, I rejoice that he loved me, and confide in his love. His goodness is my sovereign and supreme delight. That God is of such a nature in himself is my infinite treasure. Being he is my friend, and delights in my honor, though I rob myself of all my happiness, he is justified. That he intended it, is his grace and glory. But it animates me, as well as comforts me, to see the perfection of his love towards me.

As things stood, he used power enough before the fall to make me happy. If he refuses to use any more since the fall, I am obliged. But he has used more. New occasions begot new abilities. He redeemed me by his Son.

If he refuses to use any more, I cannot complain. If he refuses to curb my perverseness unless I consent, his love was infinitely showed. He desires that I should, by prayers and endeavors, clothe myself with grace. If in default of mine, he does it himself—freely giving his Holy Spirit to me—it is an infinite mercy, but infinitely new and superadded. If he refuses to overrule the rebellion of other men, and to bring me to honor, notwithstanding their malice; or refuses to make them love me, whether they will or no, I cannot repine. By other signs, he has plainly shown that he loves me infinitely, which is enough for me, and that he desires my obedience.

My Present Estate is the Best

This estate wherein I am placed is the best for me though encompassed with difficulties. It is my duty to think so, and I cannot do otherwise. I cannot do otherwise without reproaching my Maker—that is, without suspecting, and in that, offending his goodness and wisdom. Riches are but tarnish and gilded vanities. Honors are but airy and empty bubbles. Affections are but winds, perhaps too great for such a ship as mine, of too light a ballast: pleasures. Yea, all these are but witches that draw and steal us away from God: dangerous allurements, interposing screens, unseasonable companions, counterfeit realities, honeyed poison, cumbersome distractions. I have found them so. At least they lull us into lethargies, and we need to be quickened. Sometimes they puff us up with vainglory and we need to be humbled. Always they delude us if we place any confidence in them, and therefore it is as good always to be without them.

But it is as good also, were it not for our weakness, sometimes to have them, because a good use may be made of them. And therefore they are not to be contemned when God does offer them. But he is to be admired that makes it good on both sides—to have them and to be without them. Riches are not to be hated nor coveted; but I am to bless God in all estates, who has given me the world, my soul, and himself, and ever to be great in the true treasures. Riches are good, and therefore is it good sometimes to want them, that we might show our obedience and resignation to God, even in being without those things that are good, at his appointment. And that also we might clothe ourselves with patience and faith and courage, which are greater ornaments than gold and silver, and of greater price, and that shall stand us instead of all the splendor of alms deeds. Assure yourself—till you prize one virtue above a trunk of money you can never be happy. One virtue before the face of God, is better than all the gold in the whole world.

Heir of the Whole World & Friend of God

Knowing the greatness and sweetness of love, I can never be poor in any estate. How sweet a thing is it as we go or ride or eat or drink or converse abroad to remember that one is the heir of the whole world and the friend of God! That one has so great a friend as God is and that one is exalted infinitely by all his laws! That all the riches and honors in the world are ours in the divine image to be enjoyed! That a man is tenderly beloved of God and always walking in his Father's kingdom, under his wing, and as the apple of his eye! Verily that God has done so much for one in his works and laws, and expressed so much love in his word and ways, being as he is divine and infinite, it should make a man to walk above the stars, and seat him in the bosom of men and angels. It should always fill him with joy and triumph, and lift him up above crowns and empires.

An Oak Flourishing in Winter

That a man is beloved of God should melt him all into esteem and holy veneration. It should make him so courageous as an angel of God. It should make him delight in calamities and distresses for God's sake. By giving me all things else, he has made even afflictions themselves my treasures. The sharpest trials are the finest furbishing. The most tempestuous weather is the best seedtime. A Christian is an oak flourishing in winter.

God has so magnified and glorified his servant, and exalted him so highly in his eternal bosom, that no other joy should be able to move us but that alone. All sorrows should appear but shadows, beside that of his absence, and all the greatness of riches and estates swallowed up in the light of his favor. Incredible goodness lies in his love. And it should be joy enough to us to contemplate and possess it. He is poor whom God hates—'tis a true proverb.

And besides that, we should so love him, that the joy alone of approving ourselves to him and making ourselves amiable and beautiful before him should be a continual feast, were we starving. A beloved cannot feel hunger in the presence of his beloved. Where martyrdom is pleasant, what can be distasteful. To fight, to famish, to die for one's beloved, especially with one's beloved, and in his excellent company, unless it be for his trouble, is truly delightful. God is always present and always sees us.

Praising God All Day Long

Knowing myself beloved and so glorified of God Almighty in another world, I ought to honor him in this always, and to aspire to it. At midnight will I rise to give thanks unto you because of your righteous judgments.[186] Seven times a day will I praise you for your glorious mercy.[187] Early in the morning will I bless you; I will triumph in your works;[188] I will delight in your law day and night.[189] At evening will I praise you. I will ever be speaking of your marvelous acts;[190] I will tell of your greatness and talk of the glorious majesty of your excellent kingdom[191]—these things ought ever to breathe in our souls. We ought to covet to live in private, and in private ever to overflow in praises. I will boast in you all the day long,[192] and be glad in the Lord.[193] My exceeding joy, my life, my glory, what shall I render to you for all your benefits? I will sing and be glad.[194] Let all nations sing unto him, for he covers the earth as it were with a shield.[195] My lips shall be fain when I sing unto you, and my soul, O Lord, which you have redeemed. God is unseen till he be so known, and David's spirit an inscrutable mystery till this is experienced.

This Life is the Most Precious Season of Eternity

Our friendship with God ought to be so pure and so clear, that nakedly and simply for his divine love, for his glorious works and blessed laws, the wisdom of his counsels, his ancient ways and attributes towards us, we should ever in public endeavor to honor him, always taking care to glorify him before men—to speak of his goodness, to sanctify his name, to do those things that will stir up others, and occasion others to glorify him. Doing this so zealously that we would not forbear the least act wherein we might serve him for all worlds.

It ought to be a firm principle rooted in us—that this life is the most precious season in all eternity, because all eternity depends on it. Now we may do those actions which hereafter we shall never have occasion to do. And now we are to do them in another manner, which in its place is the most acceptable in all worlds: namely, by faith and hope, in which God infinitely delights, with difficulty and danger, which God infinitely commiserates and greatly esteems. So piecing this life with the life of heaven, and seeing it as one with all eternity, a part of it, a life within it—strangely and stupendously blessed in its place and season.

You Must Continually Visit & Practice These Principles

Having once studied these principles, you are eternally to practice them. You are to warm yourselves at these fires, and to have recourse to them every day. When you think not of these things, you are in the dark.

And if you would walk in the light of them, you must frequently meditate. These principles are like seed in the ground—they must continually be visited with heavenly influences, or else your life will be a barren field. Perhaps they might be cast into better frame, and more curiously expressed; but if well cultivated, they will be as fruitful as if every husk were a golden rind. It is the substance that is in them that is productive of joy and good to all.

Our Souls Are Made for Action

It is an indelible principle of eternal truth, that practice and exercise is the life of all. Should God give you worlds and laws and treasures and worlds upon worlds, and himself also in the divinest manner—if you will be lazy and not meditate, you lose all. The soul is made for action, and cannot rest till it be employed. Idleness is its rust. Unless it will up and think and taste and see, all is in vain. Worlds of beauty and treasure and felicity may be round about it, and itself desolate. If therefore you would be happy, your life must be as full of operation as God of treasure. Your operation shall be treasure to him as his operation is delightful to you.

Become Familiar With These Principles

To be acquainted with celestial things is not only to know them, but by frequent meditation to be familiar with them. The effects of which are admirable. For by this, those things that at first seemed uncertain become evident. Those things which seemed remote become near. Those things which appeared like shady clouds become solid realities. Finally, those things which seemed impertinent to us and of little concernment, appear to be our own according to the strictest rules of propriety and of infinite moment.

The Secret Strength of the Soul

General and public concernments seem at first unmanageable, by reason of their greatness; but in the soul there is such a secret sufficiency, that it is able upon trial, to manage all objects with equal ease—things infinite in greatness as well as the smallest sand. But this secret strength is not found in it but merely upon experience, nor discerned but by exercise. The eternity of God himself is manageable to the understanding, and may be used in innumerable ways for its benefit; so may his almighty power and infinite goodness, his omnipresence and immensity, the wideness of the world and the multitude of kingdoms.

Which argues a peculiar excellency in the soul, because it is a creature that can never be exceeded. For bodily strength by this is perceived to be finite—that bulk is unwieldy, and by the greatness of its object may easily be overcome. But the soul through God that strengthened her is able to do all things. Nothing is too great, nothing too heavy, nothing unwieldy; it can rule and manage anything with infinite advantage.

Spiritual Things are Greatest & Spiritual Strength is Most Useful and Delightful

Because the strength of the soul is spiritual, it is generally despised. But if ever you would be divine, you must admit this principle: **That spiritual things are the greatest, and that spiritual strength is the most excellent, useful, and delightful.** For which cause it is made as easy as it is endless and invincible.

Infinity is but one object; almighty power is another; eternal wisdom is another which it can contemplate. From infinity it can go to power, from power to wisdom, from wisdom to goodness, from goodness to glory, and so to blessedness, and from these to any object or all whatsoever, contemplating them as freely as if it had never seen an object before. If any one say, that though it can proceed thus from one object to another, yet it cannot comprehend any one of them, all I shall answer is this: It can comprehend any one of them as much as a creature can possibly do. And the possibility of a creature depends purely upon the power of God—for a creature may be made able to do all that which its Creator is able to make it to do. So if there be any defect in his power, there must of necessity a limit follow in the power of his creature, which even God himself cannot make a creature to exceed. But this, you will say, is an argument only of what may be, not of what is.

Though considering God's infinite love, it is sufficient to show what is possible; because his love will do all it can for the glory of itself and its object. Yet further to discover what is, we may add this: that when a soul has contemplated the infinity of God, and passes from that to another object—all that it is able to contemplate on any other, it might have added to its first contemplation. So that its liberty to contemplate all shows its unlimitedness to anyone. And truly I think it pious to believe that God has without a metaphor infinitely obliged us.

Can the Soul Enjoy the Universal Beauty of God's Kingdom?

The reason why learned men have not exactly measured the faculties of the soul, is because they know not to what their endless extent should serve. For till we know the universal beauty of God's kingdom, and that all objects in the omnipresence are the treasures of the soul, to inquire into the sufficiency and extent of its powers is impertinent.

But when we know this, nothing is more expedient than to consider whether a soul be able to enjoy them. Which if it be, its powers must extend as far as its objects. For no object without the sphere of its power, can be enjoyed by it. It cannot be so much as perceived, much less enjoyed. From whence it will proceed, that the soul will to all eternity be silent about it—a limitation of praises, and a stinginess in love following thereupon, to the endangering of the perfection of God's kingdom.

What Results From Understanding & Appreciating the Soul

Upon the infinite extent of the understanding and affection of the soul, strange and wonderful things will follow:

1. A manifestation of God's infinite love.
2. The possession of infinite treasures.
3. A return of infinite thanksgivings.
4. A fullness of joy which no thing can exceed.
5. An infinite beauty and greatness in the soul.
6. An infinite beauty in God's kingdom.
7. An infinite union between God and the soul (as well in extent, as fervor).
8. An exact fitness between the powers of the soul, and its objects—neither being desolate, because neither exceeds the other.
9. An infinite glory in the communion of saints—everyone being a treasure to all the residue and enjoying the residue, and in the residue all the glory of all worlds.
10. A perfect indwelling of the soul in God, and God in the soul. So that as the fullness of the Godhead dwells in our Saviour, it shall dwell in us; and the Church shall be the fullness of him that fills all in all—God being manifested thereby to be a king infinitely greater, because reigning over infinite subjects. To whom be all glory and dominion forever and ever. Amen.

VI.
CONTINUING BEYOND BOUNDS OR RESTRAINTS

CHAPTER 29
INFINITE ROOM FOR OUR IMAGINATIONS

God is the Object of Felicity & The Way of Enjoying It

The objects of felicity, and the way of enjoying them, are two material themes—wherein to be instructed is infinitely desirable, because as necessary as profitable. Whether of the two, the object or the way, be more glorious, it is difficult to determine. God is the object, and God is the way of enjoying.

God in all his excellencies, laws, and works, in all his ways and counsels, is the sovereign object of all felicity. Eternity and time, heaven and earth, kingdoms and ages, angels and men are in him to be enjoyed. In him the fountain, in him the end, in him the light, the life, the way, in him the glory and crown of all. Yet for distinction sake we will speak of several eminent particulars, beginning with his attributes.

The Infinity of God is the Kingdom of Our Souls

The infinity of God is our enjoyment because it is the region and extent of his dominion. Barely as it comprehends infinite space, it is infinitely delightful—because it is the room and the place of our treasures, the repository of joys, and the dwelling place, yea the seat and throne and kingdom of our souls. But as it is the light wherein we see, the life that inspires us, the violence of his love and the strength of our enjoyments, the greatness and perfection of every creature, the amplitude that enlarges us and the field wherein our thoughts expatiate without limit or restraint, the ground and foundation of all our satisfactions, the operative energy and power of the Deity, the measure of our delights and the grandeur of our soul, it is more our treasure and ought more abundantly to be delighted in.

It surrounds us continually on every side; it fills us and inspires us. It is so mysterious that it is wholly within us, and even then it wholly seems and is without us. It is more inevitably and constantly, more nearly and immediately, our dwelling place, than our cities and kingdoms and houses. Our bodies themselves are not so much ours or within us, as that is. The immensity of God is an eternal tabernacle.

Why then we should not be sensible of that as much as of our dwellings, I cannot tell, unless our corruption and sensuality destroy us. We ought always to feel, admire, and walk in it. It is more clearly objected to the eye of the soul, than our castles and palaces to the eye of the body. Those accidental buildings may be thrown down, or we may be taken from them, but this can never be removed—it abides forever. It is impossible not to be within it; nay, to be so surrounded as evermore to be in the center and midst of it, wherever we can possibly remove, is inevitably fatal to every being.

Infinity Gives Us Room for Our Imaginations

Creatures that are able to dart their thoughts into all spaces can brook no limit or restraint; they are infinitely indebted to this unlimited extent, because were there no such infinity, there would be no room for their imaginations—their desires and affections would be cooped up, and their souls imprisoned. We see the heavens with our eyes, and know the world with our senses. But had we no eyes nor senses, we should see infinity like the holy angels. The place wherein the world stands, were it all annihilated, would still remain—the endless extent of which we feel so really and palpably, that we do not more certainly know the distinctions and figures and bounds and distances of what we see, than the everlasting expansion of what we feel and behold within us.

It is an object infinitely great and ravishing, as full of treasures as full of room, and as fraught with joy as capacity. To blind men it seems dark, but is all glorious within, as infinite in light and beauty as extent and treasure. Nothing is in vain, much less infinity. Every man is alone the center and circumference of it. It is all his own, and so glorious, that it is the eternal and incomprehensible essence of the Deity—a cabinet of infinite value, equal in beauty, luster, and perfection to all its treasures. It is the bosom of God, the soul and security of every creature.

The Infinite Capacity of God's Power, Goodness, & Wisdom

Were it not for this infinity, God's bounty would of necessity be limited. His goodness would want a receptacle for its effusions. His gifts would be confined into narrow room, and his almighty power for lack of a theatre magnificent enough, a storehouse large enough, be straitened.

But almighty power includes infinity in its own existence. For because God is infinitely able to do all things, there must of necessity be an infinite capacity to answer that power, because nothing itself is an obedient subject to work upon. And the eternal privation of infinite perfections is to almighty power a being capable of all. As sure as there is a space infinite, there is a power, a bounty, a goodness, a wisdom infinite, a treasure, a blessedness, a glory.

A Painter's Table

Infinity of space is like a painter's table, prepared for the ground and field of those colors that are to be laid thereon. Look how great he intends the picture, so great does he make the table. It would be an absurdity to leave it unfinished, or not to fill it. To leave any part of it naked and bare, and void of beauty, would render the whole ungrateful to the eye, and argue a defect of time or materials, or wit in the limner.

As the table is infinite so are the pictures. God's wisdom is the art, his goodness the will, his word the pencil, his beauty and power the colors, his pictures are all his works and creatures. Infinitely more real and more glorious, as well as more great and manifold than the shadows of a landscape.

But the life of all is that they are the spectator's own. He is in them as in his territories, and in all these views his own possessions.

The Everlasting Duration of Infinite Space

One would think that besides infinite space there could be no more room for any treasure. Yet to show that God is infinitely infinite, there is infinite room besides, and perhaps a more wonderful region making this to be infinitely infinite. No man will believe, besides the space from the center of the earth to the utmost bounds of the everlasting hills, there should be any more. Beyond those bounds perhaps there may, but besides all that space that is unlimited and present before us, and absolutely endless every way, where can there be any room for more?

This is the space that is at this moment only present before our eye, the only space that was, or that will be, from everlasting to everlasting. This moment exhibits infinite space, but there is a space also wherein all moments are infinitely exhibited, and the everlasting duration of infinite space is another region and room of joys. Wherein all ages appear together, all occurrences stand up at once, and the innumerable and endless myriads of years that were before the creation, and will be after the world is ended, are objected as a clear and stable object—whose several parts, extended out at length, give an inward infinity to this moment, and compose an eternity that is seen by all who comprehend and enjoy.

CHAPTER 30

TRAVELING INTO GOD'S ETERNITY & OMNIPRESENCE

An Immovable Duration Containing All Moving Durations

Eternity is a mysterious absence of times and ages: an endless length of ages always present and forever perfect. For as there is an immovable space wherein all finite spaces are enclosed, and all motions carried on and performed, so is there an immovable duration that contains and measures all moving durations.

Without which first the last could not be; no more than finite places, and bodies moving without infinite space. All ages being but successions correspondent to those parts of the eternity wherein they abide, and filling no more of it than ages can do. Whether they are commensurate with it or not, is difficult to determine. But the infinite immovable duration is eternity, the place and duration of all things, even of infinite space itself—the cause and end, the author and beautifier, the life and perfection of all.

The Influence of Eternity

Eternity magnifies our joys exceedingly, for whereas things in themselves began and quickly end; before they came, were never in being; do service but for few moments, and after they are gone pass away and leave us forever. Eternity retains the moments of their beginning and ending within itself—and from everlasting to everlasting those things were in their times and places before God, and in all their circumstances eternally will be, serving him in those moments wherein they existed, to those intents and purposes for which they were created.

The swiftest thought is present with him eternally: the creation and the day of judgment, his first consultation, choice and determination, the result and end of all just now in full perfection, ever beginning, ever passing, ever ending—with all the intervals of space between things and things, as if those objects that arise many thousand years one after the other were all together. We also were ourselves before God eternally; and have the joy of seeing ourselves eternally beloved and eternally blessed, and infinitely enjoying all the parts of our blessedness—in all the durations of eternity appearing at once before ourselves, when perfectly consummate in the kingdom of light and glory.

The smallest thing by the influence of eternity, is made infinite and eternal. We pass through a standing continent or region of ages, that are already before us, glorious and perfect while we come to them. Like men in a ship we pass forward, the shores and marks seeming to go backward, though we move and they stand still. We are not with them in our progressive motion, but prevent the swiftness of our course, and are present with them in our understandings. Like the sun, we dart our rays before us, and occupy those spaces with light and contemplation which we move towards, but possess not with our bodies. And seeing all things in the light of divine knowledge, eternally serving God, rejoice unspeakably in that service, and enjoy it all.

God's Omnipresence Is Our Field of Joys & So Much More

His omnipresence is our ample territory or field of joys, a transparent temple of infinite luster, a strong tower of defense, a castle of repose, a bulwark of security, a palace of delights, an immediate help and a present refuge in the needful time of trouble, a broad and a vast extent of fame and glory, a theatre of infinite excellence, an infinite ocean by means whereof every action, word, and thought is immediately diffused like a drop of wine in a pail of water, and everywhere present, everywhere seen and known, infinitely delighted in, as well as filling infinite spaces.

It is the spirit that pervades all his works, the life and soul of the universe, that in every point of space from the center to the heavens, in every kingdom in the world, in every city, in every wilderness, in every house, every soul, every creature, in all the parts of his infinity and eternity sees our persons, loves our virtues, inspires us with itself, and crowns our actions with praise and glory. It makes our honor infinite in extent, our glory immense, and our happiness eternal. The rays of our light are by this means darted from everlasting to everlasting.

This spiritual region makes us infinitely present with God, angels, and men in all places from the utmost bounds of the everlasting hills, throughout all the unwearied durations of his endless infinity, and gives us the sense and feeling of all the delights and praises we occasion, as well as of all the beauties and powers and pleasures and glories which God enjoys or creates.

Perfecting & Completing Our Bliss & Happiness

Our bridegroom and our king being everywhere, our lover and defender watchfully governing all worlds, no danger or enemy can arise to hurt us, but is immediately prevented and suppressed in all the spaces beyond the utmost borders of those unknown habitations which he possesses. Delights of inestimable value are there preparing, for everything is present by its own existence.

The essence of God therefore being all light and knowledge, love and goodness, care and providence, felicity and glory, a pure and simple act, it is present in its operations, and by those acts which it eternally exerts is wholly busied in all parts and places of his dominion, perfecting and completing our bliss and happiness.

EPILOGUE

THOMAS TRAHERNE &
THE DISCOVERY OF *CENTURIES OF MEDITATION*

Who was Thomas Traherne?

Thomas Traherne was a British writer, born 1637 in Hereford, near the Welsh border. He was the son of a shoemaker, and it is likely that he lived at least part of his childhood with a wealthier relative, Philip Traherne.

Traherne received a first-class education at Brasenose College, Oxford, completing a Bachelor of Arts in 1656 and a Master of Arts in 1661. He then went on to serve as an Anglican parish priest for six years in the little village of Credenhill. In Credenhill, he was able to devote himself to writing in addition to the many practical responsibilities of a parish priest. It was probably also during his time in Credenhill that Traherne first met Susanna Hopton, for whom *Centuries of Meditation* was written. He returned to Brasenose and completed a Bachelor of Divinity in 1669.

In the same year, Traherne moved from Credenhill to London to serve as a private domestic chaplain to Sir Orlando Bridgeman, who was, at the time, Lord Keeper of the Great Seal under King Charles II. While in London, Traherne devoted much of his time to reading and writing. When Bridgeman retired to Teddington, after a falling out with Charles II, Traherne joined him and his family. Up until Traherne's death in 1674, he remained in service to Bridgeman.

Traherne balanced his highly-developed imagination with his fine-tuned intellect. Throughout his adult life, he commingled his pastoral roles with concentrated studies and periods of solitude. He viewed himself, in the spirit of Jesus, as a physician and healer. It is not surprising then that *Centuries of Meditation* speaks powerfully to the intuition and addresses the healing of the soul.

In addition to *Centuries of Meditation*, Traherne's books include *Roman Forgeries* (published anonymously in 1673), *Christian Ethics* (published posthumously in 1675), *A Serious and Pathetical Contemplation of the Mercies of God* (published posthumously in 1699), collections of his poetry (published posthumously throughout the twentieth century), and *Select Meditations* (published posthumously in the twentieth century). *Select Meditations* is possibly an early draft of *Centuries of Meditation*.

The History of *Centuries of Meditation*.

The history of *Centuries of Meditation* is a fascinating story. In the 240-odd years that elapsed from the time Traherne penned the manuscript to its first publication in 1908, it likely touched the lives of several loyalists and in this way assured its survival.

Thomas Traherne wrote *Centuries of Meditation* for Susanna Hopton as a guide to spiritual formation. By "spiritual formation," I mean the shaping of the heart and soul with attention to the way one views God, the world, and the heavens. This book was probably written with one reader in mind—thus accounting for the intimate emotion one often feels when reading it. As a spiritual primer, this book is one of the most affirming, poetic, and captivating books of its kind.

Susanna Hopton and her husband, Richard, lived as a wealthy and influential couple in Herefordshire. Mrs. Hopton took her faith very seriously—so seriously that her home became the center of a religious society. It is likely that Traherne was a part of that society and that his *Centuries of Meditation* was a contribution to that society through Susanna.

During his lifetime, Traherne left some of his other devotional writings with Mrs. Hopton. A few of these were mistakingly published under her name. The book that came to be known 200 years later as *Centuries of Meditation*, however, had been given no title. Nor did the author reveal his own name anywhere in the manuscript. The book was merely a small octavo containing 140 leaves. Traherne wrote on leaves 5-91 (or pages 1-172). Leaves 92-140 were left blank.

The text was divided into four sets of one hundred numbered paragraphs. The manuscript concluded with a fifth set of only 10 paragraphs. Because the numbered paragraphs were initially viewed as separate meditations, the name, *Centuries of Meditation*, was logically derived from the grouping of several hundred (ie. Centuries of) meditations. However, the reader should not view these as isolated meditations; rather, there is a clear connection from one to the next. The title of this edition, *Waking Up in Heaven*, better conveys the thematic progression from cover to cover.

Although Susanna Hopton never published this manuscript, she kept it well protected and preserved. After Traherne's death in 1674 and Susanna Hopton's death in 1709, this manuscript disappeared from public notice for nearly two centuries until 1895.

The discovery of the manuscript played itself out through four key men. The first was William T. Brooke, a bibliophile with a special interest in seventeenth-century verse. He found two old unpublished manuscripts in a secondhand bookbarrow in London. The one that interested him most contained poetry. The other one, written in the same handwriting, contained prose. Neither of them disclosed either the author or the title.

William Brooke sold the manuscripts to Dr. Alexander Grosart, a well-known literary editor in London at the turn of the century. Grosart attributed these writings to Henry Vaughan, another seventeenth-century poet. Grosart died in 1899, before he could publish Traherne's writings under any name.

After Dr. Grosart's death, Charles Higham purchased Grosart's library, which included the Traherne manuscripts. Higham was a well-known bookseller and a friend of Bertram Dobell, another successful London bookseller. Higham loaned, and later sold, the two manuscripts to Dobell.

As far as we know, Dobell was the first person who seriously questioned Henry Vaughan's authorship of the manuscripts. Dobell embarked on a mission to discover the true author. After years of collecting and piecing together clues, Dobell determined that a seventeenth-century author by the name of Thomas Traherne was the true author. After modernizing the text, Dobell published the volume of poems in 1903. In 1908, Dobell published a modernized version of Traherne's prose manuscript, giving it the title *Centuries of Meditation*.

The Dobell version of *Centuries of Meditation* was reprinted in 1927, 1934, 1948, and 1950. Then, in 1958, H. M. Margoliouth completed the editing of an authoritative version of *Centuries of Meditation* with the original spelling, capitalization, and punctuation—along with many useful notes and appendices. Anyone who has a serious interest in *Centuries of Meditation* should refer both to the Dobell version and the Margoliouth version.

Since Dobell's first publication of the manuscript in 1908, Traherne has been likened to Wordsworth, Blake, Whitman, and Thoreau for his joyful, poetic writing about nature and man; to St. Augustine, St. Thomas Aquinas, Julian of Norwich, and Thomas à Kempis for his theology; to Dante, Milton and Bunyan for his imagination; and to the seventeenth-century metaphysical poets—George Herbert, Henry Vaughan, and John Donne—for his devotional, meditative poetry. He is also echoed in the 20th century voices of writers like C. S. Lewis, T. S. Eliot, Annie Dillard, and Dallas Willard.

APPENDICES

APPENDIX A:
NOTES
(as footnoted in the Preface & Introduction)

Preface

1. Josef Pieper, *Happiness and Contemplation,* trans. Richard and Clara Winston (New York: Pantheon Books Inc., 1958), p. 74.
2. C. S. Lewis, *The Letters of C.S. Lewis to Arthur Greeves (1914-1963),* ed. Walter Hooper (New York: Macmillan Publishing Company, 1979), p. 560.
3. Thomas Merton, *Mystics and Zen Masters* (New York: Farrar, Straus and Giroux, 1967), p. 132.
4. Dorothy L. Sayers, "The Beatrician Vision in Dante and Other Poets," *Nottingham Mediaeval Studies* 2 (1958) : p. 23.

Introduction

1. C. S. Lewis, *The Letters of C.S. Lewis to Arthur Greeves (1914-1963),* ed. Walter Hooper (New York: Macmillan Publishing Company, 1979), pp. 368-369.

APPENDIX B:
SCRIPTURE REFERENCES
(as footnoted in Sections I-VI)

I am indebted to H. M. Margoliouth for identifying, in his 1958 edition of *Centuries, Poems, and Thanksgivings*, the references for many of Traherne's Scripture quotations. Traherne used the King James Version of the Bible, although I have edited these Scripture quotations in the same way that I edited the rest of Traherne's text.

1.	Matthew 13:35; Psalms 78:2	22.	Revelations 1:7
2.	Romans 4:13	23.	Isaiah 11:12
3.	Ephesians 3:9	24.	Isaiah 26:4
4.	1 Peter 5:10	25.	Luke 8:39
5.	Isaiah 40:12; Psalms 90:4	26.	John 8:56
6.	Psalms 119:130	27.	Philippians 2:5
7.	Matthew 25:23	28.	Romans 8:9
8.	Genesis 28:16-17	29.	John 19:38-40
9.	Psalms 82:5	30.	Colossians 2:9
10.	Psalms 82:5	31.	Genesis 1:28
11.	Psalms 82:5	32.	Psalms 8:3-5
12.	Psalms 19:10	33.	Psalms 19:10
13.	Psalms 39:6	34.	Psalms 119:72
14.	Isaiah 63:9	35.	John 13:34
15.	Acts 17:28	36.	Psalms 16:2-3
16.	Psalms 103:22	37.	Matthew 27:51-52
17.	Matthew 24:28	38.	Matthew 27:51
18.	John 12:32	39.	Exodus 13:21
19.	Jeremiah 38:6-13	40.	Ephesians 3:18-19
20.	Acts 10:10-16	41.	Leviticus 24:2-4
21.	Hosea 11:4	42.	Psalms 45:2

43.	Psalms 135:15-18		71.	Hebrews 7:27
44.	Hebrews 2:10		72.	Hebrews 10:7
45.	Psalms 43:3		73.	Hebrews 5:5
46.	Ephesians 3:15-19		74.	Acts 20:28
47.	Psalms 68:18		75.	Revelations 7:9-10
48.	Ephesians 3:17		76.	Revelations 5:8-10
49.	John 13:34		77.	Revelations 15:2-4
50.	Romans 15:30-31		78.	Revelations 5:11-13
51.	John 6:56-57		79.	1 Kings 18:44
52.	John 14:17		80.	Ephesians 3:19
53.	1 John 3:1		81.	John 4:24
54.	1 Peter 2:9		82.	Psalms 104:2
55.	Luke 17:21		83.	Psalms 84:7
56.	Revelations 15:3		84.	Ephesians 3:18
57.	Revelations 2:5		85.	2 Corinthians 6:16
58.	Isaiah 66:1		86.	Isaiah 22:1
59.	Psalms 71:8		87.	1 Corinthians 13:12
60.	Psalms 48:9		88.	1 Timothy 6:10
61.	Ezekiel 1:4-28		89.	Romans 8:38-39
62.	Book of Wisdom 13:1-5 (Apocrypha)		90.	John 3:3
			91.	Mark 10:15
63.	Romans 1:20		92.	Colossians 3:5
64.	Song of Solomon 8:6		93.	Ephesians 2:12
65.	Hebrews 5:4		94.	Psalms 103:22
66.	Hebrews 5:5,6		95.	Romans 8:28
67.	Philippians 2:6-9		96.	2 Corinthians 11:14
68.	Romans 8:32		97.	Psalms 102:7
69.	Philippians 3:8		98.	Psalms 45:13
70.	Psalms 49:7, 8		99.	Romans 6:10-11

100.	Proverbs 27:8	129.	Psalms 50:7-15
101.	Acts 17:23	130.	Psalms 40:6;
102.	Ephesians 4:18		Hebrews 10:5
103.	Deuteronomy 33:13-16	131.	Psalms 51:16-17
104.	Genesis 28:17	132.	Isaiah 22:1
105.	Genesis 13:14-15; 15:5	133.	Psalms 58:10
106.	Psalms 19:10	134.	Psalms 59:16
107.	1 Samuel 13:14	135.	Psalms 63:1-5
108.	Psalms 8:3-8	136.	Psalms 65:2
109.	Psalms 19:1-6	137.	Psalms 65:4
110.	Psalms 19:7-10	138.	Psalms 66:1-5
111.	Psalms 22:23-31	139.	Psalms 74:12-14
112.	Psalms 24:1	140.	Psalms 74:16-17
113.	Psalms 28:5	141.	Psalms 84:1
114.	Psalms 33:6-9	142.	Psalms 84:10
115.	Psalms 35:10	143.	Judges 5:11
116.	Psalms 36:5-9	144.	Psalms 86:8-10
117.	Psalms 45:10-11	145.	Psalms 107:43
118.	Psalms 45:13-16	146.	Psalms 35:13
119.	Psalms 46:4	147.	Psalms 69:12
120.	Psalms 46:8	148.	Psalms 150:3-5
121.	Psalms 47:1-2	149.	Ephesians 2:12
122.	Psalms 47:4	150.	Colossians 2:8
123.	Psalms 48:2-3	151.	2 Corinthians 3:18
124.	Psalms 48:12-14	152.	Hebrews 1:3
125.	Psalms 49:6-8	153.	1 Corinthians 1:24
126.	Psalms 49:10-11	154.	Colossians 3:3
127.	Psalms 49:13-14	155.	Colossians 2:3
128.	Psalms 49:20	156.	1 Corinthians 14:20

157.   Colossians 2:2

158.   Proverbs 2:4

159.   Proverbs 4:7-9

160.   Philippians 3:20

161.   2 Corinthians 6:12

162.   Psalms 102:6, 7

163.   Acts 20:35

164.   Matthew 10:15

165.   Psalms 29:2

166.   Psalms 46:1

167.   Matthew 25:40

168.   Psalms 132:9

169.   Proverbs 3:17

170.   Hebrews 10:23

171.   James 2:23

172.   Proverbs 4:23

173.   Acts 20:35

174.   Leviticus 19:18

175.   1 Corinthians 13

176.   Matthew 25:40

177.   Romans 8:9

178.   Revelations 1:8, 11

179.   Revelations 1:5

180.   John 17:22

181.   Colossians 2:9

182.   Ephesians 1:22, 23

183.   Psalms 139:17, 18

184.   Psalms 8:5

185.   Song of Solomon 4:12

186.   Psalms 119:62

187.   Psalms 119:164

188.   Psalms 92:4

189.   Psalms 1:2

190.   Psalms 9:1

191.   Psalms 145:12

192.   Psalms 44:8

193.   Psalms 104:34

194.   Psalms 67:4

195.   Psalms 47:9

APPENDIX C:
BIBLIOGRAPHY

I. Traherne's Published Works
(relevant to this edition of *Centuries of Meditation*)

Traherne, Thomas. *Centuries of Meditation.* Edited by Bertram Dobell. London, 1908.

Traherne, Thomas. *Centuries, Poems, and Thanksgivings.* Edited by H. M. Margoliouth. 2 vols. Oxford: Clarendon Press, 1958.

II. Biographical Sources

Wade, Gladys. *Thomas Traherne: A Critical Biography.* Princeton: Princeton University Press, 1944.

III. Secondary Sources

Clements, A. L. *The Mystical Poetry of Thomas Traherne.* Cambridge: Harvard University Press, 1969.

Day, Malcolm M. *Thomas Traherne.* Boston: Twayne Publishers, 1982.

Dowell, Graham. *Enjoying the World: The Rediscovery of Thomas Traherne.* Harrisburg: Morehouse Publishing, 1990.

Martz, Louis L. *The Paradise Within: Studies in Vaughan, Traherne, and Milton.* New Haven: Yale University Press, 1964.

Salter, K. W. *Thomas Traherne: Mystic and Poet.* London: Edward Arnold, 1964.

Sayers, Dorothy L. "The Beatrician Vision in Dante and Other Poets." *Nottingham Mediaeval Studies* 2 (1958): 3-23.

Sherrington, Alison J. *Mystical Symbolism in the Poetry of Thomas Traherne.* St. Lucia, Australia: University of Queensland Press, 1970.

Stewart, Stanley. *The Expanded Voice: The Art of Thomas Traherne.* San Marino, Calif.: Huntington Library, 1970.

APPENDIX D:
DETAILED TABLE OF CONTENTS

The sections originally noted in Dobell's 1908 edition of *Centuries of Meditation* are identified in this table with the Century (main section) in Roman numerals followed by a colon and the Meditation (subsection) in Arabic numerals. For example Century 1, Meditation 2 would be noted as 'I:2'.

SECTION I: MY CHALLENGES TO YOU   page 1
CHAPTER 1: CONSIDER SECRET INFLUENCES ON   page 3
YOUR SOUL

Truths You Love Without Knowing Them	I:1	page 3
Attraction to Unknown Things	I:2	page 3
Making You Possessor of the World	I:3	page 3
Advancing Gently	I:4	page 4
Communing with God	I:5	page 4
Seated in the Highest Happiness	I:6	page 5

CHAPTER 2: THINK WELL   page 6

Two Worlds	I:7	page 6
Thinking Well	I:8	page 6
Imagining the World	I:9	page 6
Enjoying the World	I:10	page 7
The Reason We Were Created	I:11	page 7
Prizing All Things	I:12	page 7
God's Thoughts	I:13	page 8
Prizing Things in Their Proper Places	I:14	page 8
God Made the World for Every Individual	I:15	page 9
Everything Points in the Same Direction	I:16	page 9
God Delights in Giving	I:17	page 10
The Heavens within the World	I:18	page 10

God's Presence and Eternity are Our   I:19   page 11
    Companions
Loving God With All the Powers of Your Soul   I:20   page 12

CHAPTER 3: ENJOY THE WORLD LIKE NEVER   **page 13**
BEFORE
Valuing Present Mercies   I:21   page 13
Man's Soul is Insatiable   I:22   page 13
God's Treasures are Free   I:23   page 15
The Fruition of the World   I:24   page 16
Everything in the World is Yours   I:25   page 16
Spiritually Enjoying the Service of Things   I:26   page 16
Seeing the Love of God in Everything   I:27   page 17
Waking Up in Heaven   I:28   page 17
Till the Sea Flows in Your Veins   I:29   page 17
Delighting in God's Goodness to All   I:30   page 18
A Mirror of Infinite Beauty   I:31   page 18
Ingratitude   I:32   page 19
Hideous Riches of Darkness   I:33   page 19
Neglecting the Heavens & the Stars   I:34   page 20
Our Inheritance   I:35   page 21
A Paradise & A Prison   I:36   page 21
Open Eyes   I:37   page 22
In the Best of Manners   I:38   page 22
Every Soul a Treasure   I:39   page 23
Free from Trivial Things   I:40   page 23

CHAPTER 4: UNDERSTAND WHAT YOU WANT   **page 25**

Wants & Supplies in Heaven	I:41	page 25
What God Wants	I:42	page 25
Learning Your Wants	I:43	page 26
God's Treasures	I:44	page 26
Being Sensible of Your Wants	I:45	page 27
Prize What You Need and Have	I:46	page 27
Heaven & Hell	I:47	page 28
Seeing & Enjoying What We Want	I:48	page 28
Ingratitude & Envy	I:49	page 29
Living in Heaven	I:50	page 29
Our Wants Bond Us to God	I:51	page 30

CHAPTER 5: CLAIM THE WORLD AS YOUR INHERITANCE   **page 31**

How You Inherit Everything	I:52	page 31
As Rich as God	I:53	page 31
Having Everything	I:54	page 32
Being Present Throughout Eternity	I:55	page 33

SECTION II: MY PRAYERS TO JESUS   page 35
CHAPTER 6: THE CROSS OF CHRIST IS THE GATE   **page 37**
OF HEAVEN: An Introduction to My Prayers

Journeys of the Soul	I:56	page 37
What Attracts Us?	I:57	page 37
The Gate of Heaven	I:58	page 38
The Cross is the Center of Eternity	I:59	page 38
A Flame that Illuminates the World	I:60	page 39
Imitating Jesus	I:61	page 40

CHAPTER 7: PRAYERS THANKING JESUS FOR ALL THE   **page 41**
           TREASURES HE HAS GIVEN US IN THE WORLD

What Return Can I Make?   I:62   page 41
Treasures of Your Goodness   I:63   page 41
You Created the World for Me   I:64   page 42
The Palace You Made for Me   I:65   page 43
The Treasures of My Body   I:66   page 44
Created in God's Image   I:67   page 44

CHAPTER 8: PRAYERS THANKING JESUS FOR   **page 46**
           HIS LOVE & FOR HIMSELF

Millions of Friends   I:68   page 46
God in Every Soul   I:69   page 47
Heavenly Mansions Around Us   I:70   page 47
Our Natures Require Love   I:71   page 47
Meeting God's Love in Everything   I:72   page 48
You Grow By Loving   I:73   page 49
Everyone is the End of All Things   I:74   page 49
Deceived In Paradise   I:75   page 50
Jesus, a Greater Treasure   I:76   page 51
The Greatness of Your Love, Jesus   I:77   page 51
You Bring Good out of Evil   I:78   page 52

CHAPTER 9: PRAYERS REQUESTING THAT I GROW   **page 53**
           IN JESUS' LOVE

Prayer for Lovingkindness   I:79   page 53
Naturally Made to Love   I:80   page 53
Delighting in God's Saints   I:81   page 54
Digging for Companions   I:82   page 55

Exchanging Souls	I:83	page 56
Turn Vices into Virtues	I:84	page 56
Be Present in All Ages	I:85	page 57

CHAPTER 10: PRAYERS REQUESTING THAT I   **page 58**
BECOME LIKE JESUS

Jesus Loves Everyone Alone	I:86	page 58
Becoming Mirrors of God's Brightness	I:87	page 58
Knowing Jesus with Hearts & Minds	I:88	page 59
With Jesus in His Sufferings	I:89	page 59
Letting God's Goodness Shine in Us	I:90	page 60
Let Nothing Divide	I:91	page 61
Inheriting Heaven & Earth	I:92	page 61
The Root of My Being	I:93	page 62
My Will & Jesus' Will	I:94	page 63
Christ's Spirit in Me	I:95	page 64
The Treasure of Love	I:96	page 65
Loving Everyone as My Friend	I:97	page 65
Never Alone	I:98	page 66
Sons of God	I:99	page 67
The Kingdom of God Within Us	I:100	page 68

SECTION III: MY VISION OF THE WORLD   **page 69**
CHAPTER 11: THE WORLD SERVES US   **page 71**

The World is a Promise of Eternal Joys	II:1	page 71
God's Gift to Every Infant	II:2	page 71
The Greatness of Sin	II:3	page 72
The End for Which We Were Created	II:4	page 72
Remember Adam's Innocence	II:5	page 72

The World is Mine	II:6	page 73
The Sun's Light Shines for You	II:7	page 73
All the Things the Sun Does for You	II:8	page 74
The Wisdom & Goodness of Night	II:9	page 75
Better to Enjoy One Sun Than Two	II:10	page 75
The Wisdom of Finite Limits	II:11	page 75
Enjoy What You Have First	II:12	page 76
Things in Their Proper Places	II:13	page 76
Enjoying God's Goodness	II:14	page 77
The World Serves You	II:15	page 77
Hidden Pleasures	II:16	page 78

CHAPTER 12: GOD CAN BE SEEN IN THE WORLD   **page 79**

Enjoying the Face of God	II:17	page 79
Enjoying the World Like God Does	II:18	page 79
All Things Flow from God	II:19	page 79
God is Invisible	II:20	page 80
God Can Be Seen in the Material World	II:21	page 81
God's Life Seen in the World's Motions	II:22	page 83
Man Made in the Image of God	II:23	page 84
God Appears to Our Understanding	II:24	page 85

CHAPTER 13: LET GOD'S LOVE RESTORE YOUR   **page 86**
PERSON TO GREATER BEAUTY

The Infinite Benefits & Rightness of Love	II:25	page 86
God's Works: The Expression of His Love	II:26	page 87
God's Works: A Gate to Seeing God's Kingdom	II:27	page 87
God's Works: His Gifts That We Must Appreciate	II:28	page 88

Our Obligation to Love	II:29	page 88
Reconciled to Your Person, Not Your Ugly Sin	II:30	page 89
Severing the Sin From the Sinner	II:31	page 89
Angels Not Bound to Die For Men	II:32	page 90
Jesus' Suffering for Man	II:33	page 90
Objects of Infinite Love	II:34	page 91
Dignity of Man	II:35	page 92
Infinite Punishments & Infinite Love	II:36	page 92
Eternal Sacrifice	II:37	page 93
Love's Suffering	II:38	page 94

CHAPTER 14: SEE GOD'S LOVE IN THE TRINITY   **page 95**

Love Begetting Love	II:39	page 95
A Love Trinity	II:40	page 95
Love in the Fountain & in the Stream	II:41	page 96
Lover Existing in Another Person	II:42	page 96
Jesus: the Wisdom & Love of the Father	II:43	page 96
Jesus and His Father	II:44	page 96
Love is the Spirit of God	II:45	page 97
Love Is the End of Itself	II:46	page 98
The Delightful Life of Love	II:47	page 98
Souls Are Made to Love	II:48	page 99
Enjoying God's Goodness to the World	II:49	page 100
God is Present By Love Alone	II:50	page 100

CHAPTER 15: EXTEND YOUR LOVE TO ALL OBJECTS   **page 101**

Love: A Candle in the Lantern of our Bodies	II:51	page 101
Living Infinitely by Loving God	II:52	page 101
God is Infinitely More Blessed	II:53	page 102

The Ironies of Love	II:54	page 102
Crowning My Friends with Glory & Happiness	II:55	page 103
Love: How a Soul Propagates Itself	II:56	page 103
Our Strong Desire to Be Good to Others	II:57	page 104
Love: The Only Throne That Exalts Us	II:58	page 104
The End of Riches	II:59	page 105
Power to Please God	II:60	page 105
Living in All	II:61	page 105
Love: How the World is Enjoyed	II:62	page 106
Contemplate the Glory of Love and Being Loved	II:63	page 106
The World Becomes Ours Through Love	II:64	page 107
Our Proneness to Love	II:65	page 107
Doting on One Person	II:66	page 108
You Can't Love Too Much	II:67	page 108
Ten Thousand Beauties in Every Woman	II:68	page 109
Managing Our Love	II:69	page 109

CHAPTER 16: GO OUT OF YOURSELF WITH THE POWER OF YOUR SOUL		**page 111**
Spiritually Multiplying Ourselves	II:70	page 111
An Infinite Wonder: Millions of Souls	II:71	page 111
Seeing & Accompanying the Endless Perfections in Every Soul	II:72	page 112
By Desire, the Soul Extends Itself	II:73	page 112
Maintaining All People in All Kingdoms as Our Joys	II:74	page 112
Our Souls' Actions in the Kingdom of Heaven	II:75	page 114
Going Out of Yourself	II:76	page 114
Seeking Riches in All Places	II:77	page 115

How Objects Make Our Soul Known   II:78   page 115
Both Enjoying Everything for Ourselves   II:79   page 116
    & Sharing All of It with Others
Filling All Time & Spaces with Our Love   II:80   page 117
Infinity is Primary, Limits Secondary   II:81   page 118
God Exerting All His Power to Show His   II:82   page 118
    Goodness
Our Cowardly & Lazy Expectations of God   II:83   page 119
The World Serves our Souls with Ideas   II:84   page 120
Our Love is Valuable & Prized   II:85   page 121
Preparing Ourselves to Speak to God   II:86   page 122
Our Souls Should Contain Heaven & Earth   II:87   page 122
God's Mercy   II:89   page 123
The Value of the World in our Thoughts   II:90   page 123

CHAPTER 17: REST & DELIGHT IN THE GREATNESS   **page 125**
    OF YOUR TRUE SELF
Continuing to Uphold our Thoughts of Heaven   II:91   page 125
The Unlimited Extent of Your Soul   II:92   page 125
Every Man Loving & Honoring You   II:93   page 126
Praises Are Transformed & Returning Benefits   II:94   page 127
Prizing Jesus' Love   II:95   page 128
Seeds of Grace & Seeds of Glory   II:96   page 129
God's Kingdom Lifts Us Above Sin   II:97   page 129
The World Makes Vices & Virtues Visible   II:98   page 130
The Sources of Happiness   II:99   page 131
How Happiness is Attained   II:100   page 132

SECTION IV: THE STORY OF MY PERSONAL JOURNEY   page 135

CHAPTER 18: MY CHILDHOOD & ADOLESCENCE   page 137

Praying for the Divine Light Wherewith I Was Born	III:1	page 137
Surrounded with Innumerable Joys	III:2	page 137
All Things Were Mine Before I Was Corrupted	III:3	page 138
With New and Open Eyes (A Poem)	III:4	page 139
Enjoying What We Naturally Saw at Our Birth	III:5	page 141
I Will Show You My Steps to Enjoying the Universe	III:6	page 141
Wholly Forgetting My Treasures	III:7	page 142
More Prone to Good & Excellent Things	III:8	page 143
The Riches of Nature	III:9	page 143
Drowning the Knowledge of Heaven and Earth	III:10	page 144
Making Children Possessors of Heaven & Earth	III:11	page 145
Indians Nearer to God in Simplicity	III:12	page 145
Making Men to Live without God in the World	III:13	page 146
Idle Talk & Worthless Vanities	III:14	page 146
Inquisitive About an Unknown Happiness	III:15	page 147
What I Imagined When I Was 4 Years Old	III:16	page 147
Questions About Earth & Heaven	III:17	page 148
Thinking About Creation	III:18	page 148
Our Greatness is Not in Our Size, But in Our Souls (A Poem)	III:19	page 149
Infinite Worth in Limited Beings	III:20	page 150
Bounding Things to Make Them Useful (A Poem)	III:21	page 150
First Visit to a Noble Dining Room	III:22	page 151

My Change from Fearing the Universe to Enjoying It	III:23	page 152
All Kingdoms Became Accessible	III:24	page 153
Learning That Every Kingdom Contains Wonders	III:25	page 154
A Poem: 'On News'	III:26	page 154
My Desire for a Book from Heaven	III:27	page 156
Thousands in the World Enjoying Communion with God	III:28	page 157
What I Found in the Bible	III:29	page 157
Giving Myself to What I Found in the Bible	III:30	page 158
Fashions & Tinselled Vanities Became Mine	III:31	page 159
My Unbelief	III:32	page 159
Reasons Why God's Manner of Revelation Was Best	III:33	page 159
Imagining the Difficulties of Being the Only Man with this Book from Heaven	III:34	page 161
Light of Heaven in this World	III:35	page 161

CHAPTER 19: MY YEARS AT THE UNIVERSITY   **page 162**

Meeting Glorious Secrets & Persons at the University	III:36	page 162
We Didn't Study Things So as to Enjoy Them	III:37	page 162
Studying with the Most Excellent Manners	III:38	page 162
My Enquiry into the Excellence of Things	III:39	page 163
Studying Things Out of Both Interest & Treasure	III:40	page 163
Studying Things in Order to See God	III:41	page 164
What I Learn by Studying Humanity	III:42	page 164

What I Learn By Studying Divinity III:43 page 166
What I Learn by Studying Natural Philosophy III:44 page 167
What I Learn By Studying Ethics III:45 page 167

CHAPTER 20: MY YEARS IN THE COUNTRY page 169
Going into the Country to Study Happiness III:46 page 169
A Poem About Overcoming Lust & Sin III:47 page 169
Descending into Humility III:48 page 171
A Poem About How Sin Destroys My Soul III:49 page 171
A Poem About My Battle with Sin: III:50 page 172
"The Recovery"
By Jesus, I Can Kill Sin III:51 page 173
I Saw Myself Like Some Traveler III:52 page 173
My Faith in God's Goodness (As Revealed III:53 page 174
in Obvious & Common Things)
Invisible Common Things III:54 page 174
The Importance of Relationships III:55 page 175
Among Things
Our Instinctive Desire for an Unknown Felicity III:56 page 176
The Perfection of Felicity's Objects and Manner III:57 page 176
I Asked About God's Treasures III:58 page 177
I Asked About How God Enjoyed His Treasures III:59 page 177
I Saw All Things in Their Proper Places III:60 page 178
I Saw the Greatest Thing God Could Make III:61 page 178
I Began to See the Richness & Greatness III:62 page 179
of Everything
Being Satisfied in God III:63 page 179
How God Exerts His Power III:64 page 180
God Has Always Propagated Himself III:65 page 180

I Discovered These Great Thoughts   III:66   page 181
Throughout the Entire Bible
Moses, Jacob, Adam & Abraham Enjoyed   III:67   page 182
Heaven & Earth
I Saw the Importance of Seeing & Loving   III:68   page 182
Things Perfectly

CHAPTER 21: MY MENTOR, DAVID   **page 184**
(A JOURNEY THROUGH THE PSALMS)
My Poetic Tribute to David   III:69   page 184
I Found a Soulmate in David   III:70   page 187
Psalm 8: Every Man's Inheritance   III:71   page 188
Psalm 19: The Glory of Heaven & Earth   III:72   page 188
Psalm 22: All Nations Praising God   III:73   page 189
Psalm 24 & 28: He Saw God's Pleasure   III:74   page 190
with the World.
Psalm 33: The Psalmist Affirms God's Works   III:75   page 191
Psalm 35 & 36: God's Mercy, Faithfulness   III:76   page 191
& Lovingkindness
Psalm 45: Entering God's Palace   III:77   page 192
Psalm 46: Praising God's Grace & His Works   III:78   page 192
Psalm 47 & 48   III:79   page 193
Psalm 49: The Vanity of False Imaginations   III:80   page 194
Psalm 50: Hindrances to Praising God   III:81   page 194
The World Created to Praise God   III:82   page 195
Psalm 51: Deep & Serious Groans   III:83   page 196
Praises & Penitence   III:84   page 197
Psalm 58 & 59: Vengeance of the Wicked   III:85   page 197
Psalm 63 & 65: Dwelling in God's Courts   III:86   page 198

Psalm 66: All Nations Praising God	III:87	page 199
Psalm 74: More of God's Treasures	III:88	page 199
Psalm 78: Celestial Light in Our Memories & Minds	III:89	page 200
Psalm 84: Preferring a Day in God's Courts	III:90	page 200
Psalm 86: The Excellency of God's Works	III:91	page 200
Psalms 103-107, 119: Living in Heaven by Enjoying God's Works	III:92	page 201
Pleasing God in Our Daily Circumstances	III:93	page 202
Psalms 145-150: The Nature of God's Kingdom	III:94	page 203
The Kingdom of God was Always Around Him	III:95	page 203
David's Faith in Prophesies	III:96	page 204
Reigning in God's Kingdom	III:97	page 204
Being Present with God's Omnipresence	III:98	page 205
Our Joy, Courage, Zeal & Fidelity	III:99	page 205
Abiding in All of God's Attributes, Thoughts, Creatures & Works	III:100	page 206

SECTION V: PRINCIPLES FOR YOUR OWN JOURNEY
page 207

CHAPTER 22: THE PRINCIPLE OF TWO KINDS OF CHRISTIANS
page 209

Principles for Action & Contemplation	IV:1	page 209
Acting on Our Principles to Do Great Things	IV:2	page 209
A Philosopher, A Christian, & A Divine	IV:3	page 209
Divine Philosophy	IV:4	page 210
Two Sorts of Christians	IV:5	page 211
Understanding & Full Assurance	IV:6	page 211
Taking Time to Study God & Happiness	IV:7	page 212

Practicing Virtue   IV:8   page 213

Two Sorts of Christians: Deferring Happiness   IV:9   page 214
or Enjoying Happiness Now

Riches Should Be Servants of Happiness   IV:10   page 215

CHAPTER 23: PRINCIPLES OF RETIREMENT & SOLITUDE   **page 216**

Enjoying Happiness After Seeking It   IV:11   page 216

Don't Boast About Your Happiness   IV:12   page 216

Why Men Despise Open Happiness   IV:13   page 217

Being Happy Alone & in Company   IV:14   page 218

Inward Apprehensions   IV:15   page 218

Things Prized Are Enjoyed   IV:16   page 219

Prizing Daily & Common Joys   IV:17   page 219

CHAPTER 24: PRINCIPLES OF CHARITY   **page 221**

Principles for Communication & Conversation   IV:18   page 221

Loving Others as Ourselves   IV:19   page 221

Thinking Oneself a Happy Physician Amidst   IV:20   page 222
a Generation of Vipers

Extracting Good out of Evil   IV:21   page 223

The Charity of Paradise   IV:22   page 223

Living Upon God's Provision   IV:23   page 224

Universal Charity Blowing Away Sins & Vices   IV:24   page 224

The Bright Star of Order & Charity   IV:25   page 225

The Worse a Person, the More to Be Loved   IV:26   page 225

Every Man a Representative of Mankind   IV:27   page 226

Treating Every Person Like Christ   IV:28   page 226

Doing the Most Good to Others (Especially   IV:29   page 226
the Poor)

Falling Short of Our Principles   IV:30   page 227
Doing the Excellent Things We Know   IV:31   page 227
Being a Blessing to Mankind   IV:32   page 228
Giving Away Riches   IV:33   page 228
His Friends' Feelings About Riches   IV:34   page 229
The Foolishness of a Miser   IV:35   page 229
The Riches of Nakedness   IV:36   page 229

CHAPTER 25: PRINCIPLES OF FREE CHOICE & EFFORT   **page 230**
Heaven Established by Principles, Not Place   IV:37   page 230
Actions to Make All Things Beautiful   IV:38   page 230
    in Their Places
The Objects of Our Joy and the Objects   IV:39   page 230
    of Our Care
God Left Man's Heart to Himself   IV:40   page 231
Keeping Your Heart   IV:41   page 231
God Made Man a Free Agent   IV:42   page 232
Our Power to Infinitely Please God Or   IV:43   page 232
    Infinitely Displease Him
Whatever Satisfies Goodness   IV:44   page 233
The Happiness of Giving   IV:45   page 234
Man's Liberty   IV:46   page 235
We Are Blessed By Being a Blessing   IV:47   page 236
Receiving & Appreciating What God Gives   IV:48   page 236
CHAPTER 26: PRINCIPLES OF SELF-LOVE   **page 238**
Self-Love & Love of God   IV:49   page 238
Receiving All Things in Heaven & Earth   IV:50   page 239
Man Was Made Good   IV:51   page 239
Being Faithful with Our Freedom   IV:52   page 239

Restored to Adam's Original Principles   IV:53   page 240
Principles of Our Blessings   IV:54   page 241
Self-Love is the Basis of All Love   IV:55   page 241

CHAPTER 27: PRINCIPLES FOR LOVING OTHERS   **page 243**
Loving Another More Than Myself   IV:56   page 243
Inheriting Others' Joys Through Love   IV:57   page 243
Love Receives What It Gives Away   IV:58   page 244
Learning From Jesus How to Love   IV:59   page 244
Love In the Midst of Disadvantages   IV:60   page 245
Allowing Room for Love   IV:61   page 246
Love Needs Expression   IV:62   page 246
A Riddle About Love   IV:63   page 247
True Glory   IV:64   page 247
How God Loves Himself and Others   IV:65   page 248

CHAPTER 28: PRINCIPLES RELATED TO LOVE & THE SOUL   **page 249**
Love's Principles   IV:66   page 249
The Visible Image of Love   IV:67   page 249
Our Love Can Be Omnipresent   IV:68   page 250
To Love All is Glorious   IV:69   page 251
Love Makes Us Sons of God   IV:70   page 251
Sitting in the Throne of God   IV:71   page 252
Our Throne is the Omnipresence &   IV:72   page 252
    Eternity of God
Objects Magnify Our Souls   IV:73   page 253
God Made Us Worthy of His Love   IV:74   page 254
God's Preparation for Creating Man   IV:75   page 256
God's Commission to Adam   IV:76   page 257

Man's Unlimited Options   IV:77   page 257
Deformity or Excellency is Within Creatures   IV:78   page 258
Man First in Intention, Last in Execution   IV:79   page 258
Love's Healing Influences   IV:80   page 259
Man is the Greatest Miracle   IV:81   page 260
The Richness of the Soul's Communications   IV:82   page 260
The Sweetest Thing in the World   IV:83   page 261
Our Souls Are Mirrors, Reflecting God's Love   IV:84   page 261
God Made Us With Our Own Love   IV:85   page 262
The Goal of Heaven and Earth   IV:86   page 263
Extending God's Grace to Sinners   IV:87   page 264
Obliging God For His Good & Generous Intent   IV:88   page 265
My Present Estate is the Best   IV:89   page 266
Heir of the Whole World & Friend of God   IV:90   page 267
An Oak Flourishing in Winter   IV:91   page 267
Praising God All Day Long   IV:92   page 268
This Life Is the Most Precious   IV:93   page 269
    Season in Eternity
You Must Continually Visit & Practice   IV:94   page 269
    These Principles
Our Souls Are Made for Action   IV:95   page 270
Become Familiar With these Principles   IV:96   page 270
The Secret Strength of the Soul   IV:97   page 271
Spiritual Things Are Greatest & Spiritual   IV:98   page 271
    Strength is Most Useful & Delightful
Can the Soul Enjoy the Universal Beauty   IV:99   page 272
    of God's Kingdom?
What Results from Understanding &   IV:100   page 273
    Appreciating the Soul

SECTION VI: CONTINUING BEYOND BOUNDS & RESTRAINTS
page 275

CHAPTER 29: INFINITE ROOM FOR OUR IMAGINATION
page 277

God is the Object of Felicity & The Way of Enjoying It	V:1	page 277
The Infinity of God is the Kingdom of Our Souls	V:2	page 277
Infinity Gives Us Room for Our Imaginations	V:3	page 278
The Infinite Capacity of God's Power, Goodness, & Wisdom	V:4	page 279
A Painter's Table	V:5	page 279
The Everlasting Duration of Infinite Space	V:6	page 280

CHAPTER 30: TRAVELING INTO GOD'S ETERNITY & OMNIPRESENCE
page 281

An Immovable Duration Containing All Moving Durations	V:7	page 281
The Influence of Eternity	V:8	page 281
God's Omnipresence Is Our Field of Joys & So Much More	V:9	page 282
Perfecting & Completing Our Bliss & Happiness	V:10	page 283

APPENDIX E:
STATEMENT OF EDITORIAL GUIDELINES

In this edition, I have attempted to re-create *Centuries of Meditation* for the contemporary reader, though with great care to preserve the poetic prose in the original version. Many aspects of the Dobell version place a burden on the contemporary reader to logically reorganize the text for himself. I believe that once a reader crosses over to this logical reordering of Traherne's text, he exits the imaginative experience of Traherne's 'heaven on earth.' Because that imaginative experience is at the heart of this edition, I have made numerous changes to the text based on the following guidelines.

A. Book Title

The title, *Waking Up in Heaven,* is derived from a frequently-quoted sentence in *Centuries of Meditation*:

"Your enjoyment of the world is never right **till every morning you awake in heaven**, see yourself in your Father's palace, and look upon the skies, the earth, and the airs as celestial joys, having such a reverend esteem of all, as if you were among the angels."

"Waking up" carries the sense of a daily possibility. It also contains the sense of gaining a new consciousness or way of seeing. Heaven is one of the most pervasive themes in Traherne's book — "heaven" in the sense of the presence of God among us and in us, rather than "heaven" as the afterlife. Traherne makes over 260 direct references to "heaven."

Thus, the title "Waking Up in Heaven" anticipates the daily possibility of seeing everything — the world, people, the Trinity, our circumstances — through the filter of God's presence. In essence, *Waking Up in Heaven* is Traherne's challenge to us — and his legacy.

B. Section and Chapter Divisions

The section divisions in this edition are consistent with the five Century divisions in Traherne's original manuscript, except that I have divided the first Century into two sections. I have divided the six sections into chapters.

C. Sub-chapter Divisions

I have replaced the original meditation numbers for each of Traherne's 410 smallers sections with a heading. These headings are intended to help the reader see the connections among the subsections as well as to summarize them.

D. Paragraph Divisions

Traherne used paragraph breaks in only two of his meditations. While my paragraph breaks are unavoidably subjective, I have attempted to break Traherne's long sections into logical groups of sentences to offer the reader more frequent breaks for processing the text.

E. Third-Person Verbs Forms and Second-Person Prounouns

In the case of third-person verb forms, I have opted for modern usage. For example, "desireth" has been changed to "desires" and "hath" has been changed to "has". In the case of second-person pronouns, I have replaced "thee" and "thou" with "you."

F. Capitalization

Dobell made liberal use of capitals in his 1908 version. I have removed the capitalization in almost all cases where a capitalized word does not refer to a specific person, place, or thing. I have also removed capitalization in pronouns used for persons of the Godhead (consistent with *The Jerusalem Bible* and *The New International Version of the Bible*).

G. Punctuation

I found over 700 colons in Dobell's edition of *Centuries*, many of the used irregularly. In many cases, I felt that a comma, semicolon, period, o em dash was more appropriate. Paragraph breaks also seemed to eliminate the need for many colons.

Whereas I rarely changed any of Traherne's root words, I have taken great liberty with his punctuation, which reflect both his own idiosyncrasies as well as the norms of seventeenth century usage. Any changes in the meaning of a sentence due to my alteration of Traherne's (or Dobell's) use of punctuation are inadvertent.

H. Incomplete Sentences

The reader will occasionally notice an incomplete sentence. In a few cases, I have completed the sentence — but, in most cases, I have left these sentences in their original form.

I. Poetry

In Traherne's poetry (which is always indented), in the interest of preserving the integrity of the original verse, I have made fewer alterations to word form and punctuation than in the prose sections.